A GUIDE TO CONDUCTING ART THERAPY RESEARCH

Harriet Wadeson, PhD, A.T.R.
Editor

Nancy Knapp, PhD, A.T.R.
Chair, AATA Research Committee
1989-1991

The American Art Therapy Association, Inc.
Mundelein, Illinois

Please write to:
The American Art Therapy Association, Inc.
1202 Allanson Road
Mundelein, Illiniois 60060
(847)949-6064 / Fax (847)566-4580

ISBN 1-882147-03-0 (paperback)

Cover Design
Janell Mousseau
Student, Graduate Art Therapy Program
Emporia State University

Book Design
Linda Gantt

FOREWORD

Frances Anderson, EdD, A.T.R., HLM
AATA Publications Chair, 1992

At the 1989 American Art Therapy Association National Conference in Chicago, Illinois, an open meeting was held to discuss the possibilities of developing a research guide. This idea had been bantered about for over a decade by Judy Rubin and Harriet Wadeson among others (see Chapter 1). Harriet Wadeson and Doris Arrington co-chaired the meeting. A real spirit of excitement and cooperation permeated this session. Enthusiasm was evident as the attendees broke into small groups, each of which would address a different facet of research for the proposed publication. I was struck by the energy in that room. *A Guide to Conducting Art Therapy Research* was a project whose time had come.

Some might say that this *Guide* has taken a long time to complete (almost three years). However, when one considers that all the contributors have very, very full jobs and also serve AATA and/or their state art therapy associations in many capacities, three years is not so very long. I also suspect that many do not understand how long it takes a manuscript to emerge as a *fait accompli*.

Many persons have labored long and hard on the *Guide*. I want to acknowledge Harriet Wadeson, the Editor, Nancy Knapp, the Production Coordinator and Research Chair of AATA from 1989 to 1991, Linda Gantt, the Copy and Production Editor, and Judy Rubin, who reviewed the text at an early stage and provided feedback and suggestions. Special note must be made of the assistance of Emporia State University's (ESU) Division of Psychology and Special Education and Word Processing. Maria Lammers served as Text Coordinator and Editorial Aide. Thanks also go to Robert Ault, David Dexter, Shari Parks, Martin Slimmer, Paul McKnab, and Billy Yates, all at ESU, who also gave so freely of their time and talents. And, of course, acknowledgment and thanks go to the contributors who wrote portions of the *Guide*.

As with any collaborative endeavor, there is the possibility that some who worked on this project may have not been properly acknowledged. So, please forgive us if this has happened.

The cooperative spirit and teamwork that pervaded the writing and production of the *Guide* personifies the very best of what our profession and professional association embodies. I applaud all of the contributors and production staff and deeply hope that this will be the beginning of many other collective endeavors.

With the publication of *A Guide to Conducting Art Therapy Research* our profession has indeed "come of age." The field of art therapy now has had a sufficient history of generating research that it has created its own knowledge base. Not only can our field "own" research, this information can be brought together in a comprehensive publication produced by our own professional association. I feel it is significant that AATA's first major publication (in addition to *Art Therapy: Journal of the American Art Therapy Association* and the *AATA Conference Proceedings*) is one devoted to research.

TABLE OF CONTENTS

PART IIII:
METHODOLOGICAL CHALLENGES SPECIFIC TO
ART THERAPY RESEARCH

PART IV:
RESOURCES FOR ART THERAPY RESEARCH

INTRODUCTION

Harriet Wadeson, PhD, A.T.R., Editor

Imagistic expression provides a unique window into human functioning. Art therapists know how to use this rich source of data to help our clients understand themselves and to improve their lives. We are less skilled in moving beyond an individual's self-story toward generalization about human functioning that must be supported by systematic investigation. Nor are we proficient in confirming the clinical efficacy of art therapy by means of well designed research studies.

For many years, art therapists have repeatedly proclaimed the need for research in our field. Much of the motivation has stemmed from the wish for substantiation of our still young discipline as it takes its place among the more established helping professions. Additionally, the permanent record art production provides is a seductive source of data, particularly as it taps unconscious reservoirs of human ideation and the exciting realms of fantasy worlds, dreams, and imagination.

Yet, most art therapists enter the field charged with their own personal experience of gratification from art expression and a wish to involve themselves with others through the intimacy of imagery. Such work is of a very different nature from the exacting methodological considerations of research design and implementation.

Additionally, the complexities of both clinical training and research training are so extensive that it is difficult, if not impossible, for a two-year Master's-level training program (our current model) to educate students in both areas adequately.

The purpose of this *Guide to Conducting Art Therapy Research (Guide)* is to address this problem. It is not our intention to furnish comprehensive training for the art therapist. There are many university courses available for that purpose. What we are hoping to provide here is a resource for individuals who wish to pursue research in art therapy and who have or will acquaint themselves with basic research methodology. From that groundwork the *Guide* will address some of the problems and potentialities specific to art therapy research. Nevertheless, it cannot be overstated that conducting research is best learned by doing. It is our hope that the *Guide* will encourage art therapists to get their feet wet in the research pool, and that it will serve as a resource to those interested in beginning and those who have already begun to design and implement art therapy research.

The *Guide* has been composed by a number of art therapy researchers who volunteered to contribute to this project. The authors of the various chapters have written about their area of expertise derived from their own individual research experience. Therefore, the material covered represents the authors' accumulated knowledge in conducting art therapy research, rather than a comprehensive compendium of all knowledge accrued in the pursuit of research in art therapy. Nor is there an attempt among the authors to speak with one voice, but rather to present their various views and recommendations. Style of presentation varies as well, from the formal to the more colloquial, from straightforward expression to poetic phraseology, from didactic exposition to personal narrative. Some chapters address beginning researchers; some will be useful to those with some degree of research sophistication. Many chapters cite valuable resources.

The *Guide* is organized in four parts. **Part I, Art Therapy Research in Perspective: Before You Begin**, reviews and orients the prospective art therapy researcher to thinking about research with an account of AATA's involvement in art therapy research, contributions from past AATA Research Chairs, and recipients of research awards compiled by Nancy Knapp. Guidance in thinking about art therapy research is represented here in a chapter by Janie Rhyne and some suggestions from Pat Allen and Linda Gantt.

Part II, Basics of Research, begins with suggestions from Cathy Malchiodi on minimizing bias in art therapy research. Recent regulations demand that investigations using human subjects, as art therapists do, adhere to certain guidelines that guarantee certain safeguards. The ethics of research with humans and its practical application are thoughtfully discussed in a chapter by Nancy Knapp. This section concludes with a description of traditional research models used in behavioral science studies outlined by Sister Dorothy McLaughlin and Richard Carolan.

Part III moves into the actual nuts and bolts of the **Methodological Challenges Specific to Art Therapy Research**. This section begins with illustrations compiled by Marcia Rosal of various research paradigms art therapists have used in studies that have been completed and published. With a continuing focus on research methodologies, Linda Gantt points out possibilities for art therapy research to use models developed by neighboring fields, such as art history, in addition to the more customary behavioral science methodologies. Continuing in this vein, Maxine Junge and Debra Linesch point out some of the newer paradigms that might be more suitable than traditional research models for art therapists to use. Beginning with the next chapter by Harriet Wadeson, this section becomes more specific in pointing out particular methodological problems posed by the nature of art therapy data and some possible solutions. Pamela Diamond describes the single-case study as a useful investigative method in art therapy, and Winnie Ferguson concludes this section with a description of the attractiveness of social action research in art therapy and its methodology.

Part IV, Resources for Art Therapy Research, includes references for many aspects of research, beginning with assessment. Linda Gantt presents an overview of art therapy assessments. Doris Arrington provides summaries of a number of assessment procedures for research, followed by charts of assessment instruments prepared by Nancy Knapp. An important chapter detailing the use of computer databases and analyses is presented by Frances Anderson with Carol Cox, David Cox, and Maxine Crouch. Potential financial resources are explored in a chapter on grants by Doris Arrington and Frances Anderson, and the *Guide* concludes with an annotated listing of references and resources prepared by Nancy Knapp.

The hallmark of our profession is our creativity. It is not limited to artistic creativity or even the encouragement of artistic creativity. Art therapy's creativity encompasses the building of therapeutic relationships, developing art therapy services, establishing training, forming local and national organizations, communicating our findings in presentations and publications, and much more. I have no doubt that the creativity that has taken our profession so far in such a short period of time will carry us further. It is the hope of all of us who have worked on this publication that this *Guide to Conducting Art Therapy Research* will serve to promote our creativity in research as well.

Part I

ART THERAPY RESEARCH IN PERSPECTIVE: BEFORE YOU BEGIN

May this Guide to Art Therapy Research *come with the hope earlier expressed by AATA's first Research Chair, Hanna Yaxa Kwiatkowska. As a first step, may it be "helpful in providing art therapists with methods for scientific investigation of as difficult an endeavor as measuring art, by itself and in combination with the intricacy of family psychopathology. The methods may be fallible; many more experimental studies are needed. But at least a start was made. These methods may also be another step in the efforts to reinforce for art therapy a respected position in the psychotherapeuetic domain."*

Hanna Yaxa Kwiatkowska (1978, p. 215). *Family therapy and evaluation through art.* Springfield, IL: Charles C. Thomas.

Chapter 1

HISTORICAL OVERVIEW OF ART THERAPY RESEARCH

Nancy Knapp, PhD, A.T.R.

Overview of Art Therapy Research

Although there has been long-term interest in the meaning behind spontaneous art products, methodical exploration of art products is more recent. MacGregor's *Discovery of the Art of the Insane* (1989) provides a current and inclusive source for background perspective on studies of patient art.

Research to evaluate the efficacy of art therapy or to understand specific art processes with particular populations has developed in many arenas and has been reviewed by numerous individuals. Although rigorous research by art therapists may have been rare historically, in some instances of art therapy practice there was not only a press for research but also support for it. For example, Mary Huntoon did formal research for 10 years beginning in 1947, funded by the Veteran's Administration at Winter Hospital in Topeka, Kansas (Casado, 1980, p. 47).

In the first publication specific to our field, Volume l, Number l, of the *Bulletin of Art Therapy*, there is evidence of an interest in research. The *News* section included an account of research into materials and methods best suited for art therapy with retarded children which was financed by a grant from the U.S Office of Education. The recognition of the importance of research was also emphasized by the inclusion of Bernard Levy, with a background as a research psychologist, on the editorial board. Levy's advocacy of research in art therapy was manifested in his teaching and mentoring as well as in his personal pursuits and writing.

From the beginning, the *Bulletin of Art Therapy*, and its subsequent format, the *American Journal of Art Therapy*, published research accounts and chronicled widely divergent work in art therapy to encourage networking. In later years, *The Arts in Psychotherapy* and *Art Therapy: The Journal of the American Art Therapy Association* joined in this tradition. At the *Bulletin's* inception, editor Elinor Ulman had hoped for a lively forum for exchange, insight, and helpful criticism. A model sequence began with the article, "An Experimental Approach to the Judgement of Psychopathology from Paintings," by Ulman and Levy (1968), followed by a critique from Rita Simon (1969) offering appreciation, criticism, and suggestions which were responded to graciously by Levy (1969).

In the absence of official records of the Research Committee, early copies of the *Bulletin* have provided a primary source for tracking the evolution of AATA's involvement in and support of research. The practice of art therapy developed simultaneously in isolated pockets throughout the country, and the formation of AATA facilitated the sharing of common goals. In the original proposal for a Constitution, Section 8 was penned into Article IV to provide for a standing Research Committee. It stated that "The research Committee will consist of five members and shall foster the development of sound research procedures in the field of art therapy." (Unpublished materials for 1971 in the AATA Archives, American Art Therapy Association, n.d.). This statement was included in the final revision of the AATA Bylaws.

According to an account of the First Annual Conference of AATA in the *American Journal of Art Therapy*, October 1970, the first Executive Board included Hanna Yaxa Kwiatkowska as Research Chair. She defined the functions of the Research Committee to include "giving help to members with problems of research design and method; advising about literature relevant to research undertaken; and putting members with similar research interests in touch with each other." (*AJAT*, 1970, Vol. 10, No. 1, p. 31). Successive chairs of that Committee have been Bernard Levy (1973-77), Gary Barlow (1977-81), Janie Rhyne (1981-85), Linda Gantt (1985-87), Harriet Wadeson (1987-89), and Nancy Knapp (1989-91). Contributions from these past Chairs are seen throughout the research represented in this *Guide*.

In addition to philosophical and theoretical advocacy, AATA has frequently provided financial support for researchers. This has been dependent upon other organizational priorities and financial stability. The awards for completed research or grants to subsidize research in progress. Other qualifications were specified according to the emphasis desired by the Research Committee. Monies came from both individual art therapists and from the organization's budget. Helen Landgarten donated prize money for the initial award in 1976. In 1986, Glady Agell provided funding for a new research award, originally intended to be earmarked for students. Other financial support has been offered by individuals specifically for particular research.

The first research competition was won by Rawley Silver for a paper, "Using Art to Evaluate and Develop Cognitive Skills," at the 1976 Seventh Annual Conference. In 1978, Harriet Wadeson was awarded the prize in what was referred to as AATA's "biennial research competition" for her paper, "Research in Art Therapy." At that time, Gary Barlow described the AATA research and publications files available for members through the National Office and the outcome of research documentation questionnaires. He also arranged for study sessions in research to be held at the National Conference, with both art therapists and a guest researcher available.

In 1979, the awards for outstanding research went to Judith O. Flesh for "Children of Holocaust Survivors — An Explorative Study Utilizing the Art Therapy Modality," and to Myra Levick for her investigation of "Group Dynamics of Dependency and Counter Dependency Manifested in Drawings of Graduate Art, Movement, and Music Therapy Students." Research assistance grants were made to Jacqueline Bachar, Georgiana Jungels, Lillian Rhinehart and Paula Englehorn, and Helayne Van Sickle (*AJAT*, 1979, Vol. 18, No. 4, p. 129). In 1980, Rawley Silver and her collaborators were given an award for their study, "Assessing and Developing Cognitive Skills Through Art."

In 1982, Janie Rhyne, as Chair of the Research Committee, reported that a survey of art therapy research articles revealed that more than two-thirds of the research reported had been undertaken by professionals in other fields rather than by art therapists (*AJAT*, 1982, Vol. 21, No. 3, p. 93). The Research Committee worked to change this situation by seeking ways to provide professional art therapists with financial assistance while they were engaged in the actual research, rather than receiving monetary recognition of past achievement. They hoped to use AATA's limited resources as seed money to attract substantial research grants from other sources. The Committee also reported that, during that year, they had developed strategies with staff at the National Institute of Mental Health to further art therapy research, reviewed criteria for the research award, and addressed issues related to research training with art therapy educators (*AATA Newsletter*,

1982, Vol. XII, No. 5, p. 1). During Rhyne's tenure as Chair, her "Ten Steps in Planning Good Research" and "Therapy" were made available to members through the AATA National Office. (This material is contained in Chapter 2 of this *Guide*.)

In 1983, a $600 grant was offered to Professional Members for original research which was not completed as part of fulfilling a master's or doctoral degree progam. The Research Award for 1983 was given to Barry Cohen, Anne Reyner, and Shira Singer to further their research into "The Diagnostic Drawing Series: A Systematic Approach to Art Therapy Evaluation and Research." Marie Caruso was commended for her study of "The Influence of Alexithymia on Symbol Formation."

In 1984, the Executive Board canceled the award for research because of a lack of response from the membership (*AATA Newsletter*, 1984, Vol. XIV, No. 4, p. 18). This was a marked contrast to the 30 reported applications in 1983. In 1985, seven applicants initially applied for the Research Award, but only two responded to the request for more detailed information (*AATA Newsletter*, 1985, Vol. XV, No. 2, p. 19). This variation in apparent interest in receiving research money may have been due to a number of factors, but possibly it reflected some general concerns about AATA's financial future during that transitional period.

Co-researchers Christy Bergland and Rosanna Moore were granted a $200 Research Assistance Award, offered to Professional Members at the 1985 Conference for "further development of a rating scale assessing correlations between patterns of score of art productions and outcome of psychiatric treatment" (*AATA Newsletter*, 1985, Vol. XV, No. 2, p. 19). Recognition was also given to David R. Henley for his proposal for an empirical study of "Incidence of Emotional Maladjustment in Hearing Impaired Children."

In 1986, Research Chair Linda Gantt announced the AATA Board's decision to temporarily suspend the Research Award and Research Assistance Grant because of budget constraints (*AATA Newsletter*, 1986, Vol. XVI, No. 4, p. 12). For the future, it was hoped that a financial contribution from Agell would be matched with other monies, and new criteria for the award's distribution would be developed. At that time, the focus of the Research Committee went to projects which did not require financial support, particularly a continuation of a demographic survey begun by Gary Barlow's committee and the cataloging of research materials written especially for art therapists begun by Janie Rhyne. Marie Caruso and Roberta Shoemaker gave the Committee permission to modify the forms they had used in independent research projects to aid in future studies for AATA.

In the same spirit of working within the existing structure, a research project was carried out at the 1986 AATA Conference in Los Angeles. In this experimental Conference, participants were aked for their responses to specific colors. Sandy Geller and Carol Cox have continued their interest in research into color, which has stemmed from the work of our second Chair, Bernard Levy, and several of his students, including Isolde Martin (1982).

In 1987, the Research Committee launched a nationwide project to collect and study artwork done immediately before a serious suicide attempt or lethal suicide. Only one member, Barbara Smiley, (Smiley, 1991) responded to a general request for participation. Linda Goldman followed through with a study group on the subject during the 1988 Conference (L. Gantt, personal conversation, June 3, 1991).

A competition was announced for a Research Assistance Award of $200 to aid in completing a current research project. The submissions were judged on "suitability of research design to the problem and the logic with which the detail of the proposal are crafted" (*AATA Newsletter*, 1987, Vol. XVII, No. 2, p. 6). Jonathan Brakarsh received a grant for his study on "The Child's Family Drawing as Measure of Stessful Family Environment," the findings of which were presented at the AATA Conference in 1988. David Henley received a grant to support research on "The Incidence of Artistic Giftedness in the Multiply Handicapped."

The Genesis of the Research Guide

In 1988, because there were no suitable entries, Research Chair Harriet Wadeson and Committee members Maxine Junge, Judy Rubin, and Nancy Knapp unanimously decided to temporarily direct the Research Award toward encouraging the development of research methodologies specific to art therapy data. Wadeson proposed compiling a manual to encourage and aid in the development of art therapy research. Rubin, a former Research Committee member, had previosuly suggested this project. Wadeson agreed to be editor, and chapters were assigned to be written. Since then, AATA's research budget and energies have been funneled into the publication of this *Guide*. Editor Wadeson dedicated countless hours to pulling divergent parts together. Two follow-up sessions at the 1990 Conference refined some problematic areas, but confirmed the need for a completed and published manual which could be supplemented or changed as dictated by future needs.

In 1990, the AATA Board of Directors was restructured so that the Research Chair, along with Chairs of other standing committees, was no longer a board member elected by the membership. At the time of this publication, overseeing research duties has been one of several responsibilities under Director Dean Wilson, to whom the Chair reports. Within this Board structure, the Research Committee is appointed by the elected Board of Directors. The Chair appoints the Research Committee, and the President is an *ex officio* member as with all standing committees. Committee concerns and business are represented on the Board by the appropriate Director. Research business may sometimes require committee liaison with other Directors, such as those responsible for ethics, publications, and awards.

In 1978, Gary Barlow, then AATA Research Chair, wrote of plans to initiate a research publication. He stated, "It is hoped that this collected information will help both the beginner and the seasoned researcher in the formulation, writing, and dissemination of quality professional research." (*AATA Newsletter*, 1978, Vol. VIII, No. 5, p. 11). His thoughts have been revisited and articulated frequently in the 13 years since. The goal of this first published guide for research in art therapy is to provide both an historical context as well as some useful current direction. The Research Committee hopes that it will be the first of a series of publications dedicated to research which, like all other seas of our profession, will ever increase in usefulness and sophistication.

References

American Art Therapy Association. (n.d.). *AATA archives*. Topeka, KS: Menninger Foundation.

Casado, M. (1980). *In search of the meaning of modern art*. Unpublished manuscript. University of Kansas, Department of History, Lawrence.

Levy, B. (1969). Experimenter's reply. [Reader's Forum.] *Bulletin of Art Therapy, 8*(3), 128, 131.

MacGregor, J. (1989). *The discovery of the art of the insane*. Princeton, NJ: Princeton University Press.

Martin, I. (1982). Universal versus learned emotional responses to colors: Afterthoughts to thesis research. *The Arts in Psychotherapy, 9*(4), 245-248.

Simon, R. (1969). Critique of an experiment. [Reader's Forum.]. *Bulletin of Art Therapy, 8* (3), 90, 127-128.

Smiley, B. (1987). *The House-Tree-Person projective test as an aid in determining suicidal intention*. Unpublished manuscript, New York University, New York.

Ulman, E., & Levy, B. (1968). An experimental approach to the judgement of psychopathology from paintings. *Bulletin of Art Therapy, 8*(1), 3-12.

Chapter 2

HOW IDEAS ARE GENERATED FOR RESEARCH

Janie Rhyne, PhD, A.T.R., HLM

Research ideas come from the minds of those who wonder—from people whose curiosity urges them to question their own observations. Research ideas come from people who want to understand—from those who know that too many answers and too few questions make for a flimsy knowledge base.

Ideas leading art therapists to do research on their own usually come from observations of the kinds of art people make in various contexts. As art therapists, we all observe similarities and differences in what and how people represent their thoughts and feelings. But art therapists are people, too, and differences among us are as great as among our clients. One of the differences is in how we interpret our clients' visual representations. We differ in what we think we know, in what sorts of things we ought to know, and in how we can go about learning more.

We differ in our present ideologies, in our background education, in what we think are "the fundamentals of art therapy," and in the directions we strive towards in the best interest of the profession of art therapy. Fortunately, there are some things on which we agree, and one of those is that we need more research in our field.

If you want, or are required to do research and evaluation, you must do a lot of learning, a good bit of independent thinking, and a stint of solid, hard work. Doing research and evaluation requires more than finding and following simple rules. The kind of learning, thinking, and working I am writing about is an anathema to many art therapists. Those who consider themselves primarily as **ARTISTIC** prefer to rely on their intuitive insights, spontaneous expressions, and empathic responses; they want nothing to do with scientific thought. I do not argue with these preferences; all of us come into this field with at least some experience and training as artists and we bring with us sensitivities and awareness of the art process that are among our most valuable assets. I do, however, get argumentative with those who claim, in the name of their artistry, that they have an inside track on the "truth," unhampered by reference to facts and figures.

On the other hand, I think a good many art therapists are overly impressed with "scientific" thinking; when they think of "research" they are intimidated and deterred by the presumption that only carefully controlled experiments in laboratory settings have any validity. I also argue with the limited views of such scientism which claims that what cannot be observed cannot be real; part of this hard-nosed experimental approach comes from the tenets of American behaviorism, and we need not be bound by a model of inquiry that precludes study of the wonderful workings of the human mind.

In between the richness of intuitive knowing and the rigor of controlled experiments, there are many ways of designing and carrying through research to add to our knowledge and to conduct evaluations of the credibility of our therapeutic approaches and techniques. The ways are various and span a wide gamut of methods, but they have one thing in common—they all require systematic study. Systematic study does not necessarily involve the use of statistics or of any numbers at all, except for dates, ages, and, perhaps, to present information about how many and how often.

All art therapists can benefit from doing self-chosen, systematic studies of whatever they are interested and involved in. To do this, you do not have to do any drastic shifting of your self-image from subjective artist to objective scientist; you simply adapt your art activities from allowing yourself spontaneous free expression to directing your perceptiveness toward creating a design. Of course, designing involves planning and structuring; your impulses may have to be curbed a bit, but there is a tradeoff. You experience tremendous satisfaction, even excitement, in recognizing that you can bring together forms that create meaningful configurations. Whether you are using painting media or conceptual thought, you can still be involving yourself in a productive, creative process.

On the other hand, many intriguing studies are not predesigned; in your observations of graphic representations you may notice something that you did not expect and were not looking for. Perhaps you detect repetitions of content, form, or color in a person's drawings or in the drawings of people in a group. You can then go back through your files and see if you can relate your observations to some patterning of time, place, or situation. If so, you then search for some plausible relationship, taking into account the full context of people and events; this is called **EX POST FACTO** research. You are systematically working backwards to find and organize information that you can build upon in future studies. Much of the "data" for documentation of observed relationships between art expression and overt behavior must be done in this after-the-fact fashion.

The "language" of the expressive arts emerges from the highly complex mind functioning of perception, memory, association, cognition, and emotion, and it resonates with multidimensional inner imagery. We know a great deal about the grammar and syntax of verbal languages; we are just beginning to learn something about how form, color, and content express meaning in visual expression. So, do not be too apologetic when you cannot "predict" what forms will emerge in visual language; just be observant and when you perceive something of interest, patiently trace it back in search of some meaningful relationship.

Before or after the fact of emerging data, much of the studying we do must be honestly designated as **EXPLORATORY**. We are venturing into the domain of art, whose wonders, mysteries, and potentials have excited and puzzled erudite philosophers for centuries; we also consider ourselves to be qualified as therapists and psychotherapists who have special expertise, innovatively combining art and science in our profession. We know that art therapy often does contribute to beneficial change but we need to understand better how, when, with whom, and in what contexts it works best. To broaden our base of understanding, we need to take the risk that goes with innovation; we need to do creative exploratory studies toward discovery of new findings. Too many of our anecdotal accounts make no attempt to draw coherent conclusions, or to point out how the work with a particular client can contribute to more generalized knowledge of art in or as therapy.

CASE STUDIES can be more than rambling accounts. Without violating the unique history of the individual client, you can do a systematic study simply by noting, recording, and thinking through all the information you can gather from and about this client. An intensive study of one person can become valid research when you put in the effort to collect data about the person's background, social status, family relationships, religious beliefs, fantasies of fear and hope, physical and medical history, sleeptime dreaming, etc. Tape recordings of the person's ideas help tremendously, especially when the person is describing and elaborating on the intended meaning in his/her art expressions. Getting all of this together, you have the richness of the drama of one person's life; put it into a coherent configuration of how the parts relate to the whole and you will have some good original research.

The issue of richness versus rigor in designing any kind of research always comes up; we would all like to have both in our studies, but usually one quality gets short shrift. The choice depends upon who is doing what kind of research and frequently under what kind of process. **EMPIRICAL** research, most often required for graduate programs in education and in the behavioral and social sciences, can and does help us build a base for documentation of some facts and figures that can be objectively supported. It is my educated guess that a larger percentage of art therapists are involved in research now than in the 1970s. To a great extent, the increase in empirical research relevant to art therapy is due to the increasing number of studies done by art therapists as a requirement for their advanced degrees in programs other than art therapy. It seems that a number of doctoral programs requiring empirical research dissertations are being attended by art therapists who continue to include artwork in their practice.

These and other empirical studies can provide observable data that are not dependent on any theoretical bias; the methods and procedures should be such that the research can be replicated by others and with other populations. Empirical studies need not be "experimental" in terms of control of all the variables, but they must follow the rules for generating data that can be organized objectively. The results are usually obtained by some sort of numerical analysis. Inferential statistics are used to provide bases for generalizations drawn from the data obtained in the study, though this can be done using the simplest descriptive statistics.

Referring back to art therapy literature in our earliest days, most of the statistically based empirical studies quoted were done by researchers in other disciplines; primarily, we turned to psychologists and psychiatrists to supply us with tested information on which we could base our assumptions. Though this is still true to some extent, especially in the reliance on projective tests, I can see changes as I read through our bibliographies. There are more entries now of current research being done by art therapists who find that they are capable of doing respectable empirical research—even when they must use statistics and face a computer terminal without flinching. One of the greatest services computers provide for research is their proficiency in coming out with statistical answers that tell you exactly what you want to know. Of course, you have to put in the right questions, but a good statistician can help you with that once you have clarified your own thinking.

Keeping in mind my earlier caveat that research requires more than following some simple rules, I have compiled a series of steps which can serve as guideposts as you develop your research ideas and projects. These guidelines are not totally of my making; with some variations they are offered in all texts used in teaching how to design and report empirical research in education and the behavioral sciences. I have put together, then, information and advice from a lot of sources; the way I have presented it to you is of my own doing. The sequence of the steps is one that I have found helpful in designing my own studies and in helping others to do theirs. Depending on the whys and wherefores of your research, you may take these steps in a different order, but do not bypass any of them. Each one directs you to recognize implicit determinants of your best options; make these options explicit in written statements. Each statement indicates sensible do's and don'ts for you to heed in planning a course of action that is wise for you to pursue.

Every research design has weaknesses of one sort or another; every person doing research has fallibilities and limitations. None of us can be interested in everything, ask every question, find all of the answers, be totally free of bias; nor can any of us become completely objective simply because we are engaged in systematic study. Your research design will reflect your personal views, foibles, and limitations; that is natural and inevitable. There will be flaws in your designs, too; other people will gladly point them out to you, mostly after you've done all the work. You can keep these frustrations to a minimum by giving yourself honest answers to straight questions about your liabilities and assets in the field of research.

You need to evaluate your situation, your background experience, training, knowledge, and capabilities. You must realize which of your **interests, questions, theories,** and **assumptions** can be sensibly integrated into a systematic study of observable phenomena, and which belong in the more philosophical realms of discourse, logic, and speculation. You must be very clear about your **purpose** and **objectives**. You must recognize **limitations** inherent in your research; and it is wise to further state restrictions that you purposely impose upon the scope of the study. These **delimitations** specify what you will avoid dealing with in your study. The **methods** and **procedures** you propose should be chosen very carefully, because the actual implementation of these steps will determine what sort of data you will collect and what form it will take. Methods and procedures provide information that can make or break the connections you expect to establish between your questions and your answers.

Only after you have finished your research will you be able to compose a coherent account of your **results** and **conclusions**. These two steps are not included in the planning stage because, obviously, you cannot know what kind of results will be obtained until you've carried through your plans, and your conclusions can be drawn only after you have studied carefully what is indicated and implied in your results. If you have done a good job of initial planning and have implemented it intelligently, then at least some of the answers to your originally posed questions should be found in the results of your procedures. After you organize and interpret these findings, you will draw conclusions, explaining and evaluating how your research has and has not fulfilled your planned objectives. You may want to point out relationships between your new data and your past theorizing. You certainly will appraise how your research findings have contributed to more understanding in your area of interest. You will recommend directions for further studies in this area. Your conclusions are a wrapup of both what you planned and expected to explore, and what, in actuality, you did discover. The writing of this section will be much facilitated by referring back to the directions you have pointed to in planning your research.

Ten Steps to Good Research

The approach, orientation, and methodology you decide on in designing your studies will predetermine the final dimensions of your constructed research. Using the 10 steps offered here, you should be able to design a framework to build on. As you proceed with the conduct of your plan you will fill in the details and probably make changes; but meanwhile, you will have a sturdy structure within which you can do further work.

Of the 10 steps outlined below, the first five are written as questions for you to ask yourself; in trying to answer them, you will clarify your own thinking. As you write your answers, you will recognize where your thinking is vague; you must give more thought and perhaps more study to these areas. In answering other questions, you will realize that your ideas are easy to put into coherent language.

The last five steps direct you to focus your thinking as you formulate the design of the research you are proposing. Delineating these steps requires some knowledge of empirical research methods; you may need to turn to someone trained in this methodology to help you choose and define methods and procedures appropriate for your study. But the other four steps in this sequence must be done by you, since only you can decide what your priorities are in doing research.

The last five steps will also lead you to search through the literature relevant to your plan. You must make decisions in defining and discriminating what is integral in the development of your research. Here, you must concentrate your designing faculties, eliminate loose-ended divergences and incorporate integrated ideas that will direct you toward convergence in reaching your research goals.

1. **In your training and practice as an art therapist, what is your major area of interest?**

With what populations have you worked and in what settings? Relate your research interest to your professional concerns. Begin with something you know about, something which attracts your attention and activates your curiosity.

2. **What sort of questions are you interested in answering?**

In your own area of experience and observation, what kind of unanswered questions keep getting in your way? What answers do you wish were written in some book, or, at least, known to some colleague? Your puzzling can motivate you to look for answers in doing your own research studies.

3. **What is your theoretical orientation?**

Most approaches to the study of art therapy are influenced by theories from more generalized fields; clarify for yourself what theories you are accepting and where they came from. Especially if you are evaluating or seeking support for theoretical views, state clearly what these are. Some current psychological approaches include: Freudian, Jungian, Adlerian, Gestalt, Phenomenological, Humanistic, etc. Others come from the practice of healing, both traditional and holistic; some originate in a study of anthropology or mythology; some research is generated from the history of art and aesthetics; and some from mysticism. Whatever your orientation is, examine and define it in explicit terms.

4. **What assumptions are you making that are to be "taken for granted" and that you will not question in your research?**

These are called *postulates,* "things assumed to be true." More candidly, these are your biases (we all have them). Here is the place where honesty is definitely the best and safest policy.

5. **What is your general purpose and what are your specific objectives in doing this research?**

In this step you begin to focus in. Your general purpose may be broad but it must not be vague. Choose specific objectives that can be achieved by your research procedures. Remember that you are committing yourself to obtaining and interpreting some kinds of definite results. Don't take on more than you can handle. If you feel up to it and plan to use an appropriate methodology, you may state your objectives as hypotheses. This appropriate methodology, you may state your objectives as hypotheses. This means that you will make predictions which will be supported or rejected, by systematic measures applied to your data. Hypotheses are simply educated guesses, and they are usually tested by simple or complex statistical analyses. To do this you must plan ahead so that you collect sufficient data that are precise enough to feed into formulas. Hypothesis testing requires you to think ahead, so that you know how you will determine the significance of your findings before you get too far into your research.

6. Review of literature

From your educational background and from reading about your area of interest, you will already be familiar with some of the literature relevant to your research. Begin with what you know and then **search** the library for other references. Learn how to use library resources efficiently. Use an index card for each book or article you read. Be sure to check current periodicals for **up-to-date** information on your subject. **Organize** the literature into related sequences. In your discussion **evaluate** what you have read. Be **selective**. Do not arbitrarily list everything you have read about your subject; present only what has a bearing on your area of inquiry. But do not disregard literature just because it presents opinions with which you differ. You can enrich your own ideas through fair-minded consideration of other viewpoints; in your written review, however, be succinct, pointing your comments toward your research goals.

7. Definitions of terms

Almost certainly you will be using terms with which your readers may be unfamiliar or whose usage differs from yours. Art therapy vocabulary is especially in need of definition because it has been adapted from so many more established disciplines. Meanings of concepts like *creativity, symbolization, imagery, universal,* etc., depend upon the context in which they are used. Define how you are using conceptual terms. Also, define terminology commonly used in your specialized field but which is unfamiliar to others outside of your field. When you use terms such as *social isolation, learning disabled, retarded, developmental stages,* etc., describe specific characteristics to which you are referring. In doing this you will hone your own thinking and you will facilitate your reader's understanding and appreciation of your research.

8. Delimitations

What restrictions are you purposely imposing on the focus and scope of your study? Be smart! Take this step early in your planning. Be realistic about what you can expect to do. Inexperienced researchers tend to take on far more than they can deal with. State clearly what populations, what kind of processes, in what settings, and what sorts of art activities you will be studying. Before you begin **delimit** the generalizations you intend to make in the conclusions you can draw at the end of your study.

9. Limitations

What restrictions are inherent in your planned research and thus beyond your control? There are many of these, of course. You can "control" the people who are your "subjects" only to a very limited extent. There is information that is unavailable to you. Some phenomena cannot be directly observed. Graphic art is too complex for precise analysis, and so on. Recognize these limitations and make them explicit for yourself before you get caught up in planning the impossible.

10. Methodology and procedures

What type of research do you plan and how will you proceed, step-by-step, in actually doing it? There are many types from which you can choose. Unless you are well trained in research methodology, you will probably need help in the details of your procedure, especially if they include statistical analysis. But you are, and must be, the designer of your own studies. Only you know what questions you are asking and what answers you are seeking, but you are not ready to make a proposal of your planning until you can organize your ideas systematically.

Like any other design, research must be constructed so that its various parts create a well-integrated whole. The methods you use must be appropriate for the phenomena you are studying. "Controlled experiments" eliciting "free expression" are, by definition, meaningless; "case histories" presenting no search for relevant historical material contribute very little to our field. "Field observations" where inferences take precedence over observations miss the point; "analytical studies" of art taken out of context betray the artist. It is up to you to choose the methods and procedures that make the most of your research explorations.

Chapter 3

GUIDELINES FOR GETTING STARTED IN RESEARCH

Pat B. Allen, PhD, A.T.R.
Linda Gantt, PhD, A.T.R.

Creative ideas often come couched in chaos, or at least lack of order; compiling lists of essential elements is one way to counter this. As with Janie Rhyne's "10 Points," the following examples were designed and used to foster methodical research by art therapists. Pat Allen listed her thoughts and choice of references for use in classes and workshops, and Linda Gantt compiled her suggestions to expand resources and to help prevent some common problems.

SOME THOUGHTS ON GETTING STARTED

Pat B. Allen, PhD, A.T.R.

I have discovered the value of art making as a metaphor for developing research in art therapy (Allen, 1988). I have used the following six points extensively in teaching and encouraging art therapists who might be reluctant to become researchers. My intention is to demystify the idea of research, to help the average art therapist identify internal resources as a researcher, to provide strategies for developing or tapping sources with complementary skills, and to point out potential areas of difficulty and suggest possible solutions.

There are specific things that art therapists can do to enhance our success in planning and conducting research. It helps to know as much as possible about ourselves and what research means to us before embarking on about ourselves and what research means to us before embarking on a research project. The following brief list of suggestions may help facilitate the process:

1. Examine your own image of what research must be. Create an image of a researcher. Do this through drawing and writing. Find out about your own fears and expectations.

2. Take a basic research methods course, usually offered on the undergraduate level in the psychology department of most colleges. Audit the course if you want to relieve anxiety and save money.

3. Do personal research with art therapy methods. Make art yourself and see what happens. Keep a journal of your results for planning studies with other subjects.

4. Consider what your motives are. If your research desire is directly related to job security, try to hook up with an existing project in your institution. It is much easier than starting from scratch and is a good learning experience.

5. Start study and support groups to sustain yourself as you undertake research. It helps to share both results and disappointments.

6. Hire experts to collaborate with and to advise you. You don't need to be an expert on every aspect of research.

I recommend the following for further reading: Bakan (1969), Barzun & Graff (1957/1985), Child (1973), Culbertson & Revel (1987), Franzella & Bannister (1977), Gantt & Schmal (1974), Green, Wehling, & Talsky (1987), Hanes (1982), Huff (1954), Isaac & Michael (1981), Miller (1972), Moore (1981), Rosenberg (1965), Rubin (1984), Tyler (1978), Wadeson & Carpenter (1976), and Willems & Raush (1969).

References

Allen, P. (1988). Art making as a metaphor for developing research in art therapy. [Abstract.] Professionalism in Practice, *Proceedings of the 19th Annual Conference of the American Art Therapy Association* (p. 85). Mundelein, IL: American Art Therapy Association.

Bakan, D. (1969). *On method: Toward a reconstruction of psychological investigation.* San Francisco, CA: Jossey-Bass.

Barzun, J., & Graff, H. (1957, rev. 1985). *The modern researcher.* New York, NY: Harcourt.

Child, I. (1973). *Humanistic psychology and the research tradition: Their several virtues.* New York, NY: Wiley.

Culbertson, F., & Revel, A. (1987). Graphic considerations of the draw-a-person test for the identification of child abuse. *Art Therapy: Journal of the American Art Therapy Association, 4,* 78-83.

Fransella, F., & Bannister, D. (1977). *A manual for repertory grid technique.* New York, NY: Academic Press.

Gantt, L., & Schmal, M. (1974). *Art therapy: A bibliography.* Rockville, MD: National Institute of Mental Health.

Green, B., Wehling, C., & Talsky, J. (1987). Group art therapy as an adjunct to treatment for chronic outpatients. *Hospital and Community Psychiatry, 38,* 988-991.

Hanes, K. (1982). *Art therapy and group work: An annotated bibliography.* Westport, CT: Greenwood Press.

Huff, D. (1954). *How to lie with statistics.* New York, NY: W.W. Norton.

Isaac, S., & Michael, W. B. (1981). *Handbook in research and evaluation* (2nd ed.). San Diego, CA: Edits Publishers.

Miller, A. (Ed.). (1972). *The social psychology of psychological research.* New York, NY: The Free Press, Collier-Macmillan.

Moore, R. (1981). *Art therapy in mental health.* Literature survey No. 3. Rockville, MD: National Institute of Mental Health.

Rosenberg, M. (1965). *Society and the adolescent self-image.* Princeton, NJ: Princeton University.

Tyler, L. (1978). *Individuality: Human possibilities and personal choice in the psychological development of men and women.* San Francisco, CA: Jossey-Bass.

Wadeson, H., & Carpenter, W. (1976). Subjective experience of acute schizophrenia. *Schizophrenia Bulletin, 2,* 302-316.

Willems, E., & Raush, H. (Eds.). (1969). *Naturalistic viewpoints in psychological research.* New York, NY: Holt, Rinehart, & Winston.

SOME SPECIFIC RECOMMENDATIONS FOR ART THERAPY RESEARCH

Linda Gantt, PhD, A.T.R.

1. Select suitable models for research—The experimental designs used in the physical sciences and in laboratory psychology are not the only research models which can be applied to art therapy problems. Art history, linguistics, and anthropology offer suitable alternative research methods and designs.

2. Emphasize structure as well as meaning—Studying the "meaning" of particular symbols or pictures is only one part of art therapy research. Structural or formal aspects (such as the use of space or degree of integration) deserve equal attention.

3. Examine and expand our vocabulary—The terms we have borrowed from other disciplines may or may not be suitable for our use. If we lack descriptive terms, we should develop them as needed so that we have a workable common vocabulary.

4. Write more careful descriptions—Our writing skills should be polished so that we can make more thoughtful and accurate statements about the art. For example, "creative" and "expressive" are words we use loosely and often inappropriately.

5. Develop a taxonomy—A classification system based on structural or formal similarities will help us sort out the characteristics which are of greatest interest and importance.

6. Study the effects of cultural and social factors on our clients' art—Art is not produced in a vacuum. We need to be able to sort out learned behavior from psychodynamic material.

7. Publish more primary material—The greater the number of pictures in published work, the more possibilities we have for future studies.

8. Look at the influence of time on art—Art should be studied both from a diachronic (across time) and a synchronic (at the same time) perspective.

9. Determine what aspects of art are the most subject to change—Certain features of art may change more rapidly than others and thus may be better indicators of a psychological state than a more enduring personality trait.

10. Establish better retrieval systems on both an individual and a national basis—Most art therapists have no systematic way of recording, filing, and retrieving pictures for comparative purposes. A slide collection of artwork (such as those used by art historians) with a computerized listing of various structural and symbolic characteristics would be an invaluable source for study.

11. Examine our individual and collective biases—Biases come in many forms (individual, cultural, philosophical) and are perhaps the greatest impediment to careful, systematic work.

12. Make a critical examination of the "received wisdom"—Many statements are offered as truisms without question. We need to specify whether such statements are based on one person's clinical impression or a carefully controlled study.

13. Participate in joint research projects—Art therapists who work in similar facilities could collaborate on ideas for research projects.

Part II

BASICS OF RESEARCH

AATA's second Research Chair expressed goals which are still pertinent, especially coming from a man who left his imprint firmly as an advocate of sound research in art therapy: "We are pleased to offer our thoughts on an issue close to all of us: attempting to define our discipline. To do so we will suggest what the outer limits of art therapy ought to be. We hope some of you share our ideas, but more than that we hope our ideas give rise to debate. It is not lost on us that this symposium initiates the professsional-scientific segment of the Association's Fifth Annual Convention. Accordingly, we hope that our ideas are provocative and the discussion lively."

Bernard I. Levy (1980, p. 3). Introduction, Symposium: Integration of divergent points of view in art therapy. In E. Ulman & C. Levy. (Eds.). *Art therapy viewpoints*. New York, NY: Schocken Books.

Chapter 4

MINIMIZING BIAS IN ART THERAPY DATA

Cathy Malchiodi, MA, A.T.R.

The effect of bias on research design, methodology, and interpretation of data is extremely important. The term *bias* can refer to many things, but is often used synonymously with the term *experimental bias*. This type of bias refers to problems in the way research is constructed or conducted. For example, when subject groups are formed on some basis other than random assignment, there may be a bias in the way the subjects were selected (sometimes referred to as sampling bias). Bias may also exist in the instrument (projective drawing task, questionnaire, etc.) used in the research to measure a response; for example, the instrument may not be accurate or appropriately standardized. Thus, the instrument itself brings its own bias into the design and can affect the results of the experimental design.

There are many texts in the social and behavioral sciences, anthropology, and related fields that explain these types of bias; the intent of this brief chapter is not to repeat what is discussed in detail in these texts. There are, however, additional types of bias that are equally important, yet less frequently discussed. These are aspects of personal bias that are often overlooked and are key to how we derive answers to the questions we are asking in art therapy research.

Before beginning any type of research, it is extremely important to consider exactly how we "know" the things we think we know. In other words, how do we arrive at our assumptions in order to develop research questions and how do we formulate answers to these questions? Helmstadter (1970) identified some common methods of knowing that researchers use to develop research questions and derive answers. He observes that tenacity, intuition, authority, the rationalistic method, and the empirical method are commonly called used to develop and answer research questions. Some additional methods that can be included in that list are personal experience, tradition, and documentation. These methods of knowing can bring strength to a research design, but also are sources of bias when relied upon too heavily.

Everyone will agree that **tenacity** is necessary for finding the answer to any difficult question. It is probably a good characteristic in a researcher, for the ability to stick to the quest and long-term goals is, in part, what makes good research achievable. However, tenacity can be less helpful when we hang onto a belief so strongly that we miss learning something new. If we are overly tenacious, we naturally exclude the possibility of gaining new knowledge that may be right in front of us. For example, when looking for a particular characteristic in a series of art products, another characteristic which was not previously considered may become evident if the researcher is open to new input. In formal research, *ex post facto* designs allow the researcher to look at aspects of the results that were not included in the original hypotheses. However, in order to use this type of design, we must be willing to let go of previous assumptions in order to re-evaluate results from a different standpoint.

Tenacity seems to be closely linked with **tradition**, the handing down of information and beliefs from one generation to another. Tradition is strong in the field of art therapy; for example, psychoanalytic influences have had a strong impact on how art therapy has been taught and practiced. Also, it seems to be a tradition in the field of art therapy to ask clients to do certain tasks such as a house-tree-person drawing or a scribble, not only because there is written information on these drawing tasks, but also because early practitioners did it this way.

Some art therapists argue that our tenacity to adhere to old traditions in research may preclude us from exploring new paradigms that would enhance our understanding of art expression and process (Junge, 1989). Sometimes tenacity is rooted in our needs to please or satisfy others who would wish us to do research in a certain way or by specific rules. On the other hand, if we tenaciously believe that we cannot learn statistics or that numbers always misrepresent the truth, an opportunity to learn some useful information may also be lost, and we may find ourselves biased to techniques that can be used to acquire additional knowledge. Art therapy educators, in particular, must be aware that students need a variety of options to do thesis research, not one paradigm that is favored by the instructor.

Helmstadter also mentions that individuals who are perceived as **authorities** are a popular source of knowledge among researchers. A good example of a perceived authority in contemporary society are the media.

However, most of us realize that what we are told on the television news or through newspapers is not always true and often is presented with a particular slant. When writing a research proposal, thesis, or dissertation, we often rely on similar authorities such as texts and scholarly journals for substantiation of a hypothesis. A review of relevant literature to support the idea we want to research is usually required as an early chapter of a research thesis or dissertation. However, as with other media, texts and articles also provide a particular perspective of the author. Some authors may openly state that they have a particular bias in the way they view things, but others may not be as forthcoming about their perspective or how they derived the information presented.

Additionally, in every profession there are people who are recognized as authorities in the field because of their achievements, work, and/or writings. The latter seems to be particularly effective in elevating one to a place of authority, even though anyone who really wants to be published can usually find a publisher to print his or her work, regardless of quality. For these reasons, when using the published work of others to substantiate one's search for answers, it is important to find out as much as possible about the authority in terms of his/her expertise with the topic (education and training) as well as the standards the publisher uses to review manuscripts.

Documentation is obviously linked closely to authority, in that books are considered authoritative in and of themselves. Academia heavily relies on books and publications and there is an edict well-known to all academicians to "publish or perish." This mandate to document produces a great deal of good information, but also may encourage publication of some information which is not so reliable, depending again on the circumstances under which it was published.

To understand and evaluate documents and their content requires patience and the ability to critically question that content. The document in which the information was published may also be considered because some books are printed in an unedited state or are self-published ("vanity press"). Some journals do not require that submissions be reviewed by an editorial board of professional peers. The term "peer review" refers to the process in which an article is critically examined by others with expertise in the topic area; this procedure usually, although not always, involves blind review (the reviewers do not know who the author is) to eliminate any bias the reviewers may have about the author. Most major journals in many professional fields use this process to insure quality and eliminate subjectivity from their publications. Also, the rate of acceptance of submissions by a particular journal may give some indication as to the scrutiny the articles have undergone by a peer review panel. When scanning the professional literature, the art therapy the art therapy researcher may want to check the journals to see if they meet such standards; such information may also be available from the reference or periodical librarian, or directly from the journal's editor.

An aspect of knowing particularly important to art therapists is **intuition**. Intuition is defined as *a priori* or metaphorical knowledge which is difficult to put into words; it is also referred to as "gut reaction." Intuition has been closely linked to creativity and art, and is a method of knowing common to the arts as well as art therapy. Certainly, intuition can be a good thing and it often leads to exciting research questions and discoveries. However, it is also potentially dangerous soil for personal bias, because of the amount of subjectivity involved.

Intuition partially arises from **personal experience**. The obvious problem with relying solely on personal experience in research is that the observations of one person are not considered generalizable. Many art therapists have relied heavily on narrative case studies, based largely on one person's observation and experience with a single subject. Although this approach teaches reporting skills, it does not encourage objectivity and does not adequately address bias. For these reasons, many researchers feel that subjectivity in the reporting process is a major drawback to the narrative case study (Rosal, 1989).

The strength of personal experience as a method of deriving knowledge is that it can provide a broader base of information than other methods. It is not as constricting as more quantitative methods and often provides the researcher with rich data on many aspects of the subject being studied. This is particularly important to art therapy research where the investigator is examining cumulative aspects of an art product or multi-faceted responses to therapeutic intervention. There are specific approaches to case study research, such as the personologic, which do rely heavily on the personal experiences of one person to derive answers (Shontz, 1985); anthropological methods of research also address ways of more objectively dealing with personal experience, both from the standpoint of the researcher and the subject. When such methods are used, at least some bias is consciously addressed and subjectivity is reduced.

Lastly, Helmstadter observes that rationalistic and empirical methods are popular ways of knowing, particularly with scientists. Although he observes these methods to be more stable, there is still a great deal of subjectivity possible as well. Deductive reasoning, the bedrock of rationalistic knowing, can be flawed in major or minor premises and resultant conclusions. The empirical method, which is currently the most highly valued way of conducting research, is not without problems either; in addition to experimental bias, empirically based research designs can limit the richness of data derived, thus affecting the results.

Conclusion

Bias is ubiquitous in research (as well as in life), but we can eliminate a great deal of it through careful self-examination, questioning the sources of our assumptions and the assumptions of others. Seeking other professionals (not only art therapists, but also social scientists, anthropologists, special educators, etc.) who are well-versed in research design can also help, both in experimental and nonexperimental areas. Such consultation can provide a necessary reality check on biases we may be blind to in our methodology and interpretation. However, regardless of how hard we try to be unbiased in conducting and discussing outcomes of our research, we all bring some bias into the process. In order to come up with a question to explore, each of us must feel strongly about some belief in order to want to take the time to find out the truth about it through the lengthy process of research. In this sense, bias seems to be a good thing, for it is personal bias that provides the momentum necessary to commit ourselves to an assumption we wish to explore.

Above all, it is important to realize that research is a way to relate the truth, not a way to prove that one thing is better than another. As art therapists, we have often felt the need to prove the efficacy of our methods to other professionals; for this reason, we may need to more closely examine the biases we may bring to our research. When we see research as a way to find the truth, we can immediately begin to eliminate the biases that each of us brings to a particular question we want to answer.

References

Helmstader, G. (1970). *Research concepts in human behavior*. New York, NY: Appleton-Century Crofts.

Junge, M. (1989). The heart of the matter. *The Arts in Psychotherapy, 16,* 77-78.

Rosal, M. (1989). Master's papers in art therapy—Narrative or research case studies? *The Arts in Psychotherapy, 16,* 71-76.

Shontz, F. (1985). A personologic approach for health psychology research. *American Behavioral Scientist, 28*(4), 510-524.

Chapter 5

ETHICS IN RESEARCH WITH HUMAN SUBJECTS

Nancy Knapp, PhD, A.T.R.

Research with human subjects is not a spectator sport; it is a complex, hands-on experience with its own set of rules, expectations, and potential pitfalls. All guidelines applicable to sound research of any type are implicit in research with people; additionally an imperative for sound, ethical human interactions exists. Research goals bring additional priorities, dilemmas, and strictures—complications which art therapists may not have been trained to confront and which may seem alien to their temperamental preferences. The label "experiment" may seem unnecessary and even evocative of Dr. Frankenstein. However, when a drawing procedure is used in original research, even if it has been previously used many times, it is considered experimental and must be used in compliance with experimental guidelines.

This chapter focuses on the ways in which the inclusion of human subjects influences research for art therapy. It provides an historical overview of ethical principles and regulatory mechanisms as well as their current role throughout the research process. Expectations are discussed within the framework of American Art Therapy Association (AATA) guidelines and American Psychological Association (APA) Ethical Principles for research with human subjects. Specific examples will be provided with emphasis on art products as the extension of the human subject.

Background

In the fourth edition of the *Comprehensive Textbook of Psychiaty*, Bernal y del Rio (1985) stated that the word *ethics* did not even appear in the first edition in 1967. Similarly, Webb commented that early guidelines now read more like "urging toward good manners than firm ethical prescriptions" (Webb, et al 1981, p. 144). One product of this was that in the early enthusiasm of learning about human behavior, a researcher could study conditioning of fear, rage, and love by borrowing a child from a foundling home as Watson did with baby Albert (Watson & Raynor, 1920) or could decide almost unilaterally to use a "captive" group such as a class of students or an institutionalized population as subjects for an experimental procedure. Extreme misuse of human subjects, such as practiced by the Nazi regime and in the withholding of treatment in Tuskegee to facilitate study of the natural course of syphilis (Annual Report of the Surgeon General, 1935, 1936, 1937), rightly elicited denunciations and ultimately led to reform. A measured attempt to quantify the risk/benefit ratio of such processes as psychosurgery led Congress to enact the National Research Act in 1974. This amendment to the Public Health Service Act was the first federal legislation aimed at preventing abuse in research with humans.

Paradoxically, other questions were unexplored because of injunctions against using human beings as subjects, perhaps in the same tradition that made it a criminal offense for Renaissance artists to study human anatomy by using cadavers. Research has become more valid and less intrusive, not because of the change in laws or ethical awareness but because of continued advances in noninvasive, low-risk techniques which provide exact diagnosis previously available only from post mortem examinations. John, et al (1988) cited the increased accuracy in differential classification in brain research with techniques such as magnetic resonance imaging and their potential use in psychiatric diagnosis and research as our understanding of the human brain increases.

The definition of ethical practice may shift with ever-changing priorities just as the AIDS crisis has precipitated conflict between the injunctions of traditional methods of research and the acute need for action (Baum & Nesselhof, 1988). In any event, experimental use of human subjects will and should continue to be an issue.

Issues with Specific Populations

All research with human subjects must be well controlled, but certain populations including infants, children, minors, and persons who are senile, psychotic, mentally retarded, or irrecoverably brain damaged require particular protection. An equitable pursuit of facts requires equitable inclusion of subjects, equitably studied; therefore, determining the criteria for choosing human subjects to study is a crucial decision. In an extension of this, Cayleff the researcher first to understand her/himself and his/her relationship with subjects, especially women, racial or ethnic minorities, lesbians, and gays.

Casas, Ponterotto, and Guiterrez (1984) reviewed the process of ethical issues relative to research with racial and ethnic minority groups and found that, although awareness has increased since 1960, racial and ethnic minorities continue to be misunderstood because of research flawed by biased paradigms, anecdotal or speculative literature, a tendency to zero in on isolated variables, attempts to formulate simplistic causal relationships, a disregard of heterogeneity between and within racial and ethnic minority groups, and the use of sample populations which are easily accessible but not representative.

Sherif (1987) is among many who have identified problematic issues in research by men about women and the assumption that a person's gender is an independent variable. In addition to facing their own biases, Ibrahim and Arredondo (1986) encouraged researchers to consider the participants' language and sociocultural experiences, and recommended obtaining consultation of experts from the group under study, not only as an ethical practice but as good scientific practice.

Aged subjects are frequently the topic of research, at times because of their accessibility but more recently because of concerns concomitant with "the greying of America." Cassel, et al. (1987) reviewed the history and concepts of research with geriatric subjects, and suggested three basic principles for justification of research with that population. They are startling in their simplicity, but apparently need to be articulated: respect for the persons, beneficence, and justice.

Regulating Factors

Layers of regulations now preclude the cavalier use of human subjects. A measured attempt to quantify the risk-benefit ratio of experimental procedures led Congress to enact the National Research Act in 1974. A National Commission for the Protection of Human Subjects of Biomedical and Behavioral Research was formed, based upon needs cited by the Belmont Report. As an amendment to the Public Health Service Act the guidelines became the first federal legislation aimed at preventing abuse in research with humans. Individual state requirements may have additional strictures in research with people; for example, there is a variation in whether or not conservators or legal guardians are allowed to consent to experimental procedures for anyone who is incompetent to sign. Custom may establish a part of a treatment plan, which is then regulated and reviewed as such.

When research is conducted by art therapists under the auspices of institutions with Human Subjects Committees, their guidelines for approval and monitoring research will be paramount. Institutions, in turn, must conform to governmental agencies, their accrediting or licensing bodies, professional requirements, and the dictates specific to their individual missions. A five-member board is required by the Department of Health and Human Services to review all research to confirm that the design is sound, that the anticipated benefits outweigh the risks involved, and that the patients or subjects give informed consent. The board also reviews proposals for validity and subsequently monitors experiments for compliance to guidelines. If it appears that a compromise must be made between human values and scientific pursuit, justification for the compromise must be well-established.

Research guidelines from AATA have become formalized as motivation for research by art therapists has increased. These and other professional considerations are part of the hierarchy of decision-making in all areas of research; AATA guidelines are in general consistent with and are subsumed under the regulations described above. Because of the relatively new entrance of art therapists into the research arena and the adjunctive status under which some art therapists work, research may require specific sponsorship by a physician or other senior staff person. Politics, therefore, might be an additional issue. Potential contradictions or conflicts may be checked with the AATA Research Committee, although where parallel guidelines exist, good practice suggests following the more conservative restrictions.

Appendix I is that portion of the Code of Ethics for Art Therapists which most directly relates to research with human subjects. Membership in the American Psychological Association (APA) constitutes a commitment to adherence to the Ethical Principles of Psychologists (American Psychological Association, 1981). Principle 9, which comprises Appendix II, provides 10 specific standards governing the conduct of research with human participants. These are consistent with all current regulations and guidelines described in this chapter. Appendix III is the Experimental Subject's Bill of Rights, based upon federal law.Research done under the umbrella of academic programs may have additional regulations. It is clear that master's level research will have different requirements from doctoral research, but standards for the use of human subjects are consistent. Differences between the student's academic considerations and priorities of the host medical, psychiatric, or educational settings have the potential for complicating research. Understanding the parameters of each component, as well as diplomatic consideration from the researcher and committee members, will facilitate the conjoint process. Again, if differing standards exist, it is prudent to follow the more rigorous protocol.

Barber (1985) described effects on research from the experimenter's personal attributes, level of sophistication, training, and orientation. Every facet of the research, its conception, the choice of target population and the individual subjects, implementation of the design, and emphasis in interpretation of and responsibility for the findings is influenced by the individual researcher. As a given, these *a priori* conditions themselves have been the subject of research and generate additional ways to study human behavior. For example, Yagoda and Wolfson (1964) found that subjects tended to draw more mustachioed figures when the examiner was mustachioed. The ubiquitous quality of the researcher's individuality may assert itself in each area of his or her research and should be recognized, or even capitalized upon. However, a researcher with a terminal illness, for example, can hardly be expected to be objective about subjects with terminal illnesses. Any bias in research has the potential to devalue both the subjects and the study, regardless of the researcher's status.

Considerations for Design

The ethical guidelines and regulations outlined above begin to be manifested from the inception of all research with human beings, no matter how unintrusive that research may seem. The process of designing the study becomes an exercise in anticipating human foibles and in projecting the worst possible scenario which might occur during even the most benign art experience. No consequence is too improbable to contemplate because it is possible that inadvertently the worst may actually occur. For example, research on unexpressed grief may precipitate an unexpected cathartic expression of sorrow; or research about anger may elicit threatening behavior. Neither the subject nor the researcher should be put at risk.

Initial plans should incorporate both adequate protective safeguards and alternate procedures appropriate for both the research population and control subjects. The safeguards are simply preventive measures which are part of sound research methodology, including clear explanations of all steps and rationale in the study. Alternate procedures include responses for subjects for whom the art elicits an inordinate reaction and for those who seem not to react at all. In this writer's experience, control subjects who actually scoffed when being informed that drawing might stir up unexpected feelings, became tearful when doing the relatively structured House-Tree-Person drawing. Some subjects spontaneously shared information which was more appropriatein a therapy session than in a research investigation. Tissues and empathy should be part of the researcher's supplies. Alternately, impaired subjects simply may be unable to respond to the expectations of the research protocol, but should not be abandoned mid-process, even if no process is evident. The research design should describe plans to provide closure for individual subjects via a simple art or verbal interaction, even though the subject may be eliminated from the research *per se*.

Criteria for Human Subjects Committee

Once the study proposal is formulated, gaining approval from a Human Subjects Committee or Institutional Review Board may be time-consuming and discouraging and provide a crucial, if humbling, lesson in the rigors of research. Early contact with this committee, awareness of its schedule and priorities, rigorous conformation to its guidelines, and a proactive ethical stance will minimize frustration and provide preventive insurance against catastrophe for the art therapist. During the process of seeking permission to do research, art therapists who previously advocated the potency of the art process may suddenly find themselves minimizing its power as a noninvasive and harmless procedure which should be quickly approved with little scrutiny. The use of art cannot simultaneously be innocuous and powerful; part of the initial challenge for art therapists in describing research with human subjects is to face the fact that the process of drawing may stir up surprising memories or unwanted feelings, and this must be articulated in the Informed Consent.

Informed Consent

The Informed Consent description is one of the research components which must pass scrutiny by the Human Subjects Committee. Specific information, written in layman's language, must be incorporated in the consent form. Standard issues include: a fair explanation of the reasons for the research and explicit permission to ask questions; an account of the procedure and methods which will take place; a description of potential benefits or risks which might reasonably result; a description of alternative procedures which might exist; permission for the subject to withdraw without prejudice or penalty at any time during the procedure; a guarantee of confidentiality; provision for care in case of injury during the research and an explanation of whose responsibility it is to deal with potentially adverse reactions; a description of how the results might be used; and information about how to contact the principal investigator. What it must not contain is even a vague implication that the subject must waive the right to sue.

Appendix IV is a sample of Informed Consent for specific research. Such forms must be reviewed with each subject or his or her parent, legal guardian, or conservator prior to research. Subjects are entitled to a copy of it along with the Human Subject's Bill of Rights. Research which involves deception or manipulation has ramifications which are both scientific and ethical. For some research, full disclosure would contaminate results. Justification for such research must be addressed in the design and finally in debriefing. An art therapist who is looking for a spontaneously drawn element in pictures would obviously not want to specify that to the subjects; the research methodology can still be described in a general but congruent way without influencing responses.

Criteria for Subjects

The researcher should understand the target population well in order to establish the criteria for individual subjects within that population. Recruitment of subjects will vary with such qualities as accessibility, but should always be free of any element of coercion. This should be carefully weighed, especially when the researcher has a dual role, such as also being the subject's therapist, teacher, or friend.

The crucial step of defining criteria leads directly to the results; when there are two groups in a study, the controls or normals must be as crisply defined as the other subjects. For example, if comparing drawings from people with head trauma, prior testing should insure that control subjects are free from any similar injury. More subjects should be recruited than are needed because of potential attrition due to confounding characteristics which appear in screening procedures before the research. For example, a control subject claiming no psychiatric history was eliminated from a study when it came out that he had "forgotten" to describe episodes which included extensive electroshock treatment. Had he been included as a control subject, his art would have had impact on the study findings, both as being thought of as characteristic of the controls' art and in contrast to the subjects' art.

Reviewing the Informed Consent with subjects or their agents may also eliminate some participants, although Smith and Berard (1982) found that human subjects judge research in different ways from Human Research Committees. In 1967, Kelman found that deception in research seemed commonplace enough to be thought of as the norm. One spouse/conservator signing a consent for his wife claimed unequivocally that she would not draw but that it was probably harmless to try. He then asked suspiciously, "What are you really going to do? There can't be this much fuss only for drawings!" Other guardians may feel a desperate need to include their family members in all possible research, although the designated subject may choose not to cooperate, despite the signed consent. It helps the researcher to be well enough grounded with the intent and safeguards of a study that the vicissitudes of human reactions can be dealt with evenly.

The family of the human subject also merits some attention. They may be too concerned or intrusive; they may press for instant feedback; they may seem overly casual about appointments and research requirements; or they may inflate the potential benefits. They may simply need to express their concerns. One distraught spouse told a researcher "If you really want to research dementia, you should just spend 24 hours at our house."

Ownership of Results

One dilemma unique to research with art is the ownership of the art product. Art therapists are not strangers to the conflictual issues when the patient/artist seeks to destroy the art which we long to study, protect, and preserve. This tension has been described in a number of poignant vignettes by art therapists; Kramer's account of Martin (Kramer, 1971, pp. 41-43) provided a model of the importance of honest exploration and personal insight when looking at the conflict which can exist between the gratification of the clinician's needs and those of the persons with whom we are working. Henley (1989) addressed related concerns in his reaction to Nadia, revisited after extensive exploration of her anomalous artistic ability.

Ultimately, of course, a case can be made for the creator's ownership of any drawing. Although one person's pictures are another person's data, art products may have more implications than most other data, and they may also be more difficult to treat anonymously. Further, artists who are enamored by their own work may not want it to be anonymous; paranoid subjects may not want their art to be used at all, and acting out subjects may destroy their pictures. The art therapist may find that this aspect of research precipitates major philosophical conflicts between artistic, therapeutic, and research agendas.

Fortunately, color photocopying and other duplication processes have facilitated compromises when the subjects want their artwork. The study protocol should include preventive planning and appropriate responses for such contingencies.

Art from the Public Domain

Research on art from people in the public domain constitutes another arena which is a correlate of the use of human subjects. Examples which illustrate the variations on this theme include Jung's initial public diagnosis of Picasso as schizophrenic after seeing his art show in 1932 (Jung, 1978); the publication of the psychological drawings of Adolph Eichmann in the *New York Times* (Selzer, 1977); Don Jones's work with Billy Milligan (Jones, 1981); Pollock's presentation of the mourning process of Kathe Kollwitz (Pollock, 1983); and Barnett's research about de Kooning as a possible victim of Alzheimer's disease (Barnett, 1989). Speculations about the art and person of Van Gogh or O'Keefe seem almost obligatory for people interested in either art or psychology. No doubt the seductive quality of art will continue to invite both thoughtless and scholarly attention. There also is little doubt that lively debate will continue as was elicited by Wilson's presentation about Nevelson (Wilson, 1985). Art will continue to be seen as an extension of the human being who created it. It may often be subjected to careless remarks and hyperbole, but it merits responsible attention from art therapists.

Perhaps the tension between endorsement and objection for the public study of art as an extension of the nonconsenting artist is similar to reservations about studies with cadavers as well as resistance to a potential challenge of popular views. Without informed consent and without personal interviews, what guidelines are appropriate for research on artists and art in the public domain? Our profession is built upon the assumption that an art product is a concrete sample of behavior which can provide a quantifiable and qualitative view of the person who produced it. Art therapists as prospective researchers in this arena have an opportunity to follow Wilson's urging to "consider the unique opportunities and obligations each individual case presents for making ethical decisions" (Wilson, 1987, p. 79). Thus, Junge's research on Kahlo and Arbus (Junge, 1988) presented both personal and universal understanding; Warick and Warick (1987) and Landgarten (1990) each revisited Munch to supplement the vast literature about him with their perspectives as art therapists; Haeseler (1988) is among those who have presented sensitive approaches to the understanding of "outsider art."

Reason and Rowen (1981) prescribed "new paradigm research." Although not technically "new," their advocation of humanistic qualities, sensitivity, and application of realistic safeguards in the experimental use of human subjects is well-suited to research by art therapists and provides a philosophic supplement to the technical guidelines of APA's Principle 9, both in the letter and the spirit of the law.

Developmentally, the field of art therapy is at the stage where its priorities and its ability can match what Wadeson (1980) predicted: to refine, modify, and adapt the methodologies traditionally employed in the behavioral sciences to the peculiar problems posed by the combination of human subjects and art. Day and Kwiatkowska (1975), and Ulman and Levy (Ulman, 1975; Ulman & Levy, 1975) published their research with human subjects in 1975. Since then our literature has grown in size and sophistication. The zeal which was demonstrated initially continues to be crucial in order to provide the catalyst and the fuel for pursuing our research goals. Within the strictures of sound design and an orientation which values people as humans beings first and then as subjects, our zeal will help us to understand each other and to elevate our profession.

References

American Psychological Association. (1981). *Ethical Principles of Psychologists*. Washington, DC: Author.

Annual Report of the Surgeon General. (1936, 1937, 1938). Public Health Services of the United States. Washington, DC: US Government Printing Office.

Barber, T. X. (1985). *Pitfalls in human research: Ten pivotal points*. New York, NY: Pergamon Press.

Barnett, C. (1989, November). The conundrum of Willem de Kooning. *Art and Antiques*, pp. 62-73.

Baum, A., & Nesselhof, S. (1988). Psychological research and the prevention, etiology and treatment of AIDS. *American Psychologist, 43*(11), 900-906.

Bernal y del Rio, V. (1985). Psychiatric ethics and confidentiality. In H. I. Kaplan, D. Freedman, & B. J. Sadock (Eds.) *Comprehensive Textbook of Psychiatry* (4th ed.). Baltimore, MD: Williams & Wilkins.

Casas, J. M., Ponterotto, J. G., & Gutierrez, J. M. (1986). An ethical indictment of counseling research and training: The cross-cultural perspective. *Journal of Counseling and Development, 64*, 347-349.

Cassel, C. K., Meier, D., & Traines, M. (1986). Selected bibliography of recent articles in ethics and geriatrics. *Journal of the American Geriatric Society, 34*(5), 399-409.

Cayleff, S. E. (1986). Ethical issues in counseling gender, race, and culturally distinct groups. *Journal of Counseling and Development, 64*, 345-346.

Day, J., & Kwiatkowska, H. (1975). The psychiatric patient and his well sibling: A comparison through their art products. In E. Ulman and P. Dachinger (Eds.), *Art therapy in theory and practice*. New York, NY: Schocken Books.

Haeseler, M. P. (1988). Outsider art: A point of view. *American Journal of Art Therapy, 26*(3), 83-88.

Henley, D. (1989). Nadia revisited: A study into the nature of regression in the autistic savant syndrome. *Art Therapy: Journal of the American Art Therapy Association, 6*(2) 43-56.

Ibrahim, F. A., & Arredondo, P. M. (1986). Ethical standards for cross-cultural counseling: Counselor preparation, practice, assessment, and research. *Journal of Counseling and Development, 64*, 349-352.

John, E. R., Prichep, L.S., Fridman, J. & Easton, P. (1988). Neurometrics: Computer-assisted differential diagnosis of brain dysfunctions. *Science, 239*, 162-169.

Jones D. (1982). Creative integration of a multiple personality: Art therapy techniques and theory [Abstract]. In A. DiMaria, E. Kramer, & I. Rosner (Eds.). Art therapy: A bridge between worlds. *The Proceedings of the 12th Annual Conference of the American Art Therapy Association* (pp. 31-32). Falls Church, VA: American Art Therapy Association.

Jung, C. G. (1978). *The spirit in man, art and literature* [R.F.C.Hull, transl.]. Bollingen Series XX. Princeton, NJ: Princeton University.

Junge, M. (1988). An inquiry into women and creativity including two case studies of the artists Frida Kahlo and Diane Arbus. *Art Therapy: Journal of the American Art Therapy Association 5*(3) 79-93.

Kelman, H. C. (1967). Human use of human subjects: The problem of deception in social psychological experiments. *Psychological Bulletin, 67*(1), I-II.

Kramer, E. (1971). *Art as therapy with children*. New York, NY: Schocken Books.

Landgarten, H. (1990). Edvard Munch: An art therapist's viewpoint. *Art Therapy: Journal of the American Art Therapy Association 7*(1), 11-16.

Pollock, G. H. (1983). The mourning-liberation process and creativity: The case of Kathe Kollwitz. In A. Di Maria, E. Kramer, & E. Roth (Eds.), Art therapy: Still growing. *The Proceedings of 13th Annual Conference of the American Art Therapy Association* (pp. 9-17). Alexandria, VA: American Art Therapy Association.

Reason, P., & Rowan, J. (1981). *Human inquiry: A sourcebook of new paradigm research*. Chichester: John Wiley.

Selzer, M. (1977). The murderous mind. *The New York Times Magazine*, 27.

Sherif, C. W. (1987). Bias in psychology. In S. Harding (Ed.), *Feminism and methodology* (Chapter 4). Bloomington and Indianapolis, IN: Indiana University Press.

Smith, C., & Berard, S. (1982). Why are human subjects less concerned about ethically problematic research than human subjects committees? *Journal of Applied Social Psychology, 12*(3), 209-221.

Ulman, E., & Levy, B. (1975). An experimental approach to the judgment of psychopathology from paintings. In E. Ulman & P. Dachinger (Eds.), *Art therapy in theory and practice*. New York, NY: Schocken.

Ulman, E. (1975). A new use of art in psychiatric analysis. In E. Ulman & P. Dachinger (Eds.), *Art therapy in theory and practice*. New York, NY: Schocken.

Wadeson, H. (1980). *Art psychotherapy*. New York, NY: John Wiley & Sons.

Warick, L., & Warick E. (1987). Edvard Munch: The creative search for self. In M. Mathews Gedo (Ed.), *Psychoanalytic Perspectives of Art* (pp. 275-304). Hillsdale, NJ: Analytic Press.

Watson, J.B., & Raynor, R. (1920). Conditioned emotional reaction. *Journal of Experimental Psychology, 3*, 1-14.

Webb, E. J., et al. (1981). *Nonreactive measures in the social sciences.* (2nd ed.). Boston, MA: Houghton Mifflin.

Wilson, L. (1987). Confidentiality in art therapy: An ethical dilemma. *American Journal of Art Therapy, 25*(3), 75-80.

Wilson, L. (1985). Louise Nevelson, the star and her set: Vicissitudes of identification. In M. Mathews Gedo (Ed.). *Psychoanalytic Perspectives of Art* (pp. 225-240). Hillsdale, NJ: Analytic Press.

Yagoda, G., & Wolfson, W. (1964). Examiner influence on projective test responses. *Journal of Clinical Psychology, 20*, 389.

Chapter 6

TYPES OF RESEARCH

Sr. Dorothy McLaughlin, RSM, EdD, A.T.R.
Richard Carolan, MA, A.T.R.

The purpose of research is to be able to make valid and reliable statements concerning the relationship between variables. The goal of efficient research is to understand, predict, and control the phenomena examined while minimizing error. Error is a measure of the gap between what one predicts will happen and what actually occurs. This is the orientation of the scientist as researcher; and it is an approach which the art therapist can develop in order to enhance knowledge of the effectiveness of art therapy, and in order to communicate that knowledge to those with other theoretical orientations. Research is an attempt to establish facts. Facts are the groundwork for understanding and agreements; facts, however, are only temporal truths. It is imperative that the art therapist interested in research be familiar with the groundwork of scientific research. It is also important that the art therapist continue to explore the art of research, which has more to do with the awakening of possibilities.

Theoretical Perspectives

The two major theoretical perspectives that influence researchers in the social sciences are **positivism** and a perspective described as **phenomenological**. These philosophies influence empirical and descriptive studies, respectively. Positivism looks at facts or causes objectively. This system sees perceptions as the basis of accurate understanding. The positivist uses questionnaires, inventories, and demography that can be statistically analyzed in order to develop a measure of relationship. According to Durkheim (1938) the social scientist is "to consider social facts as things" (p. 14). The positivist seeks facts and causes of social phenomena, "things" that exercise influence on people (Taylor & Bogdon, 1984, p. 1).

The second major theoretical perspective, described as phenomenological, seeks to understand the perceptions of others by examining their motives and beliefs as aspects of their actions. In the phenomenological view, how the individual experiences and understands his/her actions is of primary importance. Social phenomena are understood by entering into the experience as an actor would. The phenomenologist seeks understanding through in-depth interviewing, observation, and other methods that present descriptive data (Taylor & Bogdon, 1984). The phenomenologist strives to understand, on a personal level, the motives and beliefs that influence a person's actions.

Methods of Research

Evolving from these perspectives are two methods of classifying data: **quantitative**—an experimental method which uses control of variables (subjects, interventions, etc.), quasi-experimental method, paper and pencil "objective" tests, multivariate statistical analysis, sample surveys, etc.; and **qualitative**—which uses case studies, ethnology, in-depth interviews, and participant observations (Cook & Reichardt, 1979). Each of these methods, quantitative and qualitative, subscribes to a different paradigm or way of breaking down the complexity of reality into a world view. The quantitative paradigm has a positivistic, objective, hypothetical, deductive, outcome-oriented, and natural science world view. The qualitative paradigm has a phenomenological, inductive, holistic, subjective, process-oriented, and social anthropological world view (Cook & Reichardt, 1979).

Qualitative methodology seeks to collect descriptive data, people's own words and behavior. In art this includes allowing the individual's images to speak in and of themselves as opposed to being quantified and compared to a pre-established system. Art therapists relate more comfortably to the phenomenological perspective of qualitative methodology because of its person-process orientation. According to Wadeson (1980), "Much of the richness in communication through art expression may be lost when the integrated results of complex processes are reduced to a collection of quantifiable elements" (p. 330).

Art therapists are challenged by the quantitative method which requires a hypothetical, deductive, and outcome-oriented process. However, it is difficult to establish the validity and reliability of information and projections without the quantification of data into a system with which individual researchers can compare their findings.

Art therapists are encouraged to go beyond the psychodynamically oriented individual case study to experimentally based research in the natural sciences and in the social, anthropological sciences. Alternative models for research design may be drawn from art history, anthropology, and linguistics, which study human behavior and its products, namely artworks, cultures, cultural institutions, and language. These models elicit generalizations about what is probable in a group and allow the researcher to explain material after it has been produced. The deductive capabilities of natural science research go beyond the social sciences in allowing the researcher to predict (Gantt, 1986).

Despite the debate about the merits of each method mentioned, a combination of the two, quantitative and qualitative, may be best suited for the research needs of art therapists (Cook & Reichardt, 1979).

Types of Research

The basic types of research presented as a guide to art therapy research are as follows:

1. Systematic investigations aimed at understanding the relationship among variables in terms of the laws of logic

A variable is any trait, attribute, function, characteristic, or factor that can change or be different (Moore, 1983). This type of research involves correlational studies. Correlation refers to the joint relationship between (or among) two or more variables. Correlational techniques answer the questions: Is there a relationship between variable X and variable Y. If so, what is the degree and direction of that relationship? Pairs of observations on different groups are obtained and arranged in tabular form. The indexed degree of relationship is recorded (Neale & Liebert, 1986). Some examples of correlational studies are:

- Correlation of art assessment instruments with standardized instruments;
- Correlation of the forms of art renderings and different populations;
- Correlation of the content of different art expressions with different populations;
- Correlation between art expressions and different personality types;
- Correlation between changes in art expression and external events, such as medication dosage, life stress, etc.; and
- Correlation between art expression and course of psychiatric condition.

2. Systematic investigations aimed at predicting the value of one variable through its relationship with another variable

This type of research would be used in assessment studies such as intelligence and psychiatric diagnosis.

3. Systematic investigations aimed at measuring the control possible through manipulating one variable so that it will produce effects on other variables

This type of study involves outcome studies, measuring the effectiveness of an art therapy intervention. Research of this type includes:

a. Experimental Design: aimed at the how and why. The experimental design approach is essential to establish generalized principles. There are two distinguishing features of experimental research. The first is that the experimenter has manipulative control over the independent variables. Control can keep a variable from changing or it can cause it to change. The second feature is that the subjects must be randomly assigned to levels of the independent variable; they can also be paired (e.g., comparable groups).

b. Quasi-experimental Design: employs experimental units of analysis and manipulated variables without comparing groups formed by random assignment. This method involves one or more manipulated independent variables (as treatments) compared by considering subjects' performance on one or more dependent variables (outcome measures). Quasi-experimental design lacks random assignment.

c. Single-subject Design: suitable for evaluating treatments that are discrete or for responses that may reverse rapidly. The nature of single-subject research may cause it to produce data from which it is difficult to generalize. There are two common designs for this type of research: a reversal design which involves establishing a baseline, introducing treatment, allowing behavior to stabilize, taking another measurement of the baseline, finally removing the independent variable and taking another measure. A second design for single-subject research is the multibaseline design. This type of design is valuable when there is more than one type of behavior that the independent variable can be used to control. Multibaseline design is more rigorous than the case study and is often more feasible than an experimental group design. (Chapter 11 of this *Guide* describes the single-subject study in detail.)

d. Descriptive Study: answers the question "What exists?" Descriptive studies usually describe the present state of things. The types of descriptive research include: **correlational or analytic**, which describes the relationship between variables; **developmental**, which describes a process of development or trends over a period of time; and **predictive**, which describes the degree of relationship between variables with correlational coefficients expressed numerically. "Descriptive data are collected by administering questionnaires, interviewing subjects, observing events or by analyzing documentary sources" (Van Dalen, 1979, p. 285). When using the observational method for collecting data, it is required that interrater reliability be established. There are other concerns to be aware of in this type of study. McNiff (1987, p. 288) says,

> *Serious problems appear in research projects when researchers use highly subjective questionnaires, interviews and observations to collect data for quantification. These projects sometimes hide bias in scientific language and research jargon, giving the impression of authenticity. Questionnaires are particularly problematic in that they limit responsiveness of the subject, often forcing the respondent into dualisms created by the researcher.*

Quantitative studies contain descriptive data via their written or spoken words and observable actions (Neale & Liebert, 1986).

e. Case Study: is a method of studying the behavior of one individual in detail. The case study is the source of descriptive information and is used as evidence for or against theories (Neale & Liebert, 1986). A primary difficulty in case studies is that there is no basis for determining what the outcome would have been without the specific intervention. In addition, little attention is paid to the threats to external and internal validity or reliability. There is little verifiable evidence of which variable is causing or related to specific change. (See Chapter 11 on singlecase studies.)

f. Survey Study: refers to the frequency of an event or characteristic in the population at large. Since it would be too unwieldy to survey an entire population, researchers systematically draw a sample from it. After the frequency of the sample has been determined, the investigator may wish to generalize back to the population surveyed. Procedures related to sampling may be found in *Science and Behavior* (Neale & Liebert, 1986).

g. Historical Research: is the study of information from the past; the historical information is the datum which is interpreted in the study. This type of research may be of growing interest to art therapists since created images are concrete documents which in the future may be referred to in order to investigate a new hypothesis. The difficulty with this type of research has to do with establishing the authenticity of documents and the accurate interpretation of their meaning. Historical research studies policy or practice and is based on the scientific method, which requires factual objectivity. The steps in historical research include the collection of sources, criticism, and hypothesis. Primary sources are best, but sometimes secondary sources are necessary.

h. Behavioral Analysis: is a method of research used when the variables being studied are clearly behavioral. One difficulty with this approach is in establishing the validity and reliability of the observer. The observer must infer from his/her observations, and these inferences might be biased or inadequate. Once objective and accurate measurements of behavior are made, the data must be viewed and organized in a systematic, objective, and quantifiable manner. One aspect of this approach which may be of value to art therapists is the emphasis on operational definitions. Creating art renderings is a behavior, and there could be value in emphasizing and analyzing how one behaves in this process.

This review of types of research indicates the complexity of research methodology. Art therapists, like scientists and master artists, must learn the tools and facts of their trade. Various research methods outlined here are presented in greater detail elsewhere in the *Guide*.

References

Cook, T. D., & Reichardt, C. J. (1979). *Qualitative and quantitative methods in evaluation research*. Beverly Hills, CA: Saga Publications.

Durkheim, E. (1938). *The rules of sociological method*. New York, NY: The Free Press.

Gantt, L. (1986). Systematic investigation of art works: Some research models drawn from neighboring fields. *American Journal of Art Therapy, 24*, 111-118.

McNiff, S. (1987). Research and scholarship in the creative arts therapies. *Arts in Psychotherapy, 14*, 285-292.

Moore, Gary W. (1983). *Developing and evaluating educational research*. Glenview, IL: Scott, Foresman & Co.

Neale, J. M., & Liebert, R. M. (1986). *Science and behavior* (3rd ed.). Englewood Cliffs, NJ: Prentice-Hall.

Taylor, S.J., & Bogdon, R. (1984). *Introduction to qualitative research methods*. New York, NY: John Wiley & Sons.

Van Dalen, Deobald B. (1979). *Understanding educational research: An introduction* (4th ed.). New York: McGraw-Hill.

Wadeson, H. (1980). *Art psychotherapy*. New York, NY: John Wiley & Sons.

Part III

METHODOLOGIAL CHALLENGES SPECIFIC TO ART THERAPY RESEARCH

"Sometimes I wonder if it is possible for a really good art therapist to be genuinely interested in research. It seems to me that many of the interpersonal satisfactions available in clinical work are also present in those indirect service areas: . . . in teaching, in supervision, and in consultation. But research, even if it involves working with subjects in order to collect data, is less likely to be rewarding clinically. It is also rarely as flexible as any of the other roles, because of the necessary controls of important variables. Research allows creativity primarily in its design and analysis, but hardly ever in the actual implementation of the study. Yet there are a few art therapists who are good clinicians and who also enjoy designing and conducting research."

Judith Rubin (1984, p. 179). *The art of art therapy.*
New York: Brunner/Mazel.

Chapter 7

ILLUSTATIONS OF ART THERAPY RESEARCH

Marcia Rosal, PhD, A.T.R.

Theoretical Perspectives

Art therapists are busy conducting various types of research using a variety of methods and paradigms. This chapter presents an overview of the types of research which art therapists are using. The research is discussed by the methodology chosen by the art therapist. The intent is to provide the novice art therapy researcher with illustrations of the types of research which art therapists have conducted or with ideas for art therapy research which could be used for future inquiry. This overview is not intended to be exhaustive or comprehensive.

The illustrations are presented according to research methodology. The types of methodologies are presented from least complex to research frameworks requiring increasingly complex methodologies and paradigms. It is impossible within the context of this short chapter to illustrate all research methods. However, the major types of research are described elsewhere in the *Guide*.

Research Methodologies

Case Studies: Case studies are in-depth studies of an individual's behavior. In art therapy, case studies are traditionally about the effect of art therapy on a client. There are several art therapists who use the case study format including Cotton (1985) who described the art therapy process of a child with leukemia. Cotton first described the disease and then specific case background of the child prior to describing the art therapy sessions and the child's artwork. Subjective information about how the therapist viewed the therapy is often included in the study.

Survey Research: Surveys help art therapists uncover information which is important to the planning and practice of the field. Surveys are primarily questionnaires sent to a sample of a population from which information is needed.

A number of art therapists conducted research which provided the field with factual information about the profession through the use of survey research. For example, in Anderson and Landgarten (1974) Landgarten surveyed the human service agencies in the Los Angeles area. Landgarten's aim was to gauge these agencies' interest in art therapy and to gather information for placing practicum students. In addition, Landgarten wanted to find out which agencies had art therapists on staff and the job descriptions of any employed art therapists. From the information she gathered, Landgarten developed a description of the job market in the Los Angeles area. She repeated the survey 10 years later (1984). Armed with updated information, she described the changing job market in her area.

Art therapy surveys can also provide information about how art therapists use techniques and media with various populations. Marrion, Landell, and Bradley (1988) surveyed art therapists who work with sexually abused children. Information concerning treatments and interventions for this population was analyzed and described.

Descriptive Research: Art therapists use descriptive research formats to gather information to substantiate common thought and practice or to describe certain phenomena.

Using several theories as her base, Rhyne (1979) asked several subjects about their constructs of feeling states. The subjects drew 15 mind or feeling states and then were asked to describe their drawings according to specific criteria. Rhyne developed predictions or hypotheses about how individuals might draw the feeling states. Her predictions were based on assumptions which art therapists have held about how to interpret the meaning of various visual elements.

After analyzing the data, Rhyne was able to ascertain some universal aspects of how individuals draw particular feelings or mind states. For example, "fearful" is generally drawn with lines "pulling inward" with the image located "around the edges," and depression is drawn with a "downward movement." This information supported the assumptions which art therapists hold concerning the meaning of visual material.

Correlation Research: Correlation research examines the relationship between two variables. Rubin and Rubin (1988) published the results of their research exploring the relationship between graphic and verbal expression in young children. They wanted to find support for the hypothesis that a relationship exists between verbal and visual expression and that that relationship is positive and predictable. The children, ages three to six years, were asked to draw and then to talk about five topics including a person, a story, and a topic of their choice.

From their exploratory research, the researchers found that some relationships between verbal and visual thinking existed for certain tasks and topics, but that other relationships were not as strong. Rubin and Rubin concluded that the relationship between verbal and visual expression is complex and that further study of the relationship is warranted. In addition, they think their findings support the use of art to help children with their language deficits.

Assessment Research: In assessment studies, researchers are attempting to discover the predictive ability of a variable or a set of variables to assess or diagnose a particular disorder or problem profile. Art therapists use this type of research to support the use of graphic diagnostic techniques. For example, Cohen, Hammer, and Singer (1988) reported on research conducted with the Diagnostic Drawing Series (DDS).

The administration of the DDS was standardized for research purposes. Several art therapists participated in gathering the DDS from clients. The drawings of 239 cases and the diagnostic information [from the *Diagnostic and Statistical Manual*, 3rd Edition (DSM-III)] from two independent clinicians for each case, preferably psychiatrists, provided the data for the study. The researchers wanted to define the drawing characteristics which then could be used as indicators of a particular disorder. The analysis of the data supported that there are specific drawing characteristics which can be predictive of schizophrenia, depression, and dysthymia.

Outcome Studies: This type of research, often called treatment effectiveness research, uses experimental designs to study the power of a treatment or therapy to change behavior or to affect therapeutic change. Art therapists have used various research designs to evaluate their treatments for different populations. Three major outcome study designs are: (1) true experimental designs, (2) quasi-experimental designs, and (3) single-subject designs.

• **True experimental designs:** True experimental designs involve the randomization of subjects to therapy and control groups. Rosal (1985) randomly assigned 36 behavior-disordered children to one of three groups: (1) a cognitive art therapy group, (2) an unstructured art therapy group, and

(1) a cognitive art therapy group, (2) an unstructured art therapy group, and (3) a no treatment control group. The children were then tested before and after the treatment period on three measures including a classroom behavior checklist.

After collecting the data, the groups were compared with one another to determine which treatment(s) was the most effective for helping behavior-disordered children to change problem classroom behavior. Children in the two art therapy groups improved significantly more, in terms of their classroom behavior, than did the control group. There were no significant differences in effectiveness between the two types of art therapy interventions for changing classroom behavior.

• **Quasi-experimental designs:** In quasi-experimental research, only one group may be used to test therapeutic effectiveness or, if two groups are used, the subjects are not randomly assigned to the experimental or the no-treatment control group. Kunkle-Miller (1982) was not able to randomly assign deaf, emotionally disturbed children and adolescents to an art therapy versus a control group. Therefore, she matched the students in both groups on IQ, age, and severity of hearing loss.

Kunkle-Miller, wanting to substantiate that art could have a therapeutic effect on deaf children, tested the children in both groups for creativity, self-concept, and behavior. The children and adolescents in the art therapy group improved significantly in terms of creativity on the free choice activity and in terms of behavior as measured by the Rubin-Kunkle-Miller Behavioral Inventory. However, there were no significant differences in self-concept as measured by the Draw-A-Person Test.

• **Single-subject designs:** As suggested by its name, single-subject designs need only one client or subject to test the effectiveness of a therapy or treatment. In this type of research, specific problem behaviors of a client are measured prior to and during the treatment. In art therapy research, it is typical that the problem behaviors will decrease as the client becomes involved in art therapy.

Bowen and Rosal (1989) used art therapy, specifically the use of guided imagery, to reduce the maladaptive behaviors of a mentally retarded woman. As a client in a sheltered workshop, the subject had difficulty with positive, work-related behaviors and had low work production averages. These behaviors were targeted and measured prior to and then during an art therapy intervention. The client's positive behaviors on the workfloor increased with the introduction of art therapy and her work production average improved during the art therapy intervention period.

Behavioral Analysis: Careful observation of client behavior is the keystone of behavioral analysis. Understanding the behavior of a subject under particular circumstances is the purpose of this type of research. At times, behavioral analysis is used in outcome research as a measure of behavior change. For example, teachers were used as observers of problem behavior in the study by Rosal (1985). Kunkle-Miller (1982) used an observational inventory during the initial art interview as a means of understanding the interactional quality of the child's behavior within the art therapy session. In the Bowen and Rosal (1989) study, work supervisors were used to observe the work-related behaviors of a client. In these studies, the behaviors observed were defined carefully and specifically. Behavioral analysis does not always have to be a part of treatment outcome research, however. It could be used by art therapists to understand the unique ways a client interacts with other members in a group art therapy setting, or to understand the different ways a client interacts with diverse art materials.

Historical Research: Reviewing events from the past is the hallmark of historical research. Conducting this type of research aids in theory formation and ideas for future research. As of today, there are no systematic historical studies of the field of art therapy. Nor are there any studies about how particular historical (social, political, cultural) events (such as federal legislation, i.e., Public Law 94-142) may have affected the art therapy profession's growth. These would be exciting research projects for some inspired researchers.

Using another aspect of historical research, Gantt (1986) suggests using the methods of art historians as a model for art therapy research. Gantt's rationale is that in both art history and art therapy, symbols and the "circumstances surrounding its making" (p. 112) are important. Gantt (1986) described her research-in-progress of the phenomenon that several pregnant women draw mother/child representations bathed in light from a window. Gantt's research is on how this phenomenon might be related to the women's exposure to traditional paintings of the Annunciation.

Phenomenological-Hermeneutic Research: Phenomenological research is a paradigm used to uncover the meaning of human experience. The major tool used in this type of research is a qualitative interview. The interview is theme-oriented and the subject is asked to describe personal meanings. The researcher is to remain unbiased, the questions are to be value free, yet the researcher is required to interpret the information.

Rhyne (1980) conducted this type of meaning-uncovering interview research using drawings as a tool. Rhyne described her thesis as, "each of us writes our own script for our personal drama of transition, that we do so congruently with our construct systems of the nature of our role in and out of the world of reality" (p. 34). Through the use of interview, art therapy students were asked to compare and contrast their personal construct drawings of feeling states and then to discuss the meanings conveyed in the drawings. Through analyzing the interviews, Rhyne was able to uncover the patterns of thinking and feeling as well as the meaning of the patterns for each individual.

Naturalistic-Ethnographic Designs: Research using the naturalistic-ethnographic approach implies that the researcher is working towards a holistic understanding of an experience to discover how individuals perceive an experience or a phenomenon. In addition, the data gathered are analyzed so that some understanding of the factors which influence behavior may be described. The researcher employing this method uses open-ended information from the subjects, as well as being a participant observer in the setting where the research is taking place.

Anderson (1991) used this type of research to study the impact of a ceramic art therapy group within a mental health agency on the treatment of women who were survivors of incest. As part of the study, Anderson asked the clients to write about each group art therapy session in what was labeled a "guided journal entry." Open-ended questions were suggested as part of the weekly journal. Sample questions included, "Did this week's ceramic session trigger any thoughts, feelings, or images? Could you describe these?"

In addition, the clients' individual therapists were interviewed to gather their perceptions of how the group affected the incest survivors' treatment. The group leaders took descriptive notes of each session and all agency staff members were asked to keep a log. Final written statements about the group experience were gathered from the group leaders and the agency staff. The clients were surveyed with an open-ended questionnaire six months after the end of the group experience.

The data gathered demonstrated the usefulness of such an art therapy group within an agency which was without this type of therapy program for the incest survivor client. In addition, the research project gathered information about a particular medium and its possible effect on this population. Finally, the research project uncovered clients' perceptions of their issues as well as how they perceived the art therapy experience in relation to these issues.

Cybernetic or Action Research: Cybernetic or action research is a model of research where practice interfaces with research and, therefore, one affects the other. In doing this type of research, the researcher's interventions change with new information gained from the clients who are being studied. Because this model is based on understanding patterns and interactions, family therapists have used this type of research paradigm to study family dynamics and family therapy. Art therapists could also use this type of research model for understanding group work or family work.

Morgan (1990) in working with a group of children ages 12 to 14 used a form of this research paradigm in studying how the use of "feelings journals" affected the understanding of feeling identification among the group art therapy participants. Morgan, who wanted to use the feelings journals as a tool in research, realized that for the most part, the group members used "happy" to describe how they were feeling each day. She mentioned that because most of the members came from "dysfunctional family systems, they learn to deny their feelings and not to talk about them" (p. 6).

Therefore, Morgan realized that she would have to intervene and help the group break through the denial. During the time when members shared their feelings journals, Morgan would ask the group to confirm or deny whether a particular member "looked or seemed" happy. Morgan also had the group members make feeling thermometers and find different words for four basic feelings: mad, sad, glad, and scared. Using the other group members as a means to confirm matches between journal entries and outward appearance then became the research target.

In this research, Morgan began with one idea (to use the feelings journals as a tool in research) but had to change her strategy (to the match between journal entry and group consensus). In addition, she used herself as a tool by intervening in the journaling process. This change in strategy and thinking by the researcher and the use of the researcher as a tool in the study are hallmarks of action research.

Summary and Conclusions

It is exciting and revealing to review the types of research which art therapists have conducted. The excitement is generated from the fact that, as a field, we have many tools for doing research and many avenues which need exploration. The revelation is generated from the fact that art therapists have already conducted a great deal of solid research and that this research is a firm foundation for further inquiry.

I hope the information in this chapter can be used in several ways. First, the material presented here may be useful as a basis for further examination of a particular research model. Second, it may be useful as an incentive to duplicate a particular study which has been completed but needs to be conducted with a different population or age group. Third, it may be useful to help form opinions about research models and encourage the development of models unique to art therapy. Finally, this chapter may be used to help form opinions about art therapy research and about the directions for future art therapy research.

References

Anderson, F.E. (1991). *Courage! Together we heal: Mural messages from incest survivors to incest survivors* (A report on a pilot project on the development and implementation of an art therapy short-term ceramics group for incest survivors). Normal, IL: Illinois State University Press.

Anderson, F.E. & Landgarten, H. (1974). Survey on the status of art therapy in the Midwest and Southern California. *American Journal of Art Therapy, 13*(2), pp. 118-122.

Bowen, C.A., & Rosal, M.L. (1989). The use of art therapy to reduce the maladaptive behaviors of a mentally retarded adult. *The Arts in Psychotherapy, 16*, 211-218.

Cohen, B., Hammer, J., & Singer, S. (1988). The diagnostic drawing series: a systematic approach to art therapy evaluation and research. *The Arts in Psychotherapy, 15*, 11-21.

Cotton, M.A. (1985). Creative art expression from a leukemic child. *Art Therapy, 2*(2), 55-65.

Gantt, L. (1986). Systematic investigation of art works: Some research models drawn from neighboring fields. *American Journal of Art Therapy, 24*, 111-118.

Kunkle-Miller, C. (1982). The effects of individual art therapy upon emotionally disturbed deaf children and adolescents. In A. DiMaria, E.S. Kramer, & E.A. Roth (Eds.), Art therapy: Still growing. *The Proceedings of the Thirteenth Annual Conference of the American Art Therapy Association* (pp. 137-142). Alexandria, VA: American Art Therapy Association.

Landgarten, H. (1984). Ten-year follow-up survey on the status of art therapy in the greater Los Angeles area. *Art Therapy: Journal of the American Art Therapy Association, 1*(2), 84-88.

Marrion, L., Landell, S., & Bradley, S. (1988). [Child sexual abuse treatment proposal: Questionnaire survey results]. Unpublished raw data, British Columbia School of Art Therapy.

Morgan, J. (1990). *Use of journal expressions in the measurement of accuracy in feeling identification: A study of a group of 12-14 year olds in a day treatment program.* Unpublished master's paper, University of Louisville, Louisville, KY.

Rhyne, J. (1979). Drawings as personal constructs: A study of visual dynamics. (*University Microfilms International* No. TX 375-487).

Rhyne, J. (1980). Personal dramas of transition. In L. Gantt & S. Whitman (Eds.), The fine art of therapy. *The Proceedings of the Eleventh Annual Conference of the American Art Therapy Association* (pp. 31-38). Alexandria, VA: American Art Therapy Association.

Rosal, M.L. (1985). *The use of art therapy to modify the locus of control and adaptive behavior of behavior disordered students.* Unpublished doctoral dissertation, University of Queensland, Brisbane, Australia.

Rubin, J.A., & Rubin, H. (1988). Words and pictures: The relationship between graphic and verbal expression of young children. *American Journal of Art Therapy, 26,* 71-82.

Chapter 8

SOME RESEARCH MODELS DRAWN FROM NEIGHBORING FIELDS

Linda Gantt, PhD, A.T.R.

Typically, art therapists demonstrate the merits of art therapy through case studies and anecdotes that emphasize a psychodynamic interpretation of symbols.[1] But sometimes a symbol, configuration, or stylistic device occurs again and again in widely diverse cases. As curious as art therapists may be about the significance of such recurrences, many protest that they are ill-equipped either by temperament or by training to undertake rigorous empirical investigations following the research model of the natural sciences (and to an extent the social sciences). Thus, art therapists do not often venture beyond the individual case study.

Between the psychodynamically oriented case study and the experimentally based research of the natural sciences, however, lie a number of other models that art therapists may find useful for investigation. In this chapter I examine some alternative models for research design and research strategies drawn not from the natural sciences but from three fields that border on our own—art history, anthropology, and linguistics—in hope of explaining how the models may contribute to art therapy research. All three of these fields study human behavior and particularly the products of human behavior—artworks, cultural institutions, and language—and each field attempts to systematically investigate the significance of these products. I shall attempt to describe a theoretical assumption about human behavior common to both anthropology and linguistics that I believe can be useful in future art therapy research

[1]Originally published in the *American Journal of Art Therapy, 24*(4), p. 111-118, 1986, with the title "Systematic Investigations of Art Works: Some Research Models Drawn from Neighboring Fields." Reprinted here by permission of Gladys Agell and the Vermont College of Norwich University. Readers should refer to the *AJAT* version for the eight illustrations which accompanied it.

Throughout I shall be emphasizing research that deals with similarities seen in art works across diverse populations (a type of correlation study) rather than research into the efficacy of the process of art therapy (outcome study). If I emphasize the societal rules and cultural factors more than psychological laws and dynamic factors, it is with the conscious intent of bringing some balance to the way we look at art and art making.

Background

It was my own attempt to systematically investigate similarities in artworks that first made me aware of the possibilities for art therapy research as well as the difficulties and limitations one may encounter in attempting such studies. My initial foray into research was prompted by Hanna Yaxa Kwiatkowksa's remark that many depressed patients drew concentric circles, whirlpools, tunnels, bull's eyes, and the like. I decided to find out for myself whether her observation was valid. Accordingly, over the course of about seven years, I collected drawings of concentric circles and other concentric forms done by art therapy patients on the psychiatric unit and the chemical dependency unit of the large general hospital where I worked. The materials used (pastels and markers) and the setting (group art therapy) were the same for all the patients. It was a simple matter to collect rudimentary demographic data, diagnostic data, and the patients' remarks about their drawings. I wanted to see if such drawings did correlate with a diagnosis of depression. While only a very small minority of my patients produced this configuration, most of those who did were indeed depressed.

Of course, missing from this informal study were many refinements of carefully designed research, not to mention the testing of my hypothesis by statistical analysis. However, my effort nonetheless contained several of the basic elements of scientific procedure: statement of hypothesis, systematic collection of data, dispassionate observation, and formulation of a conclusion or principles. (The study also can be considered a replication of another basic element of scientific procedure in that I did not merely accept the assertion of another but looked for myself.) Had I employed objective measurement and experimentation as well, my study would have qualified as an exercise in scientific method.

This first brush with systematic investigation made me eager for advanced instruction in research methods and principles of scholarly investigation. With this in mind, I enrolled in an interdisciplinary doctoral program at the University of Pittsburgh. I soon learned in my courses that art history, anthropology, and linguistics shared with art therapy certain scientific problems. Perhaps investigators in these fields had arrived at some solutions that art therapists could use. Two practical and philosophical problems that we discussed frequently in my courses are important to note here: the difficulty of controlling variables in research with human subjects and the failure of such research to achieve predictive power equal to that of the physical sciences.

Difficulty in Controlling Variables

Laboratory studies and controlled experiments, which are the heart of physics, chemistry, and medicine   present tremendous problems for researchers in the social sciences. Simply stated, human behavior and its vagaries will not easily yield to controlled experiments. The more complicated the behavior, the more difficult it is to divide into its constituent parts or to isolate or manipulate a single variable in an experiment. Powerful sociological and psychological influences confound the results of experiments with people, and researchers have difficulty detecting such influences and controlling for them.

For example, a confounding influence known as the Hawthorne effect (often encountered in social science research) might operate as well in art therapy research. Investigators have found that the very fact of being selected as a subject for a research project can alter the subject's attitude and hence his or her behavior. In art therapy, supervisors who assign students to work with individual patients sometimes see those patients react in a variety of unpredictable but understandable ways. One common reaction is that the patient consciously or unconsciously tries to "do well" for the student's sake so the student will earn a good evaluation. Other patients, on finding they are being accorded something that others on the unit are not, have a sinking feeling that their condition is much worse than they had realized. The placebo effect is another confounding factor in research with human subjects. When sick people hope they are going to get better, are told they are going to get better, and are given potions that are supposed to make them better, many of them *do* get better. The placebo effect depends in large part on the expectations of both the patient and the therapist. The job of weeding out such extraneous or confounding influences as the Hawthorne effect and the placebo effect from research design is probably the most overwhelming task a beginner must face.

Failure to Achieve Predictive Power

The natural sciences, with their emphasis on the discovery of lawful and regular events and processes, have predictable capabilities far beyond those of the social sciences. Anyone who has worked in a psychiatric facility knows that while it is possible to "explain" occurrences of violence or suicide *after the fact*, it is virtually impossible to *predict* them with any certainty in an individual case. Because of the many chance factors involved in each single case, researchers can make generalizations only about what is probable in a group or class. For example, on the basis of the data I collected I might conclude that "in a group of people who draw concentric circles, 85 percent will be depressed" (a probabilistic generalization that could be tested by another researcher). However, I could not make the deductive generalization that "a person who draws concentric circles is depressed." Unfortunately, probabilistic generalizations are "substantially weaker than deductive explanation" (Nachmias and Nachmias, 1976, p. 5). As long as art therapy lacks the power to predict lawful and regular occurrences, art therapists can only explain and understand material *after* it has been produced.

Because art history, anthropology, and linguistics share with art therapy these problems in the study of human behavior, the research models and methods these fields have developed may prove useful to us.

Art History

Art history and art therapy share similar raw material as subject matter for their investigations: the completed artwork, its symbolism (both overt and covert), and the circumstances surrounding its making. Unlike art therapists, however, art historians devote much effort to the description and classification of art works and their iconography. Furthermore, while art therapy approaches interpretation mainly from a psychological orientation, art historians are trained to make interpretations that synthesize observations about the formal characteristics of the work and its symbolism within an historical context. The art therapist looks within the artist's unconscious for what influenced his or her creative inspiration, while the art historian assumes that the artist was, for the most part, working consciously in a particular tradition and was influenced by peers, teachers, and patrons.

Erwin Panofsky (1939), who was instrumental in moving art history from a purely descriptive endeavor (classifying styles and dating and authenticating individual works) to an interpretive enterprise, delineated three major processes in the "investigation and interpretation of a work of visual art."

The first is "pre-iconographical description—that is, "the identification of the primary or immediately apparent subject matter" and a description of the formal characteristics of the work. Thus a pre-iconographic study might identify the "immediate content" of a painting as "a woman with a child" and describe such formal aspects as the color or the kind of line used.

The second process an art historian would apply to an artwork is "iconographical analysis—the identification and description of the secondary or allegorical and symbolic content of the artwork. Using the example mentioned above, the "woman with a child" might be identified as "Mary and the Christ Child." An iconographic study draws on existing tradition for the source of those symbols an artist chooses to use. The traditions such a study encompasses are broad; they include literature and other cultural artifacts. (In the present day, television and movies must certainly be considered as possible sources of symbolism.)

The third process, according to Panofsky, is "iconological interpretation" or synthesis—a study of both the primary (immediate) and the secondary (symbolic) content to determine integrated meaning. To this end, the art historian takes into account *both* the stylistic treatment of the subject and the underlying cultural premises from which the work is drawn and which the artist may express consciously or unconsciously. The emphasis is on putting the art into historical context. In seeking this synthesis, the art historian leaves no stone unturned to find historical evidence to aid in understanding a picture or sculpture. It is this strong emphasis on historical sources (including some outside the "visual tradition," such as literary sources) that art therapists frequently overlook in their discussions of clients' art.

Art therapists can learn from the pre-iconographic studies of art historians how to classify art works according to immediate subject or certain formal characteristics. Rita Simon (1970), in her descriptions of various styles of art, and Heinz Lehmann and F. Risquez (1953), in their study of fingerpaintings done by psychotic and nonpsychotic patients, exemplify pre-iconographic investigations. Art therapists, too, can undertake iconographic studies of overt symbols, their frequency, their sources, their use by a specific population to better understand a particular population or a particular diagnostic group. For example, one might study the symbols of popular rock music groups for information about the images that adolescents are drawn to, both consciously and unconsciously. This, in turn, may help us to understand what comes from a cultural or artistic tradition and what comes from unconscious inspiration in the work of a particular adolescent. Dee Spring's study of the symbols used by sexually abused and chemically dependent women (1985) and Diane Devine's study of paintings by alcoholic men (1970) are examples of the iconographic approach to art. The current significance of enduring images, such as the unicorn or the rainbow, might be studied in light of earlier uses and meaning, for surely the meaning of a unicorn today is considerably removed from what it was for the makers of medieval paintings and tapestries. Such studies could enrich our understanding of the effects of tradition on present-day imagery.

Currently, I am engaged in an iconologic study of the connections between a recurring symbol in the present-day drawings of various people who worked apart from each other (and hence did not see each other's work) and the influence of a specific religious tradition in painting. I was prompted to do this study by noticing similarities in drawings made under the same circumstances by two pregnant women, neither of whom saw the other draw. They were participating in a pilot study on mother and child relationships. The artists were asked to draw a picture of themselves and their expected babies. Both women drew pictures in which light streams through a window into the room where the mother is with her child. This use of light, rare in the work of my adult psychiatric patients, appears frequently in paintings of the Annunciation. My task became one of collecting as many drawings as I could of women and children bathed in a shower of light from a window, studying and synthesizing any written material on the topic, and, finally, drawing some conclusions about both the psychological and historical aspects of this image.

The art historian Carla Gottlieb (1981) includes many examples of such imagery in her fascinating book on window symbolism. Notable among her examples are Annunciation paintings from the 15th and 16th centuries. But the theme is not simply a religious one, for Gottlieb shows a 17th-century Dutch painting that features the same image (light streaming in the window of a room where a mother and baby are) yet is clearly secular. I have found, as well, recent paintings on this theme, some of which have a religious content and others that do not. Much work remains to be done on this project before I can draw conclusions about how exposure to traditional art on this theme may have affected the contemporary artists whose drawings caught my interest. At the same time, I may learn more about the influence of psychological considerations on the artists in question.

Anthropology

The field of anthropology, like art history, draws upon vast collections of material in its studies of different cultures. Like art therapy, anthropology relies on case studies (not of individuals but of societies) and, again like art therapy, has been plagued in the past by such difficulties as unevenness of data, subjective evaluation of data, and the impossibility of generalizing beyond a single case.

A vast improvement in the possibilities for research has been realized with the development of centralized collections of anthropological data, such as the Human Relations Area File, begun by anthropologist George Peter Murdock. These files provide the requisite material for sophisticated cross-cultural studies. For example, Herbert Barry (1957) drew on such a file to test his hypothesis that child training practices correlate with the type of artwork produced in a society. Similarly, John Fischer (1961) studied the association of various types of social organization with design elements in a culture's art work.

A similar data bank that art therapists should know about is the Archives for Research in Archetypal Symbolism, housed in the Jung Institute in New York City. Included are thousands of photographs of religious symbols and artworks from all over the world and from all the ages, along with an extensive library on symbolism. Art therapists might well give some thought to developing a comparable resource file of pictures done by members of particular social, national, or diagnostic groups, with comments from the artists and the art therapist and pertinent demographic and diagnostic data. Such a data bank would provide a repository for much material that falls through the cracks or otherwise fades from the memory of individual art therapists.

Anthropological research provides us not only with a model for the collection and use of data, but, more important, with theoretical models for human behavior that can help art therapists differentiate between culturally determined and psychologically determined aspects of artwork. Anthropologists (and linguists to an even greater extent) have used a model that does not attribute all human behavior to biological or psychological laws. In addition to recognizing innate laws that biologists say govern human behavior, this model is *rules*-based (that is, cultural in nature) and allows for the observed extraordinary variability of human behavior. A rules-based model attributes most of the variety in social institutions and everyday behavior to the different rules that prevail in different cultures. For example, social ritual is rule-governed behavior; in certain countries, a suitable expression of delight in a repast is a belch, while the very same behavior in other countries may bring looks of disapproval and disdain.

Laws are invariable—everywhere on earth the law of gravity operates in the same way; *rules*, however, are highly variable and are determined by the culture in which one lives. We have only begun to ask questions about how cultural practices or attitudes have an effect on what our clients draw. In her work with Hispanic patients, Julie Lomoe-Smith (1982) observed that cultural attitudes and expectations influenced both the art and the verbal responses of her clients. Denise Evans Lofgren (1981) notes that in working with patients from another culture, "differences in traditions of visual symbolism . . . can emerge distinctly and dramatically for those who care to look for them" (p. 30). Ana Gardano (1986) found some evidence that cultural factors can have an effect on the intensity of emotional response to colors. (p. 30). Ana Gardano (1986) found some evidence that cultural factors can have an effect on the intensity of emotional response to colors.

It is not hard to find examples of rules for art in other cultures and in other ages that are considerably different from the current rules in our culture. Some rules are taught formally (for example, the rule for creating one-point perspective); others are passed on informally or may be derived from other rule systems within a culture, such as religion. (Moslems, for example, are prohibited from depicting the human form in art.) Franz Boas (1955), one of the first anthropologists to make a careful study of primitive art, shows that art that seems to break all Western stylistic conventions nonetheless adheres to a set of easily described rules.

Linguistics

To make the most effective use of art therapy products, we need to know the rules our clients are using to make art. Linguists have provided an excellent structure for investigating rules-based behavior. Other scholars have adapted their concepts and methods to shed light on the mechanisms of transmitting cultural practices. For example, Peter Roe (1980), an anthropologist working with the Shipibo Indians of Peru, while attempting to determine whether one woman's art would be influenced by the work of other members of her same residence group, sought to devise a means for determining the "best" and "worst" art in the group without injecting his Western aesthetic preferences. Roe privately asked each group member to tell him whom she considered to be the "best artist" and the "worst artist," then commissioned works from both of those artists. Comparing the two, Roe was able to determine the Shipibos' rules for good art. [Roe derived his method of working from that of the linguist Noam Chomsky (1957).] Roe found that the woman acknowledged to be the "best" had used a total of 91 rules in four xxxxx different designs, whereas the "worst" artist had used only 14 rules to produce a single design. Roe concluded that:

> . . . a good artist is one who not only produces designs loaded with more elements and uses more rules than a bad artist does, but the superior artist's designs are higher-order solutions in the hierarchy of style. The designs of the inferior artists will, conversely, be much further down the hierarchy. . . . (p. 61)

So Roe was able to determine the rules of art making without asking the artists. If he had asked the artists what rules they used, it is likely that they would have been unable to tell him. The same thing happens in language; while most while most people can use the rules correctly, it takes a trained linguist to write a grammar of a given tongue.

Roe's general principle of a *hierarchy of solutions* is, in my opinion, a valuable tool for comparing artworks in art therapy. For example, *The Bellelli Family* (c. 1862), a well-known family portrait of a mother, father, and two young daughters by Edgar Degas, can be compared with a family drawing done by a 10-year-old child (published by Burns and Kaufman, 1972, p. 42). These two pictures demonstrate two different artistic solutions to the same problem: how to portray the psychological relationships in a family. The child drew (from left to right) his mother, father, sister, brother, and self, each engaged in a different activity. Separating each figure from the others are vertical lines spanning the whole page. Burns and Kaufman see such "barriers" as indicative of avoidance. As if to emphasize the psychological separateness, the child shows himself building a fence which is set between him and the rest of the family. Degas places the mother and one daughter on the left and the second daughter in the middle of the picture. The father is on the far right, seated in an arm chair. Degas achieves the same effect of separating one member from the rest of the family but in a much more subtle way. He has placed the edges of the mirror, fireplace, and table to create a line that cuts off the husband and father from his wife and daughters. Arranging the composition of a painting to isolate one person from others is a higher-order solution than simply drawing a line between them.

Both artists accomplished the task of portraying a family, yet there is no doubt that in our culture Degas would be judged the better artist. Degas has at his disposal an extensive "grammar" of Western art: color, proportion, perspective, composition, light, and shadow. Degas employed other devices as well to solve the problem of how to portray psychological relationships. He has enveloped one daughter within the voluminous outline of the mother. There is a similar picture (again in Burns and Kaufman, p. 43) in which a child depicts herself as occupying the same visual space as her father. In both works this device indicates emotional closeness. In the Degas painting, the sharply drawn features of the mother and daughters contrast with the somewhat indistinct face of the father, who has his back turned to the viewer. Louise Bates Ames, in her introduction to the Burns and Kaufman book, describes a picture by a third child in which she "pictured [her father] as sitting at his desk so that only his arm showed," a solution almost identical to that of Degas. The net effect in both pictures is that the father is emotionally removed or inaccessible. Each of the three child artists used one device to achieve a certain effect, whereas Degas used all three in one work. Of course, Degas used many other devices as well; thus, his work ranks very high in the hierarchy of solutions for both psychological and technical problems. Letters and other historical material confirm that relationships within the Bellelli family were as Degas portrayed them. Indeed, the art critic John Canaday (1958) proclaimed this painting one of the finest psychological portraits ever made.

Understanding the principle of the hierarchy of solutions can give us insight into the art productions in art therapy. A patient calls upon his intuitive responses to a situation in order to represent it. If he has at his command only the most rudimentary artistic solutions or rules, he can portray psychological truths in only the most rudimentary ways. Can an art therapist help a patient expand his repertoire? As his options expand and increase, can the patient find for himself richer and more subtle solutions to psychological dilemmas? This is a question of utmost importance to art therapists who are considering options for their clients in the hope of promoting favorable change. Will providing our patients with more conscious options *in their artwork,* more higher-order aesthetic and technical solutions, likewise promote change for the better?

Implications for Art Therapy

Art making stands on the borderline between law-governed and rule-governed behavior. Part of our difficulty as art therapists is that we have not distinguished which is which—how much is "nature" and how much is "nurture" in an artist's work. What part of artistic activity proceeds according to developmental laws? Do children progress from the scribble stage to the preschematic stage regardless of where they live? Alexander Alland (1983), an anthropologist who studied drawings of children from six cultures, questions our assumption that the development of children's drawing skills proceed in an orderly fashion from scribbles to representation. Furthermore, he suggests that representation and symbolism in drawing are consciously or unconsciously taught to children by adults and other children. He concludes:

> . . . that certain principles of attack [in the drawing process] are held in common by children everywhere and these general principles interact with specific conscious and unconscious culturally-based rules to govern what kind of pictures children will make. (p. 215).

In *The Painted Message*, Otto Billig (1978) asks the same questions about the artwork of adults—how much is culturally influenced and how much is psychologically determined? Gathering his evidence in New Guinea, where he could be certain to get a number of subjects who had not been influenced by Western culture (or, presumably, by Western art), Billig studied what happened in a person's artwork when he or she became psychotic. He found that, in effect, the cultural rules about how to draw dropped away, that the work of schizophrenic artists in New Guinea closely resembled that of schizophrenic artists in the West.

It is fairly easy to determine that some behaviors in art are indeed *law*-governed. The regular omission of one side of a figure by a person who has suffered a stroke certainly suggests lawful behavior. But is the repeated use of dark, somber colors by a depressed patient law-governed or *rule*-governed that is, accessible to the conscious control of the artist?

Conclusion

As art therapists eager to investigate the apparent similarities we find in the artwork of diverse populations, we need to devise ways to determine which characteristics are the result of biological or psychological laws, which of cultural rules, and which of independent invention. The experimental and quasi-experimental designs which are the foundation of research in the biological and physical sciences are crucial in the search for psychological laws (cause and effect). However, these designs cannot be used for certain types of questions. The research strategies and theoretical models of other fields in the humanities may be of real utility in this endeavor. Like many art therapists, I place great stress on dynamic processes and interpretations. However, my ideas are now tempered by influences from the fields of study discussed above. To understand our clients more completely, I believe we must consider their cultural rules and their visual and literary traditions, as well as their intrapsychic processes.

References

Alland, A., Jr. (1983). *Playing with form: Children draw in six cultures.* New York, NY: Columbia University Press.

Barry, H., III. (1957). Relationships between child training and the pictorial arts. *Journal of Abnormal and Social Psychology, 54,* 380-383.

Billig, O. (1978). *The painted message.* New York, NY: Halsted Press, John Wiley & Sons.

Boas, F. (1955). *Primitive art.* New York, NY: Dover.

Burns, R., & Kaufman, S. (1972). *Actions, styles and symbols in kinetic family drawings (K-F-D): An interpretive manual.* New York, NY: Brunner/Mazel.

Canaday, J. (1958). *Composition as expression* (Portfolio 7, Metropolitan Seminars in Art). New York, NY: Metropolitan Museum of Art.

Chomsky, N. (1957). *Syntactic structures.* New York, NY: Humanities Press.

Devine, D. (1970). A preliminary investigation of paintings by alcoholic men. *American Journal of Art Therapy, 9,* 115-128.

Fischer, J. (1961). Art styles as cultural cognitive maps. *American Anthropologist, 63,* 79-93.

Gottlieb, C. (1981). *The window in art: From the window of God to the vanity of man.* New York, NY: Abaris Books.

Lehmann, H., & Risquez, F. (1953). The use of fingerpainting in the clinical evaluation of psychotic conditions: A quantitative and qualitative approach. *Journal of Mental Science, 99,* 763-777.

Lofgren, D. (1981). Art therapy and cultural difference. *American Journal of Art Therapy, 21,* 25-30.

Lomoe-Smith, J. (1982). Cultural influences in art therapy with Hispanic patients. In L. Gantt & A. Evans (Eds.), Focus on the future. *The Proceedings of the Tenth Annual Conference of the American Art Therapy Association* (pp. 17-22). Falls Church, VA: American Art Therapy Association.

Nachmias, D., & Nachmias, C. (1976). *Research methods in the social sciences.* New York, NY: St. Martin's Press.

Panofsky, E. (1939). *Studies in iconology: Humanistic themes in the art of the Renaissance.* New York, NY: Oxford University Press.

Roe, P. (1980). Art and residence among the Shipibo Indians of Peru: A study in microacculturation. *American Anthropologist, 82,* 42-69.

Simon, R. (1970). The significance of pictorial styles in art therapy. *American Journal of Art Therapy, 9,* 159-175.

Chapter 9

ART THERAPISTS' WAYS OF KNOWING: TOWARD CREATIVITY AND NEW PARADIGMS FOR ART THERAPY RESEARCH

Maxine Borowsky Junge, PhD, LCSW, A.T.R.
Debra Linesch, MA, MFCC, A.T.R.

For our students in academic training programs and for ourselves as professional art therapy clinicians, the word "research" all too often evokes waves of insecurity and images of scientific laboratories and white coats. This is because it is generally associated with the single predominant paradigm of Western science, positivism, and the empirical, quantitative model. In this essay, we argue for both the naturalness and the necessity of an expanded range of lenses through which art therapists can approach research. The dominance of the positive, empirical model in the human sciences is described as a sociocultural construction. Challenges to it are rapidly emerging in the form of new paradigms which offer many cultures of inquiry and diverse ways of knowing and which, most importantly, may be more resonant with art therapists' talents, interests, and world views. The fabled paradigm shift is now in front of us.

We situate the field of art therapy as philosophically and epistomologically aligned with the empirical research tradition out of its perception of the need to validate its theory and methods within the prevailing acceptable framework.

---

[1] We have borrowed the term "cultures of inquiry" from the *Research Study Guide* of the Fielding Institute's Human and Organizational Development Program.

We suggest that this has not always provided a comfortable fit for art therapists who, emphasizing creativity and subjective ways of knowing, may find their affinities with qualitative, descriptive, phenomenological, metaphorical, and interpretive methods of inquiry. One reason that art therapists have not emphasized research nor significantly introduced and tested their own methodologies may lie in the inherent conflicts and incongruities between the assumptions of the natural science model and art therapists' typical approaches to human experience. After discussing these issues, we lay out a range of cultures of inquiry indicating a diversity of research philosophies and paradigms and provide a beginning bibliography.

During the 19th century, psychiatrists and psychologists interacted with their patients to develop comprehensive case histories which sought to illuminate human behavior, psychopathology, and the subjective experience. Despite this history, in the 20th century the human sciences have been strongly dominated by a current of thought emphasizing their similarity to the natural sciences, called positivism. Positivism maintained that there was a single scientific method—that of the natural sciences—which was valid everywhere, in all situations at all times, and in all domains of knowledge. Only the result of applying that method could count as *true knowledge*. In this way of thinking, human beings are studied through experimental methods to find the underlying "truth" of the laws of human behavior.

Historically, art therapists have been naturally concerned with the process of legitimizing ourselves both clinically and theoretically as a profession. But in an era that has predominantly valued the model of empirical, quantifiable research science dealing with causality and predictability and is based on the assumption that the world and the human being are objectively knowable and, if we know enough, we can predict the future, art therapists too often fit uncomfortably, if at all. Art therapists are people who engage in the metaphorical creation of meaning. As researchers within this Western science tradition, we have often found ourselves out of synchrony with our own talents, interests, and proclivities. For the art therapist, research has been and remains problematic and fraught with hazards which both emerge from and have an impact on our professional self-image.

Based on our perception of having to "prove" the value of art therapy, we have tended to align ourselves with the most mainstream research traditions where empirical analytical science has dominated. This one "truth" approach assumes a right way and a wrong way to conduct inquiry, and that there is only one legitimate kind of knowing. Our need to validate ourselves as a profession has placed us in a research framework which sometimes seems like a straitjacket. Although we continue to engage in descriptive, exploratory, and case study research, we have not yet done much in developing our own methodologies. We may not regard ourselves as "real" researchers, as we conflictually retain our identity as artists who help others through the wonderfully rich and evocative subjectivity of the creative process.

We can never fit easily into this model of empirical science because the artistic nature of our work and ourselves assumes that we can work out of many different ways of looking at the world, as many as the multitude of varieties of lines and shapes and colors our clients create, and that there are many different kinds of knowing. A consequence of this has been that we have frequently felt uncomfortable doing research and have sidestepped the endeavor, concentrating instead on the development of clinical skills in our training programs. We currently exist in a state in which we are troubled by our dissatisfaction with research, and yearn for models of inquiry that have more meaning to our work and more congruence with our personalities as artists/clinicians/researchers.

Research paradigms, like everything else, are sociocultural constructions embedded in a particular contextual network based on explicit and implicit assumptions about the nature of the world, of truth, and of meaning. For a long while now, and particularly in the last 20 years since Thomas Kuhn's *The Structure of Scientific Revolutions* (1970), there has been a tremendous amount of criticism of traditional research philosophies and methods. Increasingly, the notion that the world is out there to be learned and separate from ourselves is under attack. Exciting new research paradigms are emerging from a variety of cultures of inquiry. These recognize that science is a socially constructed endeavor emerging from our own assumptions and biases. Research does not simply observe, describe, and measure. The concurrent subjective and implicit experience and the researcher as active participant in creating the experience under consideration must be understood. Art therapists are particularly adept at implicit ways of knowing.

The exciting and expanding understanding that there are many cultures of inquiry and ways of knowing evoked by the new research paradigm welcomes us as art therapists to participate in research endeavors that are more natural to us, more creative, and which may be vastly more fruitful to us as clinicians and to our profession.

In essence, our attraction to objective, empirical science was part of our need to validate ourselves as a profession within the acceptable and prevailing research tradition of the psychologies. Our shift toward new research paradigms recognizes our development and our sense of our own identity and opens the doors wide for us to value and express our own creativity confidently. In particular, questions and methodologies which concern themselves with metaphor and meaning in its many forms will prove useful and intriguing. As researchers we have a rich and exciting future to look forward to. As we approach research systematically, rigorously, and from our own creative framework, we have unique contributions to make.

Now we have the opportunity to broaden our perspective of examining the materials in which we are interested and create new methods out of our sense of who we are. The following delineation of eight cultures of inquiry includes the positivistic, natural science model but offers research philosophies that may engage the style and curiosity of the art therapist more readily.[2]

1. Phenomenological
2. Hermeneutic
3. Ethnographic, including participant observation, naturalistic inquiry, and other forms of field studies
4. Empirical/Analytical, including quantitative methods generally, such as experimental, quasi-experimental, and survey research
5. Action Research
6. Comparative/Historical Research
7. Theoretical, including critical theory
8. Evaluation research

Each of these cultures of inquiry addresses primary questions in different ways including: a) analysis of the relationship the researcher has to the subject, b) exploration of underlying assumptions, and c) acknowledgement of personal style.

It is crucial that we broaden our range of inquiry and develop our own identity as art therapy researchers. An investigation into new developments and paradigms in human sciences research will help us do that. Our natural tendencies to work intuitively and metaphorically do not have to be sacrificed for quality research. And our training programs (particularly, the now developing post-Master's curricula) need no longer contain the troubling contradiction between excellence in clinical training (emphasizing creativity, relationship, and subjectivity) and traditional research methods (emphasizing analysis, measurement, and objectivity).

---

[2] Editor's Note: Some of these research models are illustrated elsewhere in the *Guide*.

Suggested Readings

These references cover basic literature which will acquaint the reader with issues discussed here and serve as an introduction to new paradigm research: Belenky, Clincy, Goldberger, and Tarule (1986); Eisner (1981); Glaser and Strauss (1967); Hoshmand (1989); Junge (1989); Kuhn (1970); Lincoln and Guba (1985); Popper (1965); Reason and Rowan (1981); Reason (1988); Taylor and Bogdon (1984); and Toulmin (1972).

References

Belenky, M.F., Clincy, B.M.V, Goldberger, N.R., & Tarule, J.M. (1986). *Women's ways of knowing*. New York, NY: Basic Books.

Eisner, E.W. (1981). On the differences between scientific and artistic approaches to qualitative research. *Educational Researcher, 10*(4), 5-9.

Glaser, B.G., & Strauss, A.L. (1967). *The discovery of grounded theory: Strategies for qualitative research*. New York, NY: Aldine Publishing.

Hoshmand, L.S.T. (1989). Alternative research paradigms: A review and teaching proposal. *The Counseling Psychologist, 17*(1), 3-79.

Junge, M. (1989). The heart of the matter. *The Arts in Psychotherapy, 16*, 77-78.

Kuhn, T. (1970). *The structure of scientific revolutions*. Chicago, IL: University of Chicago.

Lincoln, Y.S., & Guba, E.G. (1985). *Naturalistic inquiry*. Beverly Hills, CA: Sage Publications.

Popper, K. (1965). On the sources of knowledge and ignorance. In *Conjectures and refutations: The growth of scientific knowledge* (pp. 3-30). New York, NY: Harper & Row.

Reason, P. (Ed.). (1988). *Human inquiry in action*. Beverly Hills, CA: Sage Publications.

Reason, P., & Rowan, J. (Eds.). (1981). *Human inquiry: A sourcebook of new paradigm research*. New York, NY: John Wiley & Sons.

Taylor, S.J., & Bogdon, R. (1984). *Introduction to qualitative research methods*. New York, NY: John Wiley & Sons.

Toulmin, S. (1972). *Human understanding: The collective use and evolution of concepts* (vol.1). Princeton, NJ: Princeton University Press.

Chapter 10

METHODOLOGICAL PROBLEMS AND SOME SOLUTIONS SPECIFIC TO ART THERAPY DATA

Harriet Wadeson, PhD, A.T.R.

One of the paradoxes of life is that our blessings are often one and the same as our curses. So it is with art therapy data. We are privileged to view the human psyche (whatever it may be) through the revealing window of imagistic expression. Through it we gain glimpses that illuminate the unconscious, dreams, fantasies, and imagination. Sometimes the worlds we behold are beautiful, sometimes bizarre, sometimes confounding, sometimes empty, seldom simple. As clinicians, we are privileged to work in realms of creativity and to encourage its growth.

As researchers, however, we are often perplexed as to how to bring systematic investigation to the rich and complex array of visual data our clients present to us. In discussing research and scholarship as "the next growth area" in the creative arts therapies, McNiff (1987) cites Arnheim's caution "against over-emphasis on quantification that can overlook the essence of a work of art by concentrating only on what can be measured" (p. 289). On the other hand, a purely descriptive or speculative approach says little from which we might generalize about human functioning. Thus, the art therapist is faced with the enormous challenge of "reading" the art in such a way that it may speak to us of the human condition with sound evidence to support our assertions, and, at the same time, convey its essential meaning without being reduced by our investigative methods.

To my mind, the major challenges in art therapy research are posed by its potential to illuminate the human condition. These would entail correlation studies (Gantt, 1986).[1] On the other hand, many art therapists feel the pressure

---

[1]See Chapter 8 for a slightly revised version of this paper.

to provide data showing that art therapy "works." These would be outcome studies (Gantt, 1986). There are problems specific to both areas. Before looking at them specifically, however, there are overriding problems that should be recognized in conducting any sort of behavioral science research. Gantt (1986) notes the difficulty in controlling variables in research with human subjects. In the natural sciences, variables are more easily controlled. For example, laboratory animals might be raised according to a strict regimen, injected with specific doses of drugs at prescribed times, killed, and autopsied to study effects on specific organ systems. Studying the effects of the same drugs on humans would be far less exact with possibilities of unknown and/or uncontrolled variables entering in. For one, their diets throughout their lives would not be constant.

Gantt (1986) also notes the failure of behavioral science research to achieve the predictive power of physical science research. She cites the Hawthorne effect in which selection as a research subject can alter the subject's attitude and the placebo effect in which the subject improves as a result of receiving an intervention, whatever it may be (for example, sugar-water that is believed to be medicine). Thus, the mind-set of the subject can influence research results.

In addition to the difficulties that face all researchers in the behavioral sciences, art therapy researchers encounter others posed by the very nature of our data. The purpose of this chapter is to articulate some of those problems.

Certainly fundamental to both art therapy practice and to art therapy research is how we understand art expression (see Wadeson, 1987, Chapter 4). From the very beginning of my art therapy practice in 1961, it became clear to me that an important differentiation we needed to make was between enduring patterns and momentary influences. It seemed to me that assessments based on a single session (such as some psychological tests using subjects' drawings) resulted in errors from confusing the two. Thus, a chaotic picture might indicate either personality disintegration or temporary disorganization due to a traumatic event, such as hospital admission. Art therapy sessions over time reveal the more enduring patterns of expression as a foundation, against which the temporary changes may be seen as an overlay. Both may be the focus of research, but it is crucial that the art therapist be clear about which is being studied. Gantt (1986) points up the cultural determinants of expressive properties and suggests that in studying similarities in the artwork of diverse populations, art therapists "need to devise ways to determine which characteristics are the result of psychological laws, which of cultural rules, which of independent invention" (p. 118).

Correlation Studies

Unfortunately (or fortunately, depending on your point of view), neither art expressions nor the individuals who create them are sufficiently simple to produce the one-to-one correlations that would make our work so much easier. For example, wouldn't we be delighted to produce research that would show that a particular symbol signals suicidal intent? Think of the lives we might save. Or, in our present search for markers of sexual abuse in children too afraid to speak of it, wouldn't art therapists provide an important service by discovering significant indisputable graphic indicators in the child's artwork?

For the present, our successful detections are of a more clinical nature than determined by research. Our methods are inexact. We rely on therapeutic relationships we have built; we try to develop trust; we seek to understand our clients' imagery; and, in some instances, our clients respond to our sensitivity and entrust us with their fears and vulnerabilities. But such results may be too little and too late. How many more people might be helped and how much more timely that help might be if the art data before our eyes might reveal itself more readily and more clearly.

As the word indicates, correlation refers to a relationship. In art therapy research, visual characteristics of the artwork are likely to be correlated with something else. For example, use of space, color, line, or content might be correlated with diagnosis. Or, change in artwork, such as more color used, more space covered, might be correlated with change in psychiatric condition, such as improvement. These examples refer to artistic style.

Style

How does one measure color used, space covered, quality of line? Unfortunately, measurement of these graphic characteristics may violate Arnheim's caution and move us far from the expressive quality of the art piece as a whole. Nevertheless, it is possible to set up measurement guidelines. For unbiased results, customary methodological strategies should be employed. For example, the raters should be independent and "blind." In other words, those rating the graphic characteristics should be "blind" to the patient's condition or medication or whatever other variables the researcher is attempting to correlate with the art style. In addition, the other variables should be assessed independently, preferably by raters other than those judging the art. If the other variable is diagnosis, it should be made by raters who have not seen the art. A further necessary strategy is assurance that the sample is large enough to obtain results of statistical significance.

Methodological considerations of sample size and independent unbiased rating may pose difficulties of feasibility, but they are not the central problem in art therapy research. The major problem is in devising a way to assess the artwork and to understand what it communicates. In evaluating style, simply counting colors used or measuring pictorial objects may not produce meaningful results. As I have stated elsewhere (Wadeson, 1979, 1980), in art expression the whole is more than the sum of its parts. The impact of an artwork cannot be fully assessed through the measurement of its individual components, no matter how precise those measurements might be. On the other hand, impressionistic judgments are imprecise.

Often, style in art expression is related to effect, an important aspect of communication in art and psychiatric assessment. Once again, it is difficult to form simple relationships. More often than not, it is the totality of the art production that conveys its emotional import rather than particular visual characteristics. For example, a picture with much empty space might express a feeling of emptiness associated with depression, or it may dramatize a small object in the picture and convey a very different sort of feeling.

This area may be even more difficult. The art therapist is on safest ground when the subject identifies the content. For example, the woman in the picture is identified as "my mother"; the clay house is "where I was born." Beyond such designations, the art therapist is in uncertain territory and unless it is identified as such, the whole research effort may be dismissed as speculative. Although various objects depicted in clients' artwork may be obvious, their particular meanings may be less so, and art therapists must be careful about making assumptions. The example I like to cite is the Star of David my bipolar patient drew repeatedly. Her Jewishness was very important to her, and since she spoke of it often I assumed that this symbol represented her Jewish identity. Many sessions later she told me that her husband's name was David and the star stood for him. The limitation in relying on clients' explanations alone, of course, is that one of the profundities of artwork is its unconscious expression, by definition, material outside the subject's awareness.

In my experience, the best solution to this problem makes use of our major strength, our clinical expertise in fostering the creation of revealing art expression and in helping clients to relate to their artwork (see Wadeson, 1987, Chapters 3 and 5). By helping clients get in touch with their unconscious processes through their art, and by a sensitive building of trust in unconscious processes through their art, and by a sensitive building of trust in the therapeutic relationship, the art therapist creates the optimal conditions for the patient to disclose meaningful data without need of the art therapist's speculative interpretation. In this way the work serves both clinical and research objectives. This is a very important consideration that will be discussed further below.

Conflict Between Research and Clinical Objectives

An important consideration in medical research with human subjects is the well-being of the research subject (see the chapter on ethics). Some studies may create conflict between research and treatment objectives. Although the encouragement of art expression is a far more benign intervention than many physical procedures, nevertheless there may be instances when an art therapy directive devised to obtain research data may run contrary to clinical goals. For example, it might be clinically inadvisable to suggest drawing experiences of abuse to an adult survivor of child abuse who is overwhelmed and suicidal as she begins to recall repressed memories of ritual abuse. In my own work with several such clients, I have felt it important to their treatment for them to remain in control of the expression of their painful pasts. As research subjects in the investigation of memories of abuse, on the other hand, they could be administered a protocol collecting data in accordance with research rather than treatment objectives. In the best of all possible worlds, of course, research and treatment goals are synergistic. When they are not, risks versus benefits must be balanced, as described in Chapter 5.

Repetitions

One of the most exciting opportunities for exploration in art therapy research presents itself when particular stylistic characteristics, symbols, or themes emerge over and over again in the art of a particular group. Such was my experience in noticing spirals appearing among suicidal patients who never saw one another's art and who were hospitalized at different times (Wadeson, 1971, 1975). What is more, these patients described their spirals as having similar meanings of entrapment and hopelessness. Linda Gantt (1986) reports that her initial interest in research was stimulated by Hanna Kwiatkowska's telling her that depressed patients drew concentric circles, whirlpools, and other concentric forms. Hanna and I both worked at the National Institute of Mental Health, she with schizophrenics and I with depressed and bipolar patients. Prompted by her remark about my work, Linda collected concentric form drawings over the next seven years.

The point here is that some of the most meaningful research often arises out of the art therapist's impressionistic observations. Although only a small minority of Linda's patients produced concentric configurations, most of those who did were depressed. All my patients were depressed so that my research was generated from the observation of many such drawings. To substantiate my observation, I collected and counted them.

Although my observations were not the result of a tightly controlled scientific study, they point up another significant aspect of art therapy research alluded to earlier. Art therapists, unlike natural science researchers, lack the ability to predict. Therefore, many of our investigations must be with *ex post facto* data; in other words, art that has already been produced. We are unable to predict that a suicidal individual will draw a spiral or a depressed patient will produce a concentric configuration. (A physiologist, on the other hand, would be able to predict that administrations of beta blockers of epinephrine from the adrenal medulla gland will lower blood pressure.)

Nevertheless, despite art therapists' inability to predict, the importance of "found" data should not be minimized. Often these observations are closest to the heart of our work. We are not imposing expectations removed from reality. Many a "green" researcher has floundered in frustration down a blind alley pursuing a naive and fruitless expectation. For example, I once attended a student presentation in which a would-be researcher described her design of having patients draw doorways to illuminate boundary issues. Although one can envision a connection here, she had nothing to report. There were no noteworthy characteristics found in the doorway drawings. The design arose from the student's ideas rather than from observations of patient art work.

Some of my own observations have come as surprises rather than from expectations, such as depression in schizophrenia (Wadeson & Carpenter, 1976), concordance in the artwork of manic patients and their spouses (Wadeson & Fitzgerald, 1971), aggression and depression in hyperkinesis changing with amphetamine dosage (Wadeson & Epstein, 1976).

In addition to staying close to what actually **is**, "found object" research has another important advantage as well. Like "found object" art, it does not require elaborate materials. Whereas many art therapists might not have access to research resources such as computerized data systems, research assistants, or sophisticated statistical consultation, all can collect artwork and observe its characteristics. A researcher with such a "prepared mind" may then carry simple observations further and design a study to test them.

Outcome Studies

Art therapists know that art therapy "works." At times we are in the position of needing to "prove" that to administrators. Jobs may depend on such studies. And yet, outcome research is fraught with problems. It may be difficult to isolate the art therapy treatment variable sufficiently to show that it alone made a difference. Additionally, "outcome" itself is a slippery variable. What is meant by a positive outcome? Fewer hospitalizations? Holding a job? A patient's self-report of feeling better? Or something even more vague that captures "quality of life"? And when we speak of "positive outcome," "positive" in whose eyes? The client's? The researcher's? Society's standards?

Certainly, assessing outcome in terms of art is even more slippery. Does more color, more detail, people drawn with happy faces, indicate a positive response? How do we show that art translates to life? We need other variables, such as patients' reports about their lives, changed conditons of life, etc., to accompany what we may see as positive work.

Where empirical substantiation is required, the art therapist would be well advised to be as specific as possible about outcome indices. For example, elimination of substance abuse is a specific treatment goal that is easily measured. Outcome studies require tight controls to isolate the art therapy variable. Therefore, a control group would need to be matched with the subject group demographically, diagnostically, for treatment interventions, etc. Probably the art therapy intervention would have to be balanced with a comparable non-art therapy intervention to demonstrate that it was the unique nature of the art therapy experience that affected increased positive outcome. As stated previously, the sample would have to be sufficiently large to produce a result of statistical significance. Rawley Silver (1976) demonstrated that art tasks could be used to develop cognitive skills in children. Outcome was evaluated through pretests and postests, a customary procedure. My impression is that it is outcome studies for which art therapists are most desirous. It has been our wish to demonstrate to the larger realm of the helping professions and to the general public that our work is valid and substantial. As art people we sometimes bear the stereotype of being adrift in a world of make-believe. Often art therapists have tried to represent themselves as being as "scientific" as psychiatrists and psychologists (who also suffer being viewed as "unscientific" by those in the natural sciences).

Art therapists should realize that there have not been adequate outcome studies conducted in any of the psychotherapies until recently. Currently, studies are being undertaken through the National Institute of Mental Health, and they are still quite limited in their scope. An art therapist might be wise to present clinical substantiation of the efficacy of art therapy at this juncture in the development of the profession. Future substantial studies demonstrating art therapy's contribution to positive outcomes will be most welcome.

Addressing the Problems

In 1979, I published a paper, and in 1980, a chapter on art therapy research (Wadeson, 1979[2]; 1980) describing some of the problems I had faced and some of the solutions I had found. At that time art therapy research was far more primitive than it is now. Today many art therapists have access to sophisticated technologies to assist them as described in the chapter on computers. Nevertheless, some of the recommendations I made in 1979 are still applicable. In addition to the suggestions already stated in connection with particular problems, the following is a sampling of possible empirical research formats that may be applied to art therapy data, or in some instances, help to elicit the desired data. Proceeding from the least structured to the most structured research methodologies, they are:

1. Observations of emerging data

Such data become apparent only after art productions have been collected and studied, as described above. An example of such findings was reported in "Impact of the Seclusion Room Experience" (Wadeson & Carpenter, 1976). Twenty out of 41 patients hospitalized for acute schizophrenia who had been placed in seclusion spontaneously made 43 pictures which they described as representing this experience. Their discussions of the pictures indicated that they represented hallucinations and delusions experienced in seclusion, intense affect associated with seclusion, and a focus on the staff member in attendance at seclusion. The subject matter of seclusion was neither suggested nor expected in the art from these patients. Its prominence in the pictures conveyed its importance to them, and the various reactions depicted suggested that attention was warranted to increase awareness of the meaning of this experience to the patient. An important consideration in this form of research is the care the art therapist must take not to encourage the production of particular art data once aware of its likelihood to appear.

2. Art tasks designed to elicit specific data

In this sort of investigation, the art therapist structures the session carefully so that the desired data will emerge. Well-known examples of this procedure are Kwiatkowska's family assessment (Kwiatkowska, 1978), the Ulman

---

[2] This paper won first prize for research from the American Art Therapy Association in

Assessment Series (Ulman, 1975), and Rhyne's visual thinking assessment (1979). In my own work, I was interested in acute schizophrenics' subjective experience of their illness. To elicit this data I asked them to draw a self image, a picture of their psychiatric illness, and pictures of any hallucinations and delusions they had had (Wadeson & Carpenter, 1976). Studies such as these require careful planning. (The door drawing exercise described previously probably did not result from a pilot trial.) Before structuring the sessions on the experience of schizophrenia, I conducted sessions with this population for six months to determine the most propitious art tasks to elicit the data I sought. A carefully planned procedure such as this can be extremely fruitful. From this simple design of a sequence of five pictures requested, 14 papers were published.

An important consideration in this sort of design is the constancy of sequence of art tasks, art materials, and instructions. Additionally, as do many art therapists using this sort of procedure, I begin each session with a "free" picture. In this way it is possible to get a base-line art expression without contamination of the researcher's instructions. As a practical matter, the "free" picture can serve as a warm-up or ice-breaker for the more focused work. A significant advantage of this sort of design is its focus and efficiency in obtaining the desired data.

3. Judgments of art made when "blind" to the independent variable

It is difficult for the art therapist to be "blind" to some kinds of variables, such as changes in the patient's condition, diagnosis, length of hospitalization, etc. Factors such as drug dosage, on the other hand, may easily be concealed if the study is "double-blind," i.e., if the patient is not allowed to know drug dosage as well. The study of "The Effect of Amphetamine on Hyperkinesis" is an example of this design (Wadeson & Epstein, 1976). I noted changes in depression and aggression while "blind" to drug dosages. Increases in both aggression and depression correlated with increase in amphetamine dosage.

4. Predictive studies

As mentioned previously, it is very difficult for art therapists to achieve predictablilty. Occasionally, however, it is possible to design such a study. In researching recovery style in acute schizophrenia, I predicted that the artwork of those who "integrated" their illness would be more expressive than those who "sealed over" the acute schizophrenic episode (McGlashen, Wadeson, Carpenter, & Levy, 1977). In order to eliminate my own bias, I employed two raters "blind" to the patients who created the art to judge the artwork for specific characteristics of expressiveness as well as a global rating of expressiveness. They achieved acceptable interrater reliability, and their judgments supported the hypothesis that "integrators" would produce more expressive art than "sealers."

Feasibility

Even armed with research expertise and imaginative designs, the art therapy researcher may be confounded by practical considerations. Research is usually extremely time-consuming. For example, many art therapy students in a two-year Master's degree program simply do not serve in a practicum long enough to collect adequate data to complete credible research. In addition to the time necessary to collect the data, often a trial period is necessary to do some pilot investigation to refine the strategies to be used. Short time is likely to produce only a small sample, thereby considerably limiting the generalizations that can be drawn from the data. Some of my own research has suffered from small sample size.

As mentioned earlier, access to support resources may also be limited. Art therapists whose primary responsibilities are clinical may also have little opportunity during the work week for the extensive effort most research demands.

A possible solution to some of these problems may be found in collaboration. Art therapists can share data with one another (see Arrington's chapter on assessment instruments listing those seeking data from other art therapists). Additionally, art therapy research can "piggy-back" and become a part of larger investigations. For example, my study of "Art and Recovery Style from Psychosis" (McGlashan, Wadeson, Carpenter, & Levy, 1977), discussed previously, was built upon the work of the other investigators who had delineated the "integrator" and "sealing over" modes of recovery. Another example was the addition of an art therapy evaluation in the family links of alcoholics (Wadeson, 1980, Chapter 18). In this instance, the major investigation consisted of interviews with family members. A family art evaluation around the issue of alcohol use in the family added an additional dimension. Linda Gantt (see Chapter 3) has suggested the development of client art data banks, an enterprise of significant collaboration within the field that would be of great benefit to art therapy researchers.

As a former AATA Publications Chair as well as a Research Chair, I would like to add a plug for clear writing. Some art therapists do excellent work, but do not know how to report it in writing. This is an additional area of time and effort for those who face this problem. The researcher may need to take a writing course, obtain tutoring, or employ an editor.

In terms of feasibility, some of the most likely prospective researchers to have motivation, research guidance, and resources are doctoral candidates.

As more and more art therapists pursue doctoral degrees, more art therapy research is likely to be produced and new standards of excellence achieved.

Challenges

Art therapy research can be ambitious or modest. Most art therapists can observe emerging patterns for particular groups of clients. Most can also design tasks to elicit specific data. Where a variable can be isolated, greater methodologic rigor can be employed. Some observations can be quantified without losing their meaning. "Blind" raters can be employed to eliminate bias.

This chapter has focused on some of the obvious problems associated with empirical investigation of art therapy data. Other kinds of studies discussed elsewhere in this text bring with them their own problems and creative solutions. As stated at the beginning of this chapter, the major challenge is the unique nature of art therapy data, the rich and fertile fields in which we toil. For the most part, art therapists have borrowed the research methodologies of the behavioral sciences. Perhaps it is time to develop our own methods, measurements, and language to describe our data. Toward that end in 1989, the AATA Research Committee offered a prize for the development of new methodologies tailored to the study of art therapy data. There were no winners. The prize money has gone into the production of this *Guide*, in the hope that it will assist and encourage substantial art therapy research and the development of suitable methodologies to answer the questions art therapy researchers seek to ask.

References

Gantt, L. (1986). Systematic investigations of art works: Some research models drawn from neighboring fields. *American Journal of Art Therapy, 24,* 111-118.

Gantt, L. (1987). Some specific recommendations for art therapy research. Upublished paper.

Kwiatkowska, H. (1978). *Family therapy and evaluation through art.* Springfield, IL: Charles C Thomas.

McGlashan, T., Wadeson, H., Carpenter, W., & Levy, S. (1977). Art recovery and style from psychosis. *Journal of Nervous and Mental Disorders, 164,* 182-190.

McNiff, S. (1987). Research and scholarship in the creative arts therapies. *The Arts in Psychotherapy, 14*, 285-292.

Rhyne, J. (1979). Drawing as personal constructs: A study in visual dynamics (Doctoral dissertation, University of Santa Cruz, 1978). *Dissertation Abstracts International, 79*, 10569.

Silver, R. A. (1976). Using art to evaluate and develop cognitive skills. *American Journal of Art Therapy, 16*(1), 11-19.

Ulman, E. (1975). A new use of art in psychiatric analysis. In E. Ulman & P. Dachinger (Eds.), *Art therapy in theory and practice*. New York, NY: Schocken.

Wadeson, H. (1971). Portraits of suicide, Pubication of exhibit, Annual Meeting, American Psychiatric Association, Washington, DC.

Wadeson, H. (1975). Suicide: Expression in images. *American Journal of Art Therapy, 14*, 75-82.

Wadeson, H. (1979). Some uses of art therapy data in research. *American Journal of Art Therapy, 18*(1).

Wadeson, H. (1980). *Art psychotherapy*. New York, NY: John Wiley & Sons.

Wadeson, H. (1987). *The dynamics of art psychotherapy*. New York, NY: John Wiley & Sons.

Wadeson, H., & Carpenter, W. (1976). Impact of the seclusion room experience. *Journal of Nervous and Mental Disorders, 163*, 318-328.

Wadeson, H., & Carpenter, W. (1976). Subjective experience of acute schizophrenia. *Schizophrenia Bulletin, 2*, 302-316.

Wadeson, H., & Epstein, R. (1976). Intrapsychic effect of amphetamine in hyperkinesis. *Mental Health in Children, 3*, 35-60. Westbury, NY: PJD Publications.

Wadeson, H., & Fitzgerald, R. (1971). Marital relationship in manic-depressive illness: Conjoint psychiatric art evaluations. *Journal of Nervous and Mental Disease, 153*, 180-196.

Chapter 11

THE SINGLE-CASE STUDY

Pamela Diamond, MA, A.T.R.

Outcome research in any therapeutic modality is not simple.[1] There are, however, techniques available that individual clinicians can use to begin to quantify the results of their work. The single-case experimental design builds on the case study and allows for an objective evaluation of an intervention. This chapter will provide an introduction to the design and analysis of single-case data in an art therapy context. Data requirements, measurement issues, and design variations will be presented. The position of single-case designs in the research continuum will be discussed with an emphasis on validity issues and the need for systematic replication. The goal of this chapter is to present a tool that art therapists can begin to use to systematically evaluate their practice and add to the research base in this field.

Evaluation Research Versus Basic Research

An example will help to clarify the difference between evaluation research and basic research. In the art therapy context, a basic research question might be: does the person's art change in form or content as behavior changes? Evaluation research, however is not concerned specifically with the structure of the art; it is concerned with the results of the treatment, which in the case of art therapy, involves the use of art. Evaluation research is very pragmatic and deals with causes and effects.

The goals of a given treatment are to change some behavior that is seen as troublesome to the individual seeking treatment. This behavior can be defined

---

[1] This material was originally presented at the Annual Symposium of the Buckeye Art Therapy Association in Cleveland, Ohio, September 16, 1988.

either broadly or narrowly, but there is always something that is to be changed as a result of the treatment. The questions for evaluation researchers are: (1) Did the change take place, and (2) Did the treatment which was offered cause the change? Usually, this second question is not answered unequivocally. Even in the best of experimental designs, there is a remote possibility that something other than the treatment caused the observed effect. What we do is try to clear away as many of these alternative explanations as possible.

Art therapists have used the case study extensively to validate their various treatment approaches. The primary problem with the case study as an evaluation tool is that it does not rule out the many conflicting explanations for the observed results which can be offered. Add to this difficulty the question of experimenter bias and the subjectivity of the observations, and you do not have a strong tool for determining cause and effect. The case study is good for developing an understanding of the processes involved in the therapy, and for developing hypotheses about what might be the curative factors in a treatment. In other words, it is a good beginning. It allows the researcher to develop better questions and more sophisticated measures and procedures for evaluation. It is not, however, good enough on its own to determine effectiveness.

Evaluation research addresses the question of cause and effect, treatment, and outcome. The most difficult problems to be addressed in evaluation research are the various threats to the internal validity of the study which allow for alternative explanations of these observed effects.[2] There are seven fairly common threats to internal validity which should be considered in any research design in which causality is to be inferred. When these threats exist, we cannot have as much confidence in the inferences made on the basis of the research as we might were these threats controlled in some way. Because these threats must be carefully considered in all research, I will discuss them in more detail.

Looking at a hypothetical research study will help to clarify these seven basic threats to internal validity. In this study, an art therapist asks her anorexic clients to draw full body portraits once a week during therapy. The primary goal of the portrait drawings is to encourage the client to come to grips with the reality of her body image. The therapeutic goal is to decrease denial and encourage the client to deal more effectively with the family problems which maintain her illness. There are several outcome measures which are collected: (a) the clients are weighed weekly, (b) psychologists use

---

[2] There are several good references which discuss the various threats to internal validity. One of the best is Cook and Campbell's *Quasi-Experimentation: Design and Analysis for Field Settings* (1979).

a rating form to note the number of times in verbal therapy each client has spoken about her weight and about her family, and (c) families provide reports on the clients' eating behavior at home. The therapy process will be judged a success if the client gains weight, speaks more in therapy about family issues and less about weight, and the family reports that the client is eating better.

The various threats to internal validity may provide alternative explanations for the observed results. Seven of these threats are described in detail in the next section.

Threats to Internal Validity

1. History

Some event, other than the treatment, has occurred and is responsible for the observed effect. The most obvious historical event is one held in common by all of the patients in this study—that of the concurrent psychological therapy. That experience could be what is causing the changes. Other events which are more idiosyncratic to the individual, such as falling in love, the death of a family member, leaving home for college, etc., might also be the causal agents. Anything that happens to the person other than the full body drawings during art therapy **could** be the cause of the observed effects.

2. Maturation

Biological or psychological processes in the individual which occur over time naturally are responsible for the effect. When we are working with young people especially we are vulnerable to the effects of maturation. People change a lot as they grow and develop, and they sometimes do just grow out of some conditions! With our anorexic patients, the physical changes of early adolescence may have precipitated the problem. Adaptation to these changes over time as the hormone levels stabilized may have eliminated the cause of the eating disorder.

3. Testing

Significant differences on pretesting and posttesting may be the result of taking the test itself. Tests are reactive instruments and may change that which they attempt to measure. In our example, the testing is not in the form of a 'test' as such but consists of ratings by others. This type of measure is still vulnerable to testing effects, however. The fact that the therapist asks certain questions at certain times, the fact that the person knows she is being evaluated, etc., all provide cues to the expected behavior, and motivation either to cooperate or not depending on the individual. The weight measure is really the best nonreactive measure in the study and the least affected by testing. This highlights one of the best reasons for having a variety of outcome measures. If one measure is less affected by testing than another, but the results correlate highly, the researcher will have more confidence in those measures which may have been affected by testing than if they had shown conflicting results. In this way it is possible to sometimes check directly on the effects of testing.

4. Instrumentation

Any change in observational technique or in the instrument itself which results in measures which are unreliable from one testing time to another will make it impossible to determine whether the observed effect is real or is an artifact of the observational techniques which were used. In our case, a change of psychologists midstudy would contribute to an instrumentation effect. Even with the best rating scale around, two observers are going to have slightly different interpretations of the observed results. Another instrumentation effect might result from a change in bathroom scales (we all know how much one scale differs from another), or a change in the procedure of weighing (with or without clothes, in the morning or at night). In our hypothetical study, if the weighing was done during morning appointments early in treatment and during afternoon appointments during the later phases, what appears to be a weight gain over time, may in fact be a normal weight variation which is related to time of day rather than to any treatment effect.

5. Statistical regression

When using data from a group of individuals who are likely to have scores which deviate significantly from the population mean on a given measure, there will be more of a shift toward that mean on later testing. For example, if we know that the **average** weight of **all** 16-year-old girls is 100 pounds, and we are obtaining weight measures from a group of 16-year-old girls that are much lower than this average value, say around 80 pounds, then when we measure these girls again, any increases in weight which appear may not be due to actual weight gain, but may in fact be a result of measurement error in the original measurement. Anorexics are more likely to appear to gain weight rather than lose it just because they are so very thin in the first place. They are at the extreme end of the distribution of weight and the probability of their weight being higher at another weighing is extremely high.

6. Mortality

Subjects may drop out of study for one reason or another. The researcher has no way of knowing how the results would have been different if they had not left the study. If all of the anorexics who are improving leave therapy and those who aren't stay in, then the data is skewed. It would also be a problem the other way around. Whenever a subject leaves a study prematurely, it leads to uncertainty because it is impossible to determine the effect that subject would have had if she had stayed. The experimenter can only speculate, but cannot know for certain.

7. Selection

In comparing two groups, it is not likely that the two groups are equivalent unless the subjects are randomly assigned to the groups. Without random assignment there may be effects that are due to the groups being different in the first place. In comparing two groups of anorexics, one that sought treatment and one that decided against it, the groups would not necessarily be equivalent just because they are both made up of anorexic clients. The same argument holds if the control group is made up of similar patients who could not afford the treatment because their insurance would not pay for it. There may be many other differences between the groups, and there is no way of knowing what they are. Random assignment is one of the best ways to protect against this problem, but it is difficult to accomplish in clinical settings.

The Research Continuum

Several research designs have been developed over the years to control for these various threats to internal validity. These designs represent a continuum which is based on how well or poorly the threats to internal validity are controlled.

At one end of the continuum is the **one-shot case study**. In this type of study, observations are made on outcome variables at one point in time, and the subjects generally form a convenience sample rather than a methodically or randomly selected one. This approach is considered a **pseudo-experimental design**, and is what best describes most of the art therapy case studies. As a pseudo-experimental design, it is more descriptive than experimental and none of the threats to internal validity are adequately controlled. The researcher can only make conjectures about the results and hopefully will be led onward to more rigorous designs.

At the other end of the continuum is the **pretest/posttest control group design**. When there is random assignment to groups, this design controls for all of the above-mentioned threats to internal validity except mortality. The effects of testing, instrumentation, history, and maturation should be equalized across all groups if they have been randomly assigned. Mortality remains the only threat of any consequence, since it is not directly controllable by the researcher.

Clinicians, however, often criticize this type of study. They feel that the results are not generalizable to the clinic because the research situation places constraints on the process that are not necessarily consistent with actual practice situations. Clinicians also question the ethics of the control group when dealing with people in need. This criticism is answered somewhat by waiting list controls; however, this is not always a viable alternative. Another criticism is that average scores, which represent average performances, do not adequately take into account individual differences. A final criticism is that administrative and time constraints often make such a project completely unfeasible for the practicing clinician.

The **single-case experimental design**, which falls somewhere near the middle of the continuum of research, does allow for some control of the threats to internal validity. This type of design is seen by many as more relevant to actual clinical practice and therefore is more likely to be used by the practicing clinician. The single-case experimental design differs from the one-shot case study and from standard group research in several ways: (a) it may or may not involve a group of subjects, (b) observations and measurements of relevant variables are taken prior to treatment and at various times during and after treatment, and (c) the process generally parallels responsible clinical practice.

Researchers have found single-case designs to be particularly useful in situations where control groups have not been possible or might be unethical. This approach allows for greater flexibility within the program being evaluated than many other designs. Changes in intervention are possible if seen to be needed. The only requirement for maintaining the integrity of the design is that the time when things changed should be carefully noted and the measures of the variables of interest should be uninterrupted. In evaluation research, single-case designs are often a good compromise between qualitative research and quantitative evaluation. In fact, single-case designs can be used in conjunction with qualitative studies to give additional credibility to the results.

The major difference between this type of design and a descriptive case study is that the measurements are precise and they are taken consistently over time. These measurements are chosen to accurately reflect the problem being investigated, and outcome is often measured in several different ways. Another distinguishing feature is the reliance of this design on clinical replication to add strength to the inferences which are made.

Through a skillful combination of precise measurements over time and clinical replication, the researcher/clinician can control for many of the worst threats to internal validity by using the single-case experimental design. The premise of this procedure is to use data which is collected prior to the beginning of treatment to predict the probable course of behavior should no treatment be given. The researcher can then look at the actual, observed behavior and compare it to that predicted trend. One case alone does not convince anyone of an experimental effect, but the same pattern observed with different clients, at different times, and in different settings is a very convincing argument that the treatment effect is real and valid and not due to some extraneous common denominator.

FIGURE 1. A Time-Series Graph Showing the Responses of Three People Who Received the Same Intervention at Different Points in Time.

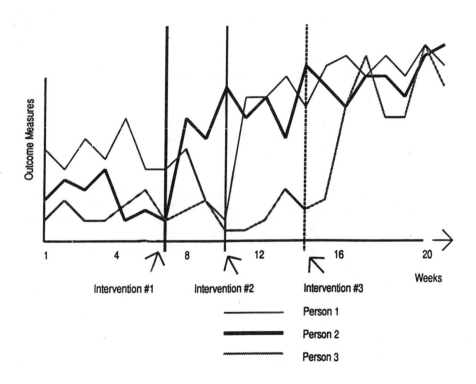

FIGURE 1. A Time-Series Graph Showing the Responses of Three People Who Received the Same Intervention at Different Points in Time.

An illustration will help to demonstrate how this design can control somewhat for the various threats to internal validity. In this example, the data for each subject are analyzed as a separate experiment. In Figure 1, the graphed lines each represent the different subjects. The vertical lines represent the time of the intervention associated with each subject. The pattern of responses indicated on this graph represents an optimal result in which there is little ambiguity. At the point of intervention, each subject shows a change in the preferred direction on the variable of interest. Results are seldom this clean, but this is the basic pattern that a researcher hopes for to demonstrate the effectiveness of a given intervention.

In the single-case experimental design with replication, several different individuals are observed and measured at different times. In this situation many of the threats to internal validity can be controlled. History and maturation are not likely explanations for the observed, similar patterns of behavior when several different cases are included. All of the subjects are unlikely to have experienced the same historical event or maturational phase at the different times. Testing and regression are less likely explanations of the observed results since repeated testing is unlikely to influence an overall trend. Selection is only a problem in group comparison studies. In the single-case design, each individual is analyzed individually as a separate study and no group comparisons are made. Instrumentation can be controlled by careful procedures and multiple and rigorous measures. Mortality is not a problem if the same attention is given to those who leave therapy as to those who remain.

The use of the single-case experimental design can produce a study in which the threats to internal validity are controlled in slightly different ways than in group comparison studies in which randomization and control groups are used. Clearly, these threats are not as completely controlled as in the true experimental design, but with enough replications which show similar patterns, the evidence of a cause-and-effect relationship becomes stronger.

To reiterate, single-case designs require objective data which is taken repeatedly and carefully on several cases undergoing the same treatment. The intervention procedure which is used should be clearly defined in order that replication by other clinicians/researchers is possible. Measures of change must be reliable and valid. And, it is as important to attend to failures as well as successes. Doing so will provide valuable information about the salient factors which led to the unexpected results.

The single-case experimental design is basically a time-series design. Much of what has been written about this approach, however, has been overlooked by our profession and by other clinicians because it has been identified with behavior therapy. The procedures are theory free, however, and, with only slight changes from what is normal clinical practice, art therapists can upgrade their research from the case study to the single-case experimental design. First, they must recognize that the design strategy is possible. Next, they must arrange to take systematic and repeated measurements on relevant outcome variables. Because measurement is such a vital issue, the next section of this chapter will address this more in depth.

Measurement

A time-series design is possible whenever measures are collected on one or several variables over time on an experimental unit. The measures must be taken prior to the treatment of interest as well as after, but other than that requirement there are many variations of the basic design. There may be one or several measures of interest; the experimental unit may be an individual, a program, or any other relevant aggregate; and the analysis of the results of the intervention may range from visual inspection of graphs of the time series to sophisticated computer modeling.

Measures used in time-series research should be relevant to the program goals. For example, if a researcher is interested in assessing the utility of a new program which was developed to decrease truant behavior in middle school children, then absence records would provide much of the relevant data. If the program is designed to aid underachievers, however, then perhaps attendance would not be the best measure. Grades and teacher evaluations might be more appropriate. The basic idea is to choose a measure that fits the specific program goals. It is preferable also to have more than one measure of the outcome of interest if possible. Hopefully, these are measures that reflect multiple points of view. For a group of truant kids, the relevant multiple measures might be weekly absence data, test grades in relevant subjects (math, language arts, etc.), six-week grades, number of encounters with law enforcement for nontruant related behavior (vandalism, runaway), teacher observations, parent observations, counselor observations, and self reports. The idea is to build a measurement package that provides a balanced picture of the problem and its resolution or nonresolution over time. These measures can be analyzed separately and studied for concomitant variation or lack of it. In this way there is information not only about global outcome, but also about the achievement of individual subgoals. In a truancy program, for example, if attendance is up but teacher attitudes are more negative, the researcher/clinician may want to recommend some changes in the treatment program to address this discrepancy.

After determining what to measure, it is important to take these measures as frequently as possible in order to establish adequate baseline and post-intervention trends. To obtain adequate observational data from multiple respondents, the forms used should be easy to fill out, nonreactive, and should be specifically designed to take advantage of the individual's specific point of view. All questionnaires should be developed with the specific program's idiosyncrasies in mind, and the instruments should never be changed during the course of the investigation.

Archival records such as absence records, grades, etc., are a good source of data for time series studies. Other sources of archival data that have proven to be useful are number of hospital stays, number of arrests for DWI (driving while intoxicated), length of stay in hospital, etc. With archival data, rates must often be calculated prior to analysis, since the time intervals between measurements often vary. For example, if arrest data are used, the appropriate rates can be calculated as number of arrests per month or per week or per year. This insures that for each interval there is a comparable number.

Another basic concern that must be addressed when considering measures for time-series designs is the reactivity of the measure. The measurement process itself often influences the results. This is especially a problem when measures are collected many times. Response sets, the guinea pig effect, the questionnaire actually influencing the attitude, all result in measurement error that will affect the results of any analysis in an unpredictable way.

It is always best to avoid measures that are too stable in time-series research. If a measure is not sensitive to small changes, it is not appropriate for this type of research. Standardized tests often have information regarding the measure's stability over time, and those measures which are highly stable should not be used in single-case research. The researcher is much more interested in 'state' than 'trait' data.

Another concern is with boredom and rote response from the respondent. Since measures are taken repeatedly, there is always a possibility that the respondents will simply remember their last responses and repeat them rather than thinking about them again. They may also be so bored with the task that they resent having to do it and merely answer randomly. Many of these problems can be avoided by careful instruction to the respondents and by developing forms that are short and to the point, rather than long and demanding.

Design Variations

There are several different design variations available in single-case research.[3] In general, the phases in which **no** treatment is applied are referred to by the letter 'A'. Those in which the **first** treatment is applied are given the letter 'B'. If there are subsequent additional treatments offered, which differ from the first, they are given the letters 'C', 'D', etc., for as many as are needed. Using these symbols then, different designs can be described which vary as to the number of different treatments, the time of application, and the number of applications.

The most common of the single-case designs is the basic A-B design. In this, the A represents a baseline period during which no treatment is offered. Data is collected on all of the variables of interest during this phase. The B phase begins when the first treatment is offered. Data collection continues during this phase on all variables. Since the baseline phase is used as an indicator of the individual's behavior prior to treatment, and will be used in the analysis to project the expected behavior, given no intervention, it is important that this phase contain as many data points as possible. In most therapy outcome studies, this presents a challenge to the researcher, since it is often difficult to justify not beginning treatment at once. Waiting lists, initial information gathering periods, and the time between the screening interview and the first appointment can all provide opportunities for having a period of time during which relevant data can be collected. Often this can be in the form of daily check lists, frequent physical measures, observations by others, etc. For some types of problems, as mentioned earlier, archival records provide extensive baseline information.

Some other variations on the basic A-B design include the A-B-A-B design in which there is a baseline condition, followed by an intervention. The intervention is discontinued after a specified time, resulting in another 'no-treatment' condition, which is then again followed by a re-application of the treatment condition. This type of design is used extensively in behavior therapy, but is not as appropriate in art therapy research.

A variation that might prove useful to art therapists is the A-B-C design in which the baseline phase is followed by two different types of treatments in sequence. The situation in which this might be useful is one in which the initial treatment is not seen as working very well and the therapist decides to make a distinct change in her procedures. If the time of change is noted carefully,

---

[3] There are many excellent references on this topic. One of the best is Bloom & Fischer's *Evaluating Practice: Guidelines for the Accountable Professional* (1982).

this will only change the original design from A-B to A-B-C. This kind of flexibility is one of the strengths of single-case research. Instead of the change invalidating the prior work, as would be the case in group research, the change can be incorporated into the design.

There are numerous variations available in the single-case design. The only absolute requirements are for some baseline condition to exist at the beginning of the process, and for a careful notation of the time when the phases are changed. This allows for great flexibility within this design paradigm.

Conclusions

The major point of this paper has been that art therapists can and should be actively involved in the evaluation of their work. Through systematic evaluation practices, the credibility and utility of the profession will be enhanced. There are many different research alternatives available to the practicing clinician, and some of the ones described in this paper are especially well suited for use by individual therapists.

References

Bloom, M., & Fischer, J. (1982). *Evaluating practice: Guidelines for the accountable professional.* Englewood Cliffs, NJ: Prentice-Hall.
Cook, T.D., & Campbell, D.T. (1979). *Quasi-experimentation: Design and analysis issues for field settings.* Boston, MA: Houghton Mifflin.

Chapter 12

SOCIAL ACTION RESEARCH

Winnie Ferguson, PhD, A.T.R.

Social action research projects are exciting to art therapists since they provide the researcher an opportunity to implement creative change in a problematic social situation (Riley, 1963). While most research entails the search for new methods and ideas, the social action project also puts the researcher in touch with current social situations which are themselves in daily flux.

Selecting an area of research requires the individual to look into him/herself in search of those issues which have strong personal interest. During the inner search, seeds of ideas often grow into research projects. Homelessness, obesity, employment, and children at risk are only a few areas which have been the subject of social action research.

An Overview of Social Action Research

Social action research data reporting differs from other research in that it reports procedures used to create a change, but does not necessarily use statistical analysis. In documenting the research the author simply reports the design, implementation, and findings of the social action research. The key to this type of work is demonstrating the development and implementation of processes which address necessary change in a problematic social issue.

One definition of the word "social" in the *American Heritage Dictionary* is "of or pertaining to society." The word "action," of course, is the active involvement in doing something. Art therapists, along with many other mental health professionals, are often involved in social problems. Issues pertaining to society are human issues and are, therefore, of concern to caring indivduals.

Social action research seems an ideal model for art therapy research, since it deals with the actual identification of a social need, planning creative interventions to address that need, implementing an actual pilot project to attempt changing the situation, and finally, evaluating the project with recommendations for further research.

Many areas appropriate for research in art therapy are identified by needs in society which are known to the researcher. Identification of a social situation warranting change is the first step in developing research directed toward this goal (Meyer, 1976). Creative approaches to problem solving are not unique to the researcher. The development of imaginative procedures for serving clients is part of most art therapists' daily routine. The identification of significant procedures for meeting needs related to a recognized social problem is the logical sequence of events in this research.

Implementation of the project using developed procedures is the next step. Organization and planning prior to the actual implementation of the project help to assure smooth operation of the research. Records, photos, and other documenting data should be carefully collected and stored for use in the evaluation phase of the work.

Evaluation of what has been accomplished in the research requires critical thinking on the part of the researcher. It is necessary to report the failures as well as the successes of the study. Data should be presented in a manner which allows readers to understand the issues. Communication of the researcher's perceptions provides others with an opportunity to replicate the project with clients.

Specific Steps

Identification of a Social Situation for Research

In searching for an area which appears to need change, the investigator first examines issues that have some personal significance. Often research is a response to a long-term interest and reflects insights developed over time.

Earlier involvements with an issue would provide the investigator with valuable personal contacts for the development of the project. Because the social action project requires implementation of the conceptual model as a pilot project, it is imperative for the researcher to have a thorough understanding of all the issues involved prior to embarking on the work.

The investigator should also consider the available resources, including not only financial resources, but also those resources which could provide ready access to the situation which will be addressed in the research. The investigator could find many challenging social situations in dire need of intervention; however, much research time might be spent attempting to gain access to clients.

One should be aware of the availability of the client group, easy access to a facility which will allow the research, and the personal time available to implement the social action project. All research requires much time from the investigator. Social action research requires the investigator to devote many hours in the actual implementation of the study. This is, of course, is in addition to the hours of library research one must complete to search for background material.

Assessment of Needs

Prior to beginning the research the investigator must completely assess the perceived problem. Reviewing the literature available regarding the social issue provides information on what others have discovered. For the literature review, one may utilize a computerized literature search available through university libraries. Information regarding the use of computerized literature searches is covered in another chapter in this *Guide*.

Surveys of the group to be served will provide the investigator with actual input from the client group. Surveys may be simple telephone interviews, or may require the subject to respond to a series of simple questions developed by the researcher. Data gathered will be useful in developing the actual form which the final social action research will use.

Development of Methods

During the assessment of needs for the research the investigator will be involved in discovering and then discarding possible methods to implement in the study. The creative development of methods which can be implemented to change the problematic condition is a major portion of social action research, and, the researcher must also complete the program with the results reported in the research document. The review of literature will provide the investigator with solutions which have been tried by others in the field. Often there will be little information available in the field of art therapy regarding one's topic.

The literature will provide a point from which the creative researcher may develop imaginative interventions. To develop a manageable research project, the investigator must identify key areas which will be the focus for change. It is enough to select one or two points of the social issue and to concentrate on those key areas.

Methods designed to implement the social action project should be unique. They should be untried by another individual with the chosen population. The methods should be based on a solid art therapy foundation.

In our small profession it is still possible to contact those individuals who have been the pioneers in the field. It would be valuable to communicate with those individuals who have been working in the area where the researcher intends to conduct the social action project. The mentor relationship which could result from this communication would be of value as the research progresses.

Implementation of a Pilot Project

Outcomes from quality research are based on the solid structure the researcher has constructed for the implementation of the pilot project. Planning cannot be overemphasized in the development of scholarly investigation. The variables of available client time, facility time, and investigator time may present a dilemma of some magnitude in initial implementation of research. Since implementation of social action research involves human subjects, the investigator is well advised to give considerable attention to planning sessions at times convenient for everyone concerned with the project.

The use of human subjects requires the investigator to obtain releases from clients and from facilities. The chapter of this *Guide* dealing with the use of human subjects is applicable to social action research.

In implementing social action projects it is necessary to conduct the research over an extended period of time. Projects which provide data encompassing a year of time will provide more relevance than those of shorter duration.

If other professionals are to be involved in the implementation of the work, it is necessary to provide an organized plan for their use. Regular meetings to keep all those active on the research team abreast of the progress will contribute to the smooth running of the project. In addition to the meetings, the researcher will find that circulating printed copies of the minutes of meetings also provides improved communication.

Actual sessions used in the research project should follow a flexible format. In all creative experiences, the therapist must be able to adapt to changes presented in the sessions. Often this flexibility uncovers unexpected and useful information. Careful documentation of all art work is essential in the collection of data. It is necessary to develop a pattern that provides the researcher time for this important part of the data collection soon after the sessions. It may be helpful to use audio tapes or video tapes to further extend the observation of the interaction during sessions. If video cameras are used, it is important that clients are comfortable with their use during sessions.

All documentation developed in the project should be included in the research report. Data not included in the body of the study should be inserted in the appendix of the report. Here, the term *documentation* would include information such as descriptions of techniques developed for the project, surveys, etc.

Assessment of Outcomes

At the completion of the social action research project, it is necessary to assess the results of the interventions to ascertain the changes brought about by the project. It is usual for the researcher to look for positive changes in the situation; however, it is equally important to report negative changes resulting from the project. If, indeed, negative changes are apparent, it is extremely important to analyze the causes of these changes. In the analysis the researcher should endeavor to ascertain what specifically caused these changes and should recommend alternative steps to rectify the problem.

Assessment of the changes resulting from the project can include both observational information and graphic examples of artwork from clients involved in the research. Assessments must be supported by concrete data which are then related to opinions in previously published work in the field. Upon conclusion of the project assessment, the researcher will have evaluated the effectiveness of the work. Questions presented at the onset of the project regarding expected changes should be answered. The investigator may wish to cite examples of specific cases which dramatically illustrate the changes generated by the work. Graphs or other visual means to illustrate the verified changes can also be used in the report.

Areas for Further Research

At this point, when the researcher has completed both the work and assessment of the project, additional directions for further investigation should be explored. During the implementation of the research it may have been obvious that another approach could have been used. In reporting the findings of the work, the researcher should suggest any techniques that should be investigated.

The researcher may believe that the work from the study would be useful with another social problem or client group. Specific recommendations reflecting these beliefs should be included in reporting the research findings.

Reporting Findings

Since social action research is based on improvement of the human condition, the findings might be reported in the form of a handbook or manual to aid others in achieving similar results. This guidebook would usually be written for a specific audience, such as other professionals or those individuals who could use the manual for self-help. The tenor of the publication would be guided by the audience selected by the author.

The resulting document might be a conventional written report or it might use an alternative medium such as video tape. Usually a video tape resulting from research would be accompanied by a manual, which would extend the usefulness of the tape. Access to facilities for production of a video tape would decrease the expense involved in this end product. If the researcher wishes to report the findings through use of video tape, it would be wise to search for funding to cover this expense. Possible sources for these costs would be grants or funding through the budget of a supporting agency.

An Example

One example of social action research revolves around the development of employability training for developmentally handicapped individuals (Ferguson, 1989). This field offered an opportunity for creative problem solving, and was the subject of an extensive social action project involving the use of art therapy, music therapy, and drama therapy. In developing the research it was necessary to see the need, assess the need, develop a program to change the situation, and implement the program.

the subject of an extensive social action project involving the use of art therapy, music therapy, and drama therapy. In developing the research it was necessary to see the need, assess the need, develop a program to change the situation, and implement the program.

In this research, I found that persons with developmental handicaps lack most of the daily living skills necessary for employment. Skills such as working together, accepting supervision, selecting appropriate clothing for work, and riding the bus are often absent in persons with developmental handicaps. Since persons with developmental handicaps respond to sensory stimulation and learn through the repetition of activities, I developed a program which presented identified employability skills through art therapy, music therapy, and drama therapy. Each skill was reinforced through repeated sensory experiences in a public school setting. Following the classroom learning experiences, the clients in the research program were placed in an actual employment situation for a three-month period. Interviews with employers and clients followed the employment period.

First, it was important to identify the information that developmentally handicapped individuals were underemployed, and that their high school training did not address employability skills. I found that these students did not understand the importance of simple skills which most people take for granted; for instance, these students did not understand the concept of team work. As a result, art therapy team work was used as a way of teaching team work skills.

The example of team work discussed in the previous paragraph led me to explore other employability skills which could be learned through expressive arts therapies. In exploring the possibilities found in the various expressive arts therapies I conceived the idea of using art, music, and drama therapy experiences in a sequential format, which would provide reinforcement for the skills to be taught.

I had had previous experience with young adults with developmental handicaps who were encouraged to become involved in arts activities in the community. Enlarging the experiences to encompass learning employability skills was an outgrowth of this earlier experience.

I interviewed school personnel in search of a program which would allow access to high school students with developmental handicaps. Following the identification of an acceptable site, I needed to secure permission from the school system, the teachers, and the students or their parents to allow the research to proceed. The research project was implemented only after nine months of planning and meetings with the school system involved.

A focus was placed on the sensory experiences as well as sequential reinforcement. Clients were given reinforcement for key employability skills through the use of art therapy, music therapy, and drama therapy experiences.

It is essential to keep the scope of the research focused and manageable. While it is impossible to attempt to effect the change of a global issue such as unemployment, it was possible, however, to effect a change in a specific facet of this social problem. For example, it was possible to address the specific issue of unemployment with developmentally handicapped persons.

Summary

Social action projects offer an opportunity to interact with people and effect change in an area important to the researcher. Almost any social problem can be amplified to provide important data. The scope of the work is limited only by the creativity and resources of the investigator. Sometimes important work is overlooked because the researcher fails to recognize the importance of his/her findings. It is important to realize that projects involving changes in serious social problems are not only significant, but are vital to our society.

References

Ferguson, W. (1989). Arts as employment training for persons with developmental handicaps. *Dissertation Abstracts International, 5,* 109, 1808.

Meyer, J. (1976). *Writing social action proposals: A practical guide.* Houston, TX: Center for Human Resources, University of Houston, College of Business.

Riley, M. (1963). *Sociological research: A case approach.* New York, NY: Harcourt, Brace, & World.

Part IV

RESOURCES FOR ART THERAPY RESEARCH

An extensive section on assessment with descriptions of a number of art therapy assessment instruments is included in this Guide *because of the important link between art therapy assessment and research. Correlational studies generally hypothesize a relationship between characteristics of art expression and some other variable, such as diagnosis, improvement, family dynamics, etc. In this way, art therapy assessments are made not only to gain an understanding of the client/patient's dynamics for treatment planning, but also to generate information that can enable art therapists to use standardized assessment instruments predictively. At this juncture in the development of the profession, most assessment procedures currrently in use have not been subjected to the sort of empirical substantiation that would permit art therapists to predict from the artwork with confidence. I hope such studies will be developed in the future. Finally, there are research aids available in our highly technological society—computerized data bases, computer programs for behavioral science research, grants, and a compendium of books and articles on research.*

Harriet Wadeson, Editor

Chapter 13

A DESCRIPTION AND HISTORY OF ART THERAPY ASSESSMENT IN RESEARCH

Linda Gantt, PhD, A.T.R.

A careful assessment or evaluation in art therapy is essential both in creating a plan for art therapy treatment and in serving as a base for art therapy research.[1] A formal art therapy assessment consists of eliciting a series of artworks that are based on "free" and/or structured tasks and noting the artist's associations and behavior. Most evaluations are done with individuals, although there are specific protocols for families (Kwiatkowska, 1978) and couples (Wadeson, 1973).

Historical Precedents

To understand better the use of contemporary art therapy assessments it is necessary to have some sense of their historical precedents. Educators, psychiatrists, anthropologists, and psychologists have used artwork in therapy, evaluation, and research for well over 100 years (MacGregor, 1989). Between 1885 and 1920, considerable work was done by educators in collecting and classifying children's art as part of the child study movement (Harris, 1963:10). Eng (1931) published an extensive bibliography of the literature on children's art, covering German, Norwegian, French, and English publications from 1892 to 1930. Harris provided an excellent review of the early descriptive and developmental studies including some ambitious international ones conducted according to standardized instructions (Harris,

---

[1] This material is based in part on a position paper on art therapy assessment written for the American Art Therapy Association in 1989, and on exerpts from a doctoral dissertation (Gantt, 1990).

1963, pp. 12-36). As a result of these efforts, sufficient evidence was amassed to show that children passed through an orderly sequence of developmental stages in their drawings (Lowenfeld, 1957). Nonverbal intelligence tests using drawings were developed from this body of knowledge (Goodenough, 1926; Harris, 1963).

A number of scientific papers published prior to 1900 in Europe and the United States (for example, Lombroso, 1882; Simon, 1888; Tardieu, 1872; and Hrdlika, 1899) described the spontaneous work of mental patients but these articles were primarily impressionistic in nature. [For a more detailed discussion of these papers and those in the first half of the 20th century see Anastasi & Foley (1940, 1941a; 1941b); Naumburg (1950, pp. 3-34, 1953, pp. 119-139); and MacGregor (1983, 1989.) In Kiell's 250-page bibliography titled *Psychiatry and Psychology in the Visual Arts and Aesthetics* (Kiell, 1965) there are many citations for the early works.]

Two Different Lines of Investigation Develop

The German investigator Fritz Mohr (1906) was the first to standardize the methods and procedures of drawing tests with psychiatric patients. He reviewed all published articles from the 19th century and "dismissed all earlier contributions, particularly those of the French, as 'merely descriptive'" (MacGregor, 1989, p. 189). Mohr's procedures were of two basic types—speific drawings requested by the investigator and drawings of the patient's own choice. In his work we can recognize the antecedents of some projective tests used by psychologists (such as the House-Tree-Person Test and the Thematic Apperception Test) as well as certain procedures used by art therapists (such as "free" drawings and the collection of drawings at various stages in a psychosis). Of particular concern to Mohr were the structural elements which he felt provided a clue to the thought processes of the artist. Art therapists would generally agree with his conclusion that "the more fragmentary the thought processes, the more fragmentary the picture" (MacGregor, 1989, p. 191).

Mohr's research design serves as a prototype for contemporary studies. "Systematizing of the testing procedure . . . provided Mohr the opportunity for making precise comparisons among the types of drawings produced by the different categories of patient. He is an attentive observer of his patient's behavior while drawing, and of the relation between the patient's other symptoms, mood, ability to concentrate, and the drawing that emerges in this context. The formal features of the drawing, as well as certain aspects of its content, could be related to his mental state" (MacGregor, 1989, p. 192).

Mohr's work both advanced the sophistication of thinking about the problems of patient art and contributed to two separate but simultaneous lines of investigation—one using free art and the other using "projective" drawings and copies of specific drawings and designs. With Mohr's work, MacGregor pointed out, "A split had opened up in the study of patient art. The two approaches were now to develop along radically different lines: on the one side the essentially diagnostic and experimentally oriented investigation of nonspontaneous drawings, in no sense 'art,' and on the other, a continuing preoccupation with the spontaneous drawings of psychotic patients produced freely outside of any test situation, either in the hospital, at home, or in rare circumstances, as an aspect of a psychotherapeutic relationship" (p. 193). While the psychologists were on one side of the split, artists (particularly the German Expressionists and the Surrealists), art historians and critics, and collectors were on the other. Art therapists should have been counted in the second group, but MacGregor did not include them by name. He acknowledged that a discussion of art therapy and diagnostic techniques using art was "outside the limits of [his] subject" (p. 8).

Comparing the Two Different Approaches

For the purposes of this chapter, it is instructive to compare and contrast the approach to patient art developed by the early art therapists and other dynamically oriented psychotherapists with that of the psychologists working at the same time.[2] Such a comparison gives us a better understanding of some problems which are crucial to present-day research. (It is also important to remember that in the 1940's and 1950's, psychological testing and therapy were usually quite separate activities; hence, there were many differences in the practioners' general orientation, philosophy, and training.)

In a chapter in Hammer's book on projective drawings, Naumburg stated, "The fundamental difference between projective drawings obtained in psychological tests and those produced in art therapy is that test designs are necessarily prompted and those in art therapy are entirely spontaneous. While certain diagnostic elements in art therapy are comparable to some aspects of projective drawing techniques, the therapeutic techniques of art therapy are related dynamically to the techniques of psychoanalysis" (Naumburg, 1958, p. 513). Psychologists (who were more likely to be administering a battery of psychological tests during the same session) offered standardized instructions and testing materials (small paper, pencils, and erasers) rather than a range of

---

[2] It is impossible, however, to draw a firm line between these two groups because there was some overlapping of method and intent. There were some psychologists using art materials and free drawings in the 1940's and 1950's.

colorful art materials (large paper, pastels, paint, and clay). They were seeking nomothetic principles (generalizations which could be made about groups of people) and enduring personality traits while the art therapists and psychoanalysts were more interested in seeing how the art reflected changes in a patient's mood. The psychologists, trained in research design and statistics, sought to demonstrate the validity and reliability of projective drawings, while the chief interest of the therapists (who had no training in research) was in how art could contribute to understanding individual patients and therefore, might assist in developing therapeutic technique. Reproductions of drawings and information about individuals were rarely published in psychological journals, but therapists published case studies which were rich in detail and were often illustrated by full-color plates (Baynes, 1940; Meares, 1957, 1958, 1960; Milner, 1969; Naumburg, 1947, 1950, 1953, 1958, 1966; Pfeifer, 1925; Pfister, 1917, 1923; Plokker, 1965; Prinzhorn, 1922/1972). The relative lack of drawings in the psychological literature made it impossible to see some of the more obvious similarities and differences which might have led to testable hypotheses.

Another major difference between the psychologists' approach and the art therapists' is in the way they looked at the completed work. Because art therapists obtained pictures with varying content, they sought global similarities and differences rather than atomistic details such as the presence or absence of small details (such as ears, buttons, or chimneys).

Problems with Earlier Studies

Since the two lines of investigation outlined above developed somewhat independently, there was relatively little cross-fertilization. It is ironic that art therapists are now embarking on research in an area which has been all but abandoned by psychologists. However, by studying the past research from both areas we can learn how to construct better art therapy studies.

On the strength of several important reviews and critical papers (Swensen, 1957; 1968; Klopfer & Taulbee, 1976; Chapman & Chapman, 1967, 1969; Wanderer, 1969) many psychologists concluded that projective drawings were not valid with respect to personality traits. Research showed that the groups under study were too variable to permit constructing generalizations. However, global ratings did prove useful in a number of studies. Despite the poor results, clinicians still seem to use the DAP and HTP. Groth-Marnat (1990, pp. 365-394) provided an even-handed review of projective drawings and a summary of the research findings with respect to reliability and validity.

Statistical Errors

Hammer (1981), the most vocal proponent of projective drawing, pointed out that in the search for group similarities, some of the importance of the observed variability of projective drawing was not appreciated. He noted that certain statistical tests which look at mean scores ignore the ends of the range: "But clinicians find that neurotic and psychotic groups tend to deviate from the norm in either direction. Thus, sick individuals will draw a figure much too large (at the grandiose end of the continuum) or much too small (reflecting direct feelings of inferiority and inadequacy); they will either draw with too light a line (reflecting anxiety, hesitancy, and uncertainty) or too heavy a line (reflecting aggression and inner tension); similarly they will erase too much or not erase at all. As with all areas of behavior, it is the deviation in either direction from the mean which is clinically noteworthy" (Hammer, 1981, pp. 177-178). [Fortunately, the Moses test of extreme reactions (Siegel, 1956, pp. 145-152) is a statistical test which can be used to measure these deviations in either direction from the mean, and such a test could be applied to art therapy research.]

Selection Bias

The earliest impressionistic studies were of those patients who drew spontaneously. If not all patients in a specific group were asked to draw, then a sampling bias resulted. This is akin to the problem of the "good subject" bias encountered by many researchers. Also, one might reasonably conclude that those subjects who were more interested in art or who had previous artistic training would be more likely to draw without encouragement, thus skewing the sample.

Improper Research Designs

Hammer observed that some research studies contradicted considerable clinical experience. ". . . I cannot help suspecting that the responsibility for the lack of statistical support for these clinical findings lies with the experimental approach rather than with the hypotheses" (Hammer, 1981, p. 176). Thus, he suggested that when looking at the correlation of certain "rare" signs with particular diagnostic categories such as schizophrenia, one should "wait to accumulate 20 such drawings [containing the sign of interest] and then determine the incidence of schizophrenia in the subjects who submitted the drawings" (p. 176).

Inadequate Temporal Controls

Many of the studies did not control for the time at which a picture was collected. Some investigators used the first picture produced but did not make certain that the art was collected from each individual at the same time in the course of an illness. Several published case studies showed striking changes in a short time in either spontaneous art (Perez & Marcus-Ofseyer, 1978) or directed drawings (such as the DAP) (Machover & Wexler, 1948; Cramer-Azima, 1956). In addition, there were studies which investigated the changes in drawings which correlated with changes in states associated with psychosis (Modell, 1951), electroconvulsive therapy (Hetherington, 1952; Stainbrook & Lowenbach, 1944), or the ingestion of hallucinogens (Maclay & Guttmann, 1941; Levine et al., 1955a, 1955b; Tonini & Montanari, 1955). These reports suggest that temporal variables should be considered critical. However, there seems to have been no review article or general discussion in the literature of the findings of these studies. Current psychiatric practice relies heavily on anti-psychotic and anti-depressant drugs which act relatively quickly (within hours, or at the most, weeks). A difference of one week in the collection of drawings could be crucial to a study's outcome.

In addition to inadequate temporal controls, other problems which plagued past research included concepts and terms which were poorly defined, considerable variation in experimental conditions, insufficient data on subjects, little quantitative data, interpretations that are "relatively vague, ill-defined, complex and mentalistic" (Anastasi & Foley, 1941, p. 232), and poor sampling techniques.

Materials and Methods for Art Therapy Assessment

Even though Naumburg outlined the theoretical distinction between projective drawings in psychological testing and the spontaneous art in art therapy, she recognized some overlap in actual practice. In her review of the literature up to the 1950's, Naumburg noted that "the line of demarcation between studies . . . that employ spontaneous art as a primary means of psychotherapy and those that deal mainly with structured art in diagnosis is not always easy to define. In some cases the therapeutic approach that uses spontaneous art may also include more formal diagnostic art elements; similarly structured art tests may include elements of free art expression as employed in art therapy. An example of this overlapping of areas of therapy and diagnosis is evident in those diagnostic papers which discuss figure and family drawings; in such cases, it can be observed that while the theme for a specific type of figure drawing is set by the therapist, spontaneity is nevertheless encouraged in the execution of this task by the patient" (Naumburg, 1953, p. 124).

Today, art therapists use a variety of structured and unstructured evaluation procedures, according to the age and general condition of the individual to be assessed. The types of art materials used vary with the specific assessment procedures, but usually consist of art paper, colored pastels, markers, pencils, collage materials, paint, and/or clay. Authors of an informal survey of art therapists working with children found a number of different types of assessments in current use, a number of them evidently passed on by an "oral tradition" (Mills & Goodwin, 1991, p. 12).

Art therapists consider form (integration/disintegration), composition, use of color, content, and the process by which the art was done in addition to specific symbolic material. The artist's verbal and nonverbal responses to various materials and procedures are noted. The artist's associations to the pictures or sculptures and behavior are as important as the art itself. A crucial part of an art therapy assessment is asking the artist to title the artwork and to talk about it (or in the case of children, to tell a story about it).

Some of the first structured procedures designed by art therapists (Ulman 1975; Kramer & Schehr, 1983) requested that the artist use specific **processes** (such as the scribble) or particular **materials** in a specific sequence. This approach seems to be an ideal compromise between asking for specific subject matter and leaving all choices up to the person being assessed.

As it became obvious that there was merit in holding the content constant, art therapy assessment procedures which use specific subject matter were developed. For example, one assessment uses a "free" drawing, a tree drawing, and a feeling drawing (Cohen, Hammer, & Singer, 1988). Kwiatkowska's family art assessment (1978) is a series of six drawings, a combination of suggested subjects and specified processes (ex., an abstract family portrait using color and shapes and a joint scribble in which individual family members make a scribble line on separate pieces of paper and then choose one of the scribbles to turn into a completed picture).

The "scribble" is designed to stimulate the production of unconscious material and to promote greater freedom in using the art materials (Cane, 1951). It is similar to the process used by artists to develop ideas for compositions and for this reason seems ideally suited to art therapy practice. According to Kramer, the scribble technique "is valuable with adults and adolescents or with mature but inhibited pre-adolescents." But, she cautions, "Younger children cannot use the scribble very well as a point of departure for their drawing. They are still bound to schematic concepts which are too rigidly defined to fit into random shapes" (Kramer, 1975, p. 37). Hays (1982) suggests the "dot-to-dot" picture as a substitute for the scribble with younger children. Some adults cannot use the scribble without becoming anxious about the content it suggests and may refuse to complete it. Persons with an organic brain syndrome, chronic alcoholism, or an acute psychosis may be unable to complete an integrated composition; therefore, the art therapist may decide not to use the scribble technique with such patients.

One investigator uses specific stimulus drawings to assess cognitive functioning (Silver, 1978, 1982, 1983; Sandburg, Silver, & Vilstrup, 1984) and depression (Silver, 1988). The most commonly used procedures and sequences are described by Ulman (1975), Kwiatkowska (1978), Rubin (1973, 1978), Kramer & Schehr (1983), Silver (1976, 1975), and Cohen, Hammer, & Singer (1988). Some other specific assessments and single-picture techniques are outlined in Hays (1981), Conger (1979), Manning (1987), and Wadeson (1973). [For details on many of these assessments see Chapters 14 & 15 of this *Guide*.]

Developing Art Therapy Assessments for Research

Choosing Between Directed or Spontaneous Art

The first decision an art therapy researcher must make is whether to study spontaneous or directed art. Each type of art has its own value and technical problems. If the choice is made to use "free" art then the next choice must be between offering only one type of art materials or a variety. Each time a decision is made to impose no limits on the art making, additional variables are introduced which must be considered in evaluating the results. Thus, art therapists find ourselves in precisely the same difficulty as Mohr when he began his work. "Faced with the difficulty of unraveling the complex spontaneous drawings . . . and wanting to isolate and identify specific areas of malfunction of the mental apparatus reflected in the more formal aspects of picture making, Mohr devised the first standardized tests to use drawings. In so doing, he moved into a different field of investigation, but with a view of obtaining insight into what he felt to be the almost impenetrable complexity of the spontaneous images" (MacGregor, 1989, p. 189-190).

Essentials of an Assessment

Lehmann and Risquez offer four principles for developing an evaluation using art:

1. The method should be applicable to any patient regardless of his degree of artistic ability, interest, cooperation and intelligence.

2. It should be possible to obtain repeated productions which are comparable in order to obtain a longitudinal view of the variations in the patient's graphic expression over a period of time.

3. The method should allow for the comparison of productions of different patients and of the same patient at different times by means of a standardized method of rating.

4. It should be possible to obtain useful and valid information on the patient's mental condition through the evaluation of his paintings without having to spend additional time in observing the patient while he is painting or in interviewing him about his finished product.

In addition it seems advisable to use as simple and direct a method of painting as possible in order to reduce to a minimum the technical difficulties connected with the handling of the various media in the making of the painting" (Lehmann & Risquez, 1953, p. 39).

Controlling Variables

Because spontaneous work can be immensely complex, measuring any aspect of it becomes technically complicated. Hanna Yaxa Kwiatkowska discussed at length the problems in quantifying art:

> *. . . Anything that affects the process of creating can make a considerable difference in the art product. There is little likelihood of uniformity in art by different patients or even in art by the same patient. The character of each patient's work depends on his mood, the circumstances preceding the art session, the sessions themselves, or even the introduction of a new medium.*
>
> *We must therefore strive for uniformity where uniformity is possible. Any degree of standardization the researcher can introduce is useful. The uniformity gained by the simple expedient of consistently using the same art materials can simplify the process of categorizing the pictures and qualifying their characteristics. Essential too is the consideration of socioeconomic status, education, intelligence and artistic talent of subjects. In addition, an adequately large sample of subjects, a clear, unambiguous rating manual, and a careful selection and training of judges are necessary.*
>
> *Statistical studies based on material obtained only from free art expression rather than from carefully designed procedures are likely to be questionable. Even more vulnerable to error is material gathered in group art therapy, where the group process inevitably affects the art products" (Kwiatkowska, 1978, p. 183-184).*

Technical Considerations

When using an assessment which does not specify subject matter, an art therapist faces certain technical problems. First, one must decide what the artist intended to draw in order to code it for subject matter. It is one thing if the picture appears to be a series of brightly colored horizontal lines but another thing entirely if the artist had the intention of drawing a cow. Second, the art therapist must find a scheme for analyzing potentially limitless subject matter. A theoretical frame which accommodates a large number of content catgories is not easy to find. The alternative is giving every distinct item its own category, but this brings with it the problem of condensing the results in order to make meaningful generalizations.

A technical consideration which must be addressed when using drawings is that the use of space must be approached differently than in a painting. A customary artistic convention permits leaving large amounts of white space as background in a drawing. Such apparently empty space must be considered on its own terms and only compared with other drawings.

Ideally, art therapists would screen for color blindness in their research subjects before proceeding to make ratings of their art. There is evidence that some groups of psychiatric patients have a higher percentage of color blind individuals (Renfroe, Velek, & Marco, 1987)[3] and strokes can effect either color perception and/or color naming.

Some Examples of Art Therapy Research Using Assessments

Since the early 1960's, the art therapy literature has increased considerably, yet the weakest area is that of empirical research. In a bibliography covering 1940 to 1973 (Gantt & Schmal, 1974) only 39 of the 1175 items were classified under the "research" section and not all of those are strictly art therapy studies. In a later bibliography covering 1974 to 1980 (Moore, 1981), 69 of the 392 listings dealt with research in some fashion, although some of these articles were more speculations and suggestions about research possibilities than carefully designed research projects.

It was only after art therapists were employed in research facilities that they, of necessity, became involved in research projects. Judith Rubin (Pittsburgh Child Guidance Center and Western Psychiatric Institute) and

---

[3] I am indebted to Carol Cox for bringing this article to my attention.

Hanna Yaxa Kwiatkowska and Harriet Wadeson (both at the National Institute of Mental Health) are some of the few art therapists who have published detailed discussions of formal research and its problems (Kwiatkowska, 1978, pp. 176-213 & 234-266; Rubin, 1978 - Appendix: Research and Assessment; Rubin, 1984, pp. 179-187; Wadeson, 1980, pp. 318-331).

In the last decade, a number of art therapists have earned doctoral degrees in psychology and related fields. Those dissertations which are specifically related to art therapy research will be a significant contribution to refining concepts and methods.

Since classification is the foundation of a true science, not surprisingly, some of the first art therapy research focused on questions about diagnostic material. Ulman and Levy did a series of studies (Ulman & Levy, 1968, 1975; Levy & Ulman, 1967) on judging psychopathology from paintings. They found that although 90% of 84 judges made correct decisions at a level better than chance as to whether a picture was done by a patient or a non-patient, there was no correlation between this ability and experience with psychiatric patients. They concluded that the art therapist judges were not better than the non-art therapist judges. There was, however, a range of accuracy among the art therapists from 55% to 77%. To study the effect of training on the judges' ability, Ulman and Levy looked at 19 subjects' judgments at the beginning, middle, and the end of a seminar on psychological assessment by graphic means. The results showed a statistically significant increase in the judges' ability to distinguish patient and non-patient art, leading the researchers to conclude that training could improve diagnostic accuracy.

Witlin and Augusthy (1988) compared the diagnostic categories assigned to 97 patients by an art therapist and a psychiatrist. The two diagnoses were the same in over 77% of the cases, with the largest percentage of agreement (100%) occurring on 5 cases of personality disorders. There was an agreement of 83.3% on 48 cases of affective disorders. However, the art therapist also saw the patients and thus, observed the patients' behavior. Therefore, not all of the diagnostic information she used came from the art. There was no mention of the criteria the art therapist used to make the diagnoses.

Rubin and Schachter (1972) found that only 3 out of 40 judges could distinguish correctly the art of schizophrenic from non-schizophrenic children at a level above chance. However, there was a significant correlation between art judged as "normal" and art which was aesthetically pleasing. Rubin, Ragans, and Schachter (1979) studied the formal properties of a series of drawings by schizophrenic and matched non-schizophrenic mothers and their school-age children. Although there was a significant difference between the art of the two groups of children on some analyses of content, there were no differences between the art of the two children's groups or the two mothers' groups on measures of formal variables such as height of figures, distance between figures, or frequencies of specific items.

Wadeson investigated depression (1971), schizophrenia (Wadeson & Carpenter, 1976a), manic/depressive illness (Wadeson & Bunney, 1969, 1970), and suicidal thoughts in art (1975) as well as the differences between the art of patients with unipolar, bipolar, and schizophrenic illnesses (Wadeson & Carpenter, 1976b). Wright and McIntyre (1982) developed a "family drawing depression scale" based on the Kinetic Family Drawing and some of Wadeson's findings about depressed individuals.

Cohen (Cohen, Hammer, & Singer, 1988) set up an ambitious project using a series of three pictures in an art therapy diagnostic procedure to be correlated with the DSM-III. Gantt (1990) had judges rate artwork from patients in four DSM-III-R categories and a control group. She found that there were statistically significant differences between two or more groups on eight of her 14 scales.

Silver developed and tested an instrument (1976; 1982) for assessing cognitive skills and applied it to the drawings of brain-damaged patients (1975) and adult psychiatric patients and adolescents (Sandburg, Silver, & Vilstrup, 1984). In addition, she developed a procedure to screen for depression (1988).

Rating Scales and Manuals

In developing rating scales and rating manuals art therapists can benefit from the successes and the failures of those devised for projective drawings. In their review of ten years of figure drawing studies Jones and Thomas (1961) found that two basic types of procedures were used: (a) matching (which generally depends on an intuitive or global impression being paired with some characteristic such as body type); and (b) coding and rating (which involved a rating scale or manual). (Ulman and Levy's work would be an example of the first type and Kwiatkowska's the second.) Several rating manuals have been developed for human figure drawings (Goodenough, 1926; Koppitz, 1968) and the House-Tree-Person Test (Buck, 1948). Harris (1963) revised and extended the Goodenough-Harris Drawing Test for children and published a detailed test manual. Because of the careful attention to standardization procedures, the "Goodenough/Harris scale" became the preferred method by which figure drawings were evaluated. However, these preferred method by which figure drawings were evaluated. However, these manuals are of limited use to art therapists unless the art being studied contains human figures, trees, and/or houses.

There have been attempts to develop rating scales and checklists of presumed attributes for psychiatric art (paintings as well as drawings) but none seem to be widely used. Schube and Cowell (1939) proposed one of the earliest measures which they called the "restraint/activity index." Elkisch (1945) used a global approach to rating the criteria of "rhythm versus rule," "complexity versus simplexity" [sic], "expansion versus compression," and "integration versus disintegration." Waehner (1946) also devised a system of scoring formal variables in children's work. Harris (1963, p. 51) expressed the opinion that the systems of Elkisch and Waehner had not been used widely "because their criteria require the examiner to learn a special set of symbols, terminology, and judgments." However, there were problems with other rating systems, too. Harris pointed out that "the 'figure drawing' approach, as loosely described by Machover, Buck, Jolles and others, appears more simple and direct, but permits the interpreter to 'project' as much as his subject!" (Harris, 1963, p. 51).

Handler and Reyher (1965) developed a scale to measure anxiety. This scale has been used with figure drawings, most recently by Evans (1984). However, a single attribute is unlikely to be much help in distinguishing between psychiatric disorders (which number over 200 in the DSM-III and DSM-III-R).

Pelto (1973) used a checklist for determining the presence or absence of 24 items culled from the literature. Russell-Lacy et al. (1973) used a similar checklist. Reiner, Tellin, and O'Reilly (1977) developed a "Pictorial Regression Scale for Adults" which consisted of 18 paired, mutually exclusive categories under the main headings of content, form, and style. No reliability studies have been reported on this scale.

Cohen judged the pictures in his Diagnostic Drawing Series for "the presence of 36 elements in 23 categories, primarily structural" (Cohen et al., 1988, p. 14). The structural categories included items such as groundline, unusual placement, space usage, and abstraction; the content categories included animals, people, and abstract symbols. Cohen was the only judge so there were no reliability statistics to be reported.

Kwiatkowska stated that the items in her rather detailed rating manual were based on two sources—extensive clinical observations and published reports in the literature on "features typical of pictures by individuals of different pathological groups" (1978, p. 186). Building on earlier work on diagnosis and formal characteristics (Gantt & Howie, 1982) Gantt used the same sources as Kwiatkowska to develop her rating scales. In addition, she postulated what might be the graphic equivalent of specific symptoms in the DSM-III-R. She devised 14 scales to measure global attributes of a single-picture assessment ("Draw a picture picking an apple from a tree"). The inter-rater reliability on the majority of the scales was within the moderately reliable to highly reliable range (Gantt, 1990, pp. 181-183).

Lehmann and Risquez constructed four separate rating scales for the finger paintings they studied: clarity, contact with reality, energy output, and affective range (Lehmann & Risquez, 1953, p. 44). However, they took care to point out problems with aesthetic bias and distortion by "the clinician's special dynamic orientation, which may lead him far afield in elaborate interpretation of every single feature of the patient's graphic product" (p. 39). No mention was made of specific tests of inter-rater reliability but the authors said they found that their rating scale "can be applied by different judges who, after a modest amount of practice, will arrive independently at fairly close scores" (p. 44).

Looking to the Future

A critical area for art therapy research is to determine what influences non-psychological factors and cultural milieu have on art. There are no large-scale studies on the art done by "normal" adults with a wide range of IQ's and educational backgrounds with no artistic training. Cameron (1938,1939) did some preliminary work with a small sample of non-patients. Thomas and her team of investigators (Harrower, Thomas, & Altman, 1975; Shaffer et al., 1986), looking for the precursors of serious physical and mental illness, did a detailed longitudinal study on projective tests (including figure drawings) with medical students. They produced a useful *Atlas of Figure Drawings* (Thomas, 1966), but one has to question if the generalizability of their findings is not biased by educational and social factors. Harris noted ". . . the growing recognition that a knowledge of the usual is essential for the recognition of the unusual. Many reputedly abnormal or unusual features in the drawings of individual children or of small, selected groups lose their apparent significance when the age and sex of the subjects and the conditions under which the drawings were made become known" (Harris, 1963, p.19). This is no less true with adults.

It appears that the psychologists' attempts to link personality traits with specific atomistic elements as hypothesized by Machover (1949) or to find a single variable (such as anxiety) which can separate one diagnostic group from another has come to a dead end. However, there is considerable evidence that global ratings and patterns or clusters of formal variables (such as color use, line quality, integration, and use of space) hold much promise for future research.

Art therapists have based their work almost exclusively on the case study model without a sufficiently detailed critique of either the methods or the results. As a result, the development of art therapy research has lagged. However, since they do see a greater number of pictures than those usually produced in testing sessions, art therapists should be able to generate testable hypotheses based on observed characteristics of the artwork (such as the sometimes dramatic fluctuations which reflect changes in psychological state).

By studying the problems researchers encountered with projective drawings, art therapists can improve their investigations. In many ways, the researchers working with projective drawings paid too little attention to the actual art and the art-making process; however, art therapists have showed little heed for or interest in generally accepted scientific principles such as experimenter bias, standardization, reliability, validity, and precise definitions. The more precise diagnostic categories which are in current use will be of great help in validity studies.

Although case studies and descriptive reports have dominated art therapy literature until recently, art therapists are now conducting basic research on assessment and evaluation. Scoring systems have been developed for several of the procedures. Some writers have investigated factors such as training (Ulman & Levy, 1973; Levy & Ulman, 1974) and personality attributes (Hersey, 1977) in raters' ability to assess drawings and paintings. Some art therapists are now collaborating with other professionals in research projects and on multi-modal evaluation procedures (Pulliam, Somerville, Prebluda, & Warja-Danielsson, 1988; Clark-Schock, Turner, & Bovee, 1988).

By understanding the history of both art therapy and projective drawing tests, art therapists can develop better assessments and rating scales for research. The relative late entry of art therapists into research may mean that it is possible to learn from the mistakes of others and to avoid ideas with dead ends. The possibilities for future research are exciting indeed.

References

Anastasi, A., & Foley, J. (1940). A survey of the literature on artistic behavior in the abnormal: III. Spontaneous productions. *Psychological Monographs, 52*(6), 1-71.

Anastasi, A., & Foley, J. (1941a). A survey of the literature on artistic behavior in the abnormal: I. Historical and theoretical background. *Journal of General Psychology, 25,* 111-142.

Anastasi, A., & Foley, J. (1941b). A survey of the literature on artistic behavior in the abnormal: Experimental investigations. *Journal of General Psychology, 23,* 187-237.

Anastasi, A., & Foley, J. (1944). An experimental study of the drawing behavior of adult psychotics in comparison with that of a normal control group. *Journal of Experimental Psychology, 34*(3), 169-194.

Baynes, H. (1940). *The mythology of the soul: A research into the unconscious from schizophrenic dreams and drawings.* London: Williams & Wilkins.

Buck, J. (1948). The H-T-P technique, a qualitative and quantitative scoring method. *Journal of Clinical Psychology Monograph, 5,* 1-20.

Cameron, N. (1938). Individual and social factors in the development of graphic symbolizations. *Journal of Psychology, 5,* 165-184.

Cameron, N. (1939). Functional immaturity in the symbolization of scientifically trained adults. *Journal of Psychology, 6,* 161-175.

Cane, F. (1951). *The artist in each of us.* [Reprinted in a revised edition, 1983. Craftsbury Common, VT: Art Therapy Publications.]

Chapman, L., & Chapman, J. (1967). Genesis of popular but erroneous psychodiagnostic observations. *Journal of Abnormal Psychology, 72,* 193-204.

Chapman, L., & Chapman, J. (1969). Illusory correlation as an obstacle to the use of valid psychodiagnostic signs. *Journal of Abnormal Psychology, 74,* 271-280.

Clark-Schock, K., Turner, Y., & Bovee, T. (1988). A multi-disciplinary psychiatric assessment: The introductory group. *The Arts in Psychotherapy, 15,* 79-82.

Cohen, B., Hammer, J., & Singer, S. (1988). The Diagnostic Drawing Series: A systematic approach to art therapy evaluation and research. *The Arts in Psychotherapy, 15,* 11-21.

Conger, D. (1979). Art therapy with elderly stroke survivors. In L. Gantt, G. Forrest, D Silverman, & R. Shoemaker (Eds.), Art therapy: Expanding horizons. *Proceedings of the Ninth Annual Conference of the American Art Therapy Association.* Baltimore, MD: American Art Therapy Association.

Cramer-Azima, F. (1956). Personality changes and figure drawings: A case treated with ACTH. *Journal of Clinical Psychology, 20*(2), 143-149.

Elkisch, P. (1945). Children's drawings as a projective technique. *Psychological Monograph, 58,* 1-31.

Eng, H. (1931). *The psychology of children's drawings: From the first stroke to the color drawing.* London: Kegan Paul, Trench, Trubner, & Company.

Evans, C. (1984). *"Draw a person . . . a whole person": Drawings from psychiatric patients and well-adjusted adults as judged by six traditional DAP indicators, licensed psychologists and the general public.* Unpublished dissertation, Temple University, Philadelphia, PA.

Gantt, L. (1990). *A validity study of the Formal Elements Art Therapy Scale (FEATS) for measuring diagnostic information through assessing formal variables in patients' drawings.* Unpublished dissertation, University of Pittsburgh, Pittsburgh, PA.

Gantt, L., & Howie, P. (1982). Diagnostic categories and art work. In L. Gantt and A. Evans (Eds.), Focus on the future: The next ten years. *The Proceedings of the Tenth Annual Conference of the America Art Therapy Association.* Falls Church, VA: American Art Therapy Association.

Gantt, L., & Schmal, M. (1974). *Art therapy: A bibliography.* Rockville, MD: National Institute of Mental Health.

Goodenough, F. (1926). *Measurement of intelligence by drawings.* New York, NY: Harcourt, Brace, & World.

Groth-Marnat, G. (1990). *Handbook of psychological assessment* (2nd ed.). New York, NY: John Wiley & Sons.

Hammer, E. (1981). Projective drawings. In A. Rabin (Ed.), *Assessment with projective techniques: A concise introduction.* New York, NY: Springer Publishing.

Handler, L., & Reyher, J. (1965). Figure drawing anxiety indices: A review of the literature. *Journal of Projective Techniques and Personality Assessment, 29*(3), 305-313.

Harris, D. (1963). *Children's drawings as measures of intellectual maturity.* New York, NY: Harcourt, Brace, & World.

Harrower, M., Thomas, C., & Altman, A. (1975). Human figure drawings in a prospective study of six disorders: Hypertension, coronary heart disease, malignant tumor, suicide, mental illness, and emotional disturbance. *Journal of Nervous and Mental Disease, 161*(3), 191-199.

Hays, R. (1981). The bridge drawing: A projective technique for assessment in art therapy. *The Arts in Psychotherapy, 8*, 207 - 217.

Hays, R. (1982). Dot-to-dot: Rationale for a "new projective" for children under ten. In L. Gantt & A. Evans (Eds.), *Focus on the future.* The Proceedings of the Tenth Annual Conference of the Art Therapy Association (pp. 116-120). Falls Church, VA: American Art Therapy Association.

Hersey, D. (1977). *Diagnostic skill in art therapy and differences in personality, art judgment, and academic background.* Unpublished doctoral dissertation, East Texas State University, Commerce, TX.

Hetherington, R. (1952). The effects of E.C.T. on the drawings of depressed patients. *Journal of Mental Science, 98*, 450-453.

Hrdlicka, A. (1899). Art and literature in the mentally abnormal. *American Journal of Insanity, 55,* 385-404.

Jones, L., & Thomas, C. (1961). Studies on figure drawings: A review of the literature (1949-1959). *Psychiatric Quarterly Supplement, 35,* 212, part 2.

Kiell, N. (1965). *Psychiatry and psychology in the visual arts and aesthetics: A bibliography.* Madison, WI: University of Wisconsin Press.

Klopfer, W., & Taulbee, E. (1976). Projective tests. In M. Rosenzweig & L. Porter (Eds.), *Annual Review of Psychology, 27.* Palo Alto, CA: Annual Reviews, Inc.

Koppitz, E. (1968). *Psychological evaluations of children's human figure drawings.* New York, NY: Grune & Stratton.

Kramer, E. (1975). Art therapy and childhood. *American Journal of Art Therapy, 14*(2), 36-38.

Kramer, E. & Schehr, J. (1983). An art therapy evaluation session for children. *American Journal of Art Therapy, 23,* 3-12.

Kwiatkowska, H. (1978). *Family therapy and evaluation through art.* Springfield, IL: Charles C Thomas.

Lehmann, H., & Risquez, F. (1953). The use of finger paintings in the clinical evaluation of psychotic conditions: A quantitative and qualitative approach. *Journal of Mental Science, 99,* 763-777.

Levine, A., Abramson, H., Kaufman, M., & Markham, S. (1955a). Lysergic acid diethylamide (LSD-25): XVI. The effect on intellectual functioning as measured by the Weschler-Bellevue intelligence scale. *Journal of Psychology, 40,* 385-395.

Levine, A., Abramson, H., Kaufman, M., Markham, S., & Kornetsky, C. (1955b). Lysergic acid diethylamide (LSD-25): XIV. Effects on personality as observed in psychological tests. *Journal of Psychology, 40,* 351-366.

Levy, B., & Ulman, E. (1967). Judging psychopathology from paintings. *Journal of Abnormal Psychology, 72,* 182-187.

Lombroso, C. (1988). *The man of genius.* London: Walter Scott.

Lowenfeld, V. (1957). *Creative and mental growth.* New York, NY: MacMillan.

Maclay, W., & Guttmann, E. (1941). Mescalin hallucinations in artists. *Archives of Neurology and Psychiatry, 45,* 130-137.

MacGregor, J.M. (1983). Paul-Max Simon: The father of art and psychiatry. *Art Therapy: Journal of the American Art Therapy Association,* 1(1), 8-20.

MacGregor, J.M. *(1989). The discovery of the art of the insane.* Princeton, NJ: Princeton University Press.

Machover, K. (1949). *Personality projection in the drawing of the human figure.* Springfield, IL: Charles C Thomas.

Machover, K., & Wexler, R. (1948). A case of manic excitment. *Rorschach Research Exchange & Journal of Projective Techniques, 12,* 179-201.

Manning, T. (1987). Aggression depicted in abused children's drawings. *The Arts in Psychotherapy, 14*, 15-24.

Meares, A. (1957). *Hypnography.* Springfield, IL: Charles C Thomas.

Meares, A. (1958). *The door of serenity.* Springfield, IL: Charles C Thomas.

Meares, A. (1960). *Shapes of sanity.* Springfield, IL: Charles C Thomas.

Mills, A., & Goodwin, R. (1991). An informal survey of assessment use in child art therapy. *Art Therapy: Journal of the American Art Therapy Association, 8*(2), 10-13.

Milner, M. (1969). *The hands of the living god: An account of a psycho-analytic treatment.* London: Hogarth Press.

Modell, A. (1951). Changes in human figure drawings by patients who recover from regressed states. *American Journal of Orthopsychiatry, 21*, 584-596.

Mohr, F. (1906). Über Zeichnungen von Geisteskranker und ihre diagnostische Verwertbarkeit. *Journal für Psychologie und Neurologie, 8*, 99-140.

Moore, R. (1981). *Art therapy in mental health* (Literature survey No. 3). Rockville, MD: U.S. Department of Health & Human Services, National Clearinghouse for Mental Health Information, National Institute of Mental Health.

Naumburg, M. (1947). *Studies of the "free" art expression of behavior problem children and adolescents as a means of diagnosis and therapy.* New York, NY: Grune & Stratton.

Naumburg, M. (1950). *Schizophrenic art: Its meaning in psychotherapy.* New York, NY: Grune & Stratton.

Naumburg, M. (1953). *Psychoneurotic art: Its function in psychotherapy.* New York, NY: Grune & Stratton.

Naumburg, M. (1958). Art therapy: Its scope and function. In E. Hammer (Ed.), *The clinical application of projective drawings.* Springfield, IL: Charles C Thomas.

Naumburg, M. (1966). *Dynamically oriented art therapy: Its principles and practice.* New York, NY: Grune & Stratton.

Pelto, V. (1973). *The use of spontaneous artwork as a means of diagnosing psychiatric patients.* Unpublished Master's thesis, California State University, Long Beach, CA.

Perez, L., & Marcus-Ofseyer, B. (1978).The effect of lithium treatment on the behavior and paintings of a psychotic patient with religious and sexual conflicts. *American Journal of Art Therapy, 17*(3), 85-90.

Pfeifer, R. (1925). *Der Geisteskranke und sein Werk: Eine Studie über Schizophrene Kunst.* Leipzig: Kröner.

Pfister, O. (1923). *Expressionism in art: Its psychological and biological basis.* (B. Low & M. Mügge, transl). New York: Dutton.

Pfister, O. (1917). Analysis of artistic production. In *The psychoanalytic method* (C. Payne, transl.). New York, NY: Moffat, Yard.

Plokker, J. (1965). *Art from the mentally disturbed: The shattered vision of schizophrenics*. Boston, MA: Little, Brown.

Prinzhorn, H. (1922/1972). *Artistry of the mentally ill*. New York, NY: Springer-Verlag.

Pulliam, J., Somerville, P., Prebluda, J., & Warja-Danielsson, M. (1988). Three heads are better than one: The expressive arts group assessment. *The Arts in Psychotherapy, 15*, 71-77.

Reiner, E., Tellin, J., & O'Reilly, J. (1977). A picture regression scale for adults. *Art Psychotherapy, 4*(3/4), 219-223.

Renfroe, J., Velek, M., & Marco, L. (1987). Dyschromatopsia in a psychiatric population. *Alabama Medicine, 56*, 20, 25-28.

Rubin, J. (1973). A diagnostic art interview. *Art Psychotherapy, 1*(1), 31-44.

Rubin, J. (1984). *The art of art therapy*. New York, NY: Brunner/Mazel.

Rubin, J. (1978/1984). *Child art therapy: Understanding and helping children grow through art* (2nd ed. - 1984). New York, NY: Van Nostrand & Reinhold.

Rubin, J., Ragins, N., & Schachter, J. (1979). Drawings by schizophrenic and non-schizophrenic mothers and their children. *Art Psychotherapy, 6*(3), 163-175.

Rubin, J., & Schachter, J. (1972). Judgments of psychopathology from art productions of children. *Confinia Psychiatrica, 15*, 237-252.

Russell-Lacy, S., Robinson, V., Benson, J., & Cranage, J. (1979). An experimental study of pictures produced by acute schizophrenic subjects. *British Journal of Psychiatry, 134*, 195-200.

Sandburg, L., Silver, R., & Vilstrup, K. (1984). The stimulus drawing technique with adult psychiatric patients, stroke patients, and in adolescent art therapy. *Art Therapy, 1*(3), 132-140.

Schube, P., & Cowell, J. (1939). Art of psychotic persons. *Archives of Neurology and Psychiatry, 41*, 707-728.

Shaffer, J., Pearson, T., Mead, L., & Thomas, C. (1986). A possible relationship between figure drawing data collected in medical school and later health status among physicians. *Journal of Clinical Psychology, 42*, 363-369.

Siegel, S. (1956). *Nonparametric statistics for the behavioral sciences*. New York, NY: McGraw-Hill.

Silver, R. A. (1983). *Silver drawing test of cognitive and creative skills*. Seattle: Special Child Publications.

Silver, R. A. (1978). *Developing cognitive and creative skills through art*. Baltimore, MD: University Park Press.

Silver, R. (1982). *Stimulus drawings and techniques*. New York, NY: Ablin Press.

Silver, R. (1988). *Draw-A-Story: Screening for depression and emotional needs*. Mamaronek, NY: Ablin Press.

Silver, R. A. (1975). Clues to cognitive functioning in the drawings of stroke patients. *American Journal of Art Therapy, 15*(1), 3-8.

Silver, R. A. (1976). Using art to evaluate and develop cognitive skills. *American Journal of Art Therapy, 16*(1), 11-19.

Simon, P.M. (1888). Les écrits et les dessins des aliénés. *Archivio di antropologia criminelle, psichiatria e medicina legale 3,* 318-55).

Stainbrook, E., & & Lowenbach, H. (1944). Writing and drawing of psychotic individuals after electrically induced convulsions. *Journal of Nervous and Mental Disease, 99,* 382.

Swensen, C. (1957). Empirical evaluations of human figure drawings. *Psychological Bulletin, 54,* 431-466.

Swensen, C. (1968). Empirical evaluations of human figure drawings: 1957-1966. *Psychological Bulletin, 70,* 20-44.

Tardieu, A. (1872). *Etudes médico-légales sur la folie.* Paris.

Thomas, C. (1966). *Atlas of figure drawings: Studies on the psychological characteristics of medical students - III.* Baltimore, MD: The John Hopkins Press.

Tonini, G., & Montanari, C. (1955). Effects of experimentally induced psychoses on artistic expression. *Confinia Neurologica, 15,* 225-239.

Ulman, E. (1975). A new use of art in psychiatric analysis. In E. Ulman & P. Dachinger (Eds.), *Art therapy in theory and practice.* New York, NY: Schocken.

Ulman, E., & Levy, B. (1968). An experimental approach to the judgment of psychopathology from paintings. *Bulletin of Art Therapy, 8*(1), 3-12.

Ulman, E., & Levy, B. (1975). An experimental approach to the judgment of psychopathology from paintings. In E. Ulman & P. Dachinger (Eds.), *Art therapy in theory and practice.* New York, NY: Schocken.

Wadeson, H. (1971). Characteristics of art expression in depression. *Journal of Nervous and Mental Disease, 153,* 197-204.

Wadeson, H. (1973). Art techniques used in conjoint marital therapy. *American Journal of Art Therapy, 12,* 147-164.

Wadeson, H. (1980). *Art psychotherapy.* New York, NY: John Wiley & Sons.

Wadeson, H., & Bunney, W., Jr. (1969). Manic-depressive art: Tested graphic characteristics and psychodynamic implications. *Psychiatry and Art,* pp. 249-252. Basel: S. Karger.

Wadeson, H., & Bunney, W., Jr. (1970). Manic-depressive art: A systematic study of differences in a 48-hour cyclic patient. *Journal of Nervous and Mental Disease, 150,* 215-231.

Wadeson, H., & Carpenter, W. (1976a). Subjective experience of acute schizophrenia. *Schizophrenia Bulletin, 2,* 302-316.

Wadeson, H., & Carpenter, W. (1976b). A comparison of art expression in schizophrenic, manic-depressive bipolar, and depressive unipolar patients. *Journal of Nervous and Mental Disease, 162,* 334-344.

Waehner, T. (1946). Interpretations of spontaneous drawings and paintings. *Genetic Psychology Monograph, 33,* 3-70.

Wanderer, Z. (1969). Validity of clinical judgments based on human figure drawings. *Journal of Consulting and Clinical Psychology, 33,* 143-150.

Witlin, B., & Augusthy, R. (1988). Comparison of art psychotherapy and discharge diagnoses of diagnostic unit patients. *Art Therapy: Journal of the American Art Therapy Association, 5,* 94-98.

Wright, J., & McIntyre, M. (1982). The family drawing depression scale. *Journal of Clinical Psychology, 38,* 853-861.

Chapter 14

ART-BASED ASSESSMENT PROCEDURES AND INSTRUMENTS USED IN RESEARCH

Doris Arrington, EdD, A.T.R.

Art therapy research focuses on using art to assess human dynamics. This chapter will present an overview of art therapy research procedures and review known art-based research instruments and procedures currently available for research projects. Some of these procedures and instruments are supported by research, some are not, and some might not need to be supported prior to relevant studies.

This chapter does not list assessment procedures or research tools that have been or are currently being used in art therapy with specific populations (ie., abused children, adults molested as children, adult children of alcoholics, battered women, etc.), due to limitations of space and time. We hope that once this information is circulated, other art therapists currently conducting or participating in research will contribute information on their assessment instruments or procedures for inclusion in future publications. Any other art-based assessment procedures and instruments omitted have been omitted unintentionally, except for those procedures and instruments used by state licensed practitioners, i.e. the Visual Motor Gestalt Test (Bender, 1946); Draw-A-Person (Machover, 1949); House-Tree-Person (Buck, 1978). For information on these instruments please refer to the original sources.

At the Spring 1990 meeting of the Board of Directors of the American Art Therapy Association the following statement on art therapy assessments was adopted:

"Art therapists use a variety of art-based assessments which include, but are not limited to, free choice and/or directed drawings, paintings, and/or sculptures. The choice of the specific art therapy assessment depends on the age of the client and the purpose for which the assessment will be used. Art therapists are aware of the most recent research on assessment and evaluation and of state laws and agency policies which govern the use of assessment procedures. All assessments are conducted according to *the Ethical Standards for Art Therapists, Art Therapy Standards of Practice*, and *Art Therapy Standards for Independent Practice.*"

Definition of Key Terms

Projective technique: refers to "any test, device or set of procedures designed to provide information about or insight into an individual's personality by allowing the individual the opportunity to respond in an unrestricted manner to art-based materials or visual constructs" (Reber, 1985).

Projective test: supports Reber's (1985) label "for any of a variety of devices used in personality assessment and clinical psychology in which an individual is presented with a standardized unstructured set of stimuli and requested to respond to them in as unrestricted a manner as possible" (p. 581).

Structured art tasks: refers to consistent devices or procedures such as drawings, construction, visual constructs or objects that elicit specific data when presented to an individual or a family. Participants may be requested to respond in an unrestricted or a specific manner.

Free or spontaneous art tasks: refers to a variety of unstructured devices or procedures such as drawings, constructions, visual constructs or objects presented to an individual or a family with the request that participants respond in as unrestricted a manner as possible. Specific data may or may not be elicited.

Background

Even before the 1900's, educators, psychiatrists, and psychologists used art and visual projective techniques as instruments to assess conscious and unconscious desires, attitudes, and intrapsychic experiences of individuals (Buros, 1978; Goodenough, 1926; Hammer, 1958; Harris, 1963; Jung, 1964;

unconscious desires, attitudes, and intrapsychic experiences of individuals (Buros, 1978; Goodenough, 1926; Hammer, 1958; Harris, 1963; Jung, 1964; MacGregor, 1983; Murray, 1935; Rorschach, 1921). According to Betensky (1973), projective tests using word or visual images reveal people's perception of their experiences and their lives in ways that paper and pencil tests or self-report tests cannot (Arrington, 1986).

Rubin (1986) points out that since 1906, art has been used as projective of people's perceptions of their lives in both clinical psychiatry and art therapy. However, "sophisticated clinicians (psychologists, psychiatrists, and art therapists) are conservative about making either diagnostic or predictive judgments" (p. 29) as to organicity or particular pathology on the basis of the art product alone. One significant reason for this conservative attitude is that data from empirical research validating symbolic meaning in human experience is almost non-existent (Anderson, 1983). A review of the literature of existing research studies in the field of visual communication and art therapy not only underscores the need for better and more systematic studies, but also identifies the gaps in the literature in the field as well (Arrington, 1986).

In an analysis of published research literature in arts for the handicapped, Anderson (1983) notes that the most widely used form of research in the field of art therapy is the case study. Although the case study is an important research strategy for building hypotheses, art therapists must begin to use other types of research methodology if they are to expand knowledge and justify the discipline to scholars. Anderson concludes that there is an urgent need to develop more appropriate and sensitive assessment tools for use in research about visual communication and art therapy with normal as well as dysfunctional populations.

Assessment Instruments

The following represents assessments and evaluation instruments currently being taught and used in art therapy research. They include both free (spontaneous) and structured art-based procedures and evaluations. A few include responses to stimulus pictures in addition to or instead of art-making.

A. ART-BASED PROCEDURES FOR ADULTS

• Diagnostic Drawing Series (DDS)
The Diagnostic Drawing Series is a three-picture tool designed by art therapists (Cohen, Hammer, & Singer, 1988). The materials consist of 18 x

24-inch white drawing paper (20 lb.) and a box of twelve square unwrapped soft chalk pastels (Alphacolor). The tasks are designed as follows: 1) Free Picture—"Make a picture using these materials"; 2) Tree Picture—"Draw a picture of a tree"; 3) Feeling Picture—"Make a picture of how you are feeling using lines, shapes, and colors."

The DDS resource library in Alexandria, Virginia stores the collection of more than 1000 drawings by over 300 adolescent and adult subjects. This material is available free of charge for year-round study.

Contributions are solicited from all inpatient and outpatient psychiatric populations ages 13 and over, controls (non-hospitalized, non-day treatment), as well as populations such as alcoholics, chemical dependency, and specialty medical researchers. To obtain a packet describing how to collect DDS samples for this collaborative project write:

Barry Cohen, MA, A.T.R.
P.O. Box 6091
Alexandria, VA 22306

• **Draw a Person Picking an Apple from a Tree**
   This procedure consists of one drawing that can be administered in a group art therapy session or in an individual session. Participants are asked to "Please draw a person picking an apple from a tree" (Lowenfeld, 1947). Materials used include 12 by 18 inch white drawing paper and a 12-color set of Mr. Sketch felt-tip markers. A rating scale and rating manual have been developed and reliability and validity studies have been done (Gantt, 1990). Contributions are solicited from normal (non-institutionalized) and inpatient psychiatric and inpatient surgery and stroke patients. To obtain a packet describing how to collect samples for this collaborative research please contact:

Linda Gantt, PhD, A.T.R.
Lake O'Woods
Bruceton Mills, WV 26525
                  or
Carmello Tabone, MA, A.T.R.
Chestnut Ridge Hospital
Morgantown, WV 26505

• **Significance of the First Product in Art Therapy**
   Shoemaker (1977) created an evaluation grid based on the assumption that observable dimensions in a patient's first art therapy sessions can provide treatment information as well as generate diagnostic information.

Patients appear to use their first art therapy session as a new way of communicating a life review of the past, the present dilemma, and goals or blocks for the future with little repression used. During the first art therapy session, therapists wishing to assess information from the patient give the following direction: "Draw or create whatever you feel like or you are presently thinking about."

The information gained in the first session with the help of the evaluation grid is shared with the patient before any formal writing is completed on the patients' charts to offer an opportunity for further therapist assessment, patient clarification, and mutual communications.

Roby & Pastushak (1978) researched and modified Shoemaker's First Picture Evaluation which consists of four vertical and seven horizontal categories. The four vertical categories are:

1) The visual product (without verbalizations);
2) The creative process (with verbalizations during creation);
3) The personal process (nonverbal and verbal); and
4) The group process (including all behavioral observations not noted under the other processes).

The seven horizontal categories of the grid, although more difficult to conceptualize, tend to be flexible and interact with other categories due to similarities and overlapping content. They include:

1) Space (Use of Area)
2) Time (Past, Present, Future)
3) Energy (Pressure, Movement, Colors)
4) Content (People, Objects, Symbols)
5) Relationship (Relativity)
6) Level of Awareness (Expressiveness)
7) Synthesis (The holistic or Gestalt idea)

Roby & Pastushak (1978) found significance to the first product both diagnostically and as a guide for treatment planning. They view the grid as a holistic view of the person and the inherent curative powers of creative expression in process.

• Ulman Personality Assessment Procedure
Ulman (1975; Agell & Ulman, 1989) developed an art therapy "diagnostic" technique which uncovered aspects of the client's personality that had been unidentified by other means. In recent years, Ulman considered that this

technique reflected personality assessment rather than a diagnostic procedure.

The Ulman Personality Assessment Procedure (UPAP) is a projective technique that consists of four drawings. The series offers a rich source of information for understanding the client's behavioral repertoire, cognitive style, and affective capacity. Each drawing is prompted by its own set of instructions that establish a particular psychological climate. For example, the first drawing is a "free drawing," producing an undirected condition. In contrast, the instructions for the second drawing furnish clear directives. Instructions for the third drawing, the scribble, invite the client to be playful ". . in actually scribbling and in using the option to free associate to the images prompted by the scribble." The fourth drawing calls for decision-making. The client is given the choice of either making another drawing from a scribble or once again drawing from unaided imagination as in the first drawing. Either way, the intervening experience of the second and third drawings may make for significant differences between the first and fourth drawings. Following the completion of the series, the drawings are reviewed by the client and therapist with an opportunity to make changes.

Contributions are solicited from all inpatient and outpatient populations. For additional information write:

Gladys Agell, PhD, A.T.R., Director
Graduate Art Therapy Program
Vermont College of Norwich University
Montpelier, VT 05602

• Wadeson—Phenomenology of Schizophrenia
Assessments with schizophrenic patients. Wadeson developed a sequence of five art tasks to gain an understanding of the subjective phenomenology of the acute schizophrenic episode. Patients participated in individual art sessions during drug-free periods shortly after admission, just prior to discharge, and at one-year follow-up (Wadeson, 1980; Wadeson & Carpenter, 1976). Materials included pastels and 18 x 24-inch paper. The five tasks were: 1) "Free" picture (patient's choice); 2) Self-portrait; 3) Picture of the psychiatric illness; 4) Hallucination experienced; and 5) Delusions experienced.

• Wadeson—Characteristics of Art Expression in Depression
Assessments with depressed and bipolar patients. With depressed and bipolar patients, Wadeson (1971; 1980) used a non-structured approach stressing "that the purpose was to provide another mode of expression in addition to words (rather than artistic accomplishment)" (p. 48). Wadeson used pictorial raters blind to information about the patient and the hypotheses

to make determinations regarding graphic style and affect associated with depression.

• Wadeson and Bunney—Manic-Depressive Art

Blind raters judged the artwork of a 48-hour cyclic manic-depressed patient in this single case study showing differences in style and affect between art produced when manic and when depressed (Wadeson & Bunney, 1969).

• Wadeson—Recovery Style from Acute Schizophrenia

Independent "blind" raters judged the art of acute schizophrenics for various graphic characteristics to predict whether their recovery style would "seal over" the psychosis or "integrate" it. In this correlational study, the hypothesis that schizophrenics who recovered from psychosis by "sealing over" the experience would be less expressive in their art than those who "integrate" the experience was supported. The rationale for this prediction was based on the belief that the same repressive processes that cause "sealing over" would inhibit expressiveness in art-making (McGlashan et al., 1977).

B. ART-BASED PROCEDURES FOR FAMILIES

• Family-Centered Circle Drawings

Individual family members are to be drawn centered in a circular matrix, the central figure is then surrounded by symbols. Burn's instructions (Burns, 1990, p. 3) are: "Draw your mother (father, sister, etc.) in the center of the circle. Visually free associate with drawn symbols around the periphery of the circle. Try to draw a whole person, not a stick or cartoon figure." Standardized descriptions and guidelines are included.

• Kwiatkowska's Family Art Evaluation

The Family Art Evaluation (Kwiatkowska, 1978) was developed for use with families with a severely disturbed hospitalized adult or adolescent member. The instrument consists of six pictures: 1) A Free Picture, which is used as an ice breaker. It allows freedom and flexibility; 2) A Family Portrait, which encourages family members to draw the family in the present; 3) An Abstract Family Portrait, which gives information about each family member's capacity for organized abstract thinking. In addition, this art-based procedure may elicit charged feelings about family members; 4) The Individual Scribble, which often brings primary process material into the open. In addition, it is a useful instrument for diagnosing the relative psychopathy and health, especially integrative capacities of individual family members; 5) A Joint Family Scribble; which allows for direct observation of how a family works together. The necessity of working on a single sheet of paper is of particular value with regard to family members' ability to tolerate closeness. Comparing

Comparing the individual and joint scribbles gives information about family dynamics; 6) A Free Picture. This is usually one of the most enlightening procedures because it seems to sum up the family's tolerance for stress aroused by uncovering aspects of the preceding pictures.

Burak (1981) developed a Conjoint Family Drawing Rating Scale which consists of a check-list of behaviors grouped according to mode of expression (verbal, physical, drawing process, and drawing content) and classified behaviors according to whether they remained stable or changed over the course of the sessions. From this check-list characteristics of each family member and of the family as a whole were identified. These characteristics were then clustered to form (systemic) behavioral patterns (p. 95).

• **Landgarten's Method**
Landgarten's (1987) art psychotherapeutic family systems diagnostic procedure is presented as somewhat gamelike. It consists of three tasks. 1) The Non-verbal Team Art Task allows the family to divide up into two teams; the composition of each unit indicates family alliances. Everyone on both teams is asked to "select a color marker that is different from the others and is to be used for the entire session. This unique color rule facilitates the therapist's observation of each person's contribution. Each team is notified that they will work together on a single piece of paper. They are not permitted to speak, signal, or write notes to each other while working on the art, and when finished, they are merely to stop. After the tasks are completed, the verbal ban is lifted, and the teams select and add a name to their product. 2) The Non-verbal Family Art Task requires that the entire family work together on a single sheet of paper. Again, they refrain from speaking until the task is complete. They may speak while titling their creations. 3) The Verbal Family Art Task allows the participants to speak while making a single piece of art. The therapist is instructed to observe and record 17 points relating to the family and individual participants.

• **Rubin's Method**
Rubin (1984) developed three specific tasks for use with families with a child or adolescent that was being seen in treatment. The tasks include: 1) The Individual Scribble introduced as a first task to put the nonartist at ease, in addition to its value as a powerful diagnostic tool; 2) Family Portraits can be either realistic or abstract and either two- or three-dimensional. Since family portraits are inevitably tension-producing, various choices are offered family members to minimize their stress; 3) Family Mural, like the joint scribble, a task which allows for direct observation of how a family works together can be an effective diagnostic assessment. Mural paper offers a larger drawing

surface than single sheets of paper and when used in the joint scribble it enables art therapists to see family interactions better although opportunity to observe the family's ability to tolerate closeness is not as great. Young children who have not developed the capacity to project an image onto a scribble can participate more fully in joint mural work.

• Wadeson's Method

Wadeson (1980; 1973) developed a variety of techniques for working with couples both diagnostically and therapeutically. Three techniques were developed to highlight the interactional processes in the marital relationship and are not presented in a fixed order as indicated by a particular diagnostic question or therapeutic issue. 1) Joint Picture without Talking. This task provides an opportunity to observe the couple work together in close proximity (single sheet or paper). Not allowing verbal communication heightens the power of the nonverbal interactions. 2) Abstract of Marital Relationship. This is a modification of the Kwiatowska Abstract Family Portrait with the same unique features. It indicates the individual's capacity for abstract thinking and elicits strong affect. 3) Self-Portrait Given to Spouse. Spouses symbolically give themselves (their self-portraits) to one another and then are given the opportunity to "do anything you want to your partner." This art-based exercise elicits intense affect and dramatizes interactions. Wadeson also uses family portraits, joint scribbles, free pictures, and a variety of other kinds of pictures when working with couples.

C. ART-BASED PROCEDURES USED WITH CHILDREN

• Kinetic Family Drawings (K-F-D)

The K-F-D procedure (Burns & Kaufman, 1970) consists of one drawing that can be administered in a group art therapy session or in an individual session. Participants are asked to "Draw everyone in the family doing something." The authors found that the addition of movement to the kinetic drawings (DAP, H-T-P) helped mobilize a child's feelings, not only as related to self-concept, but also in the area of interpersonal relations. The K-F-D often reflects primary disturbances much more quickly and adequately than interviews or other probing techniques (Burns & Kaufman, 1972).

• Dot-to-Dot

Hays (1982), working with four- to 10-year-old children, compared the Dot-to-Dot projective technique with the scribble technique. The data collected indicated that the Dot-to-Dot technique assessed associative material more quickly than the scribble technique. This assessment model has implications for future studies with children.

• The Bridge Drawing

Hays (1981) chose 150 adolescents, 14 to 18 years old, to assess how a normal population going through a difficult change would draw a bridge going from one place to another. Adolescents were chosen because developmentally they represented a population in a tumultous period of adjustment. "The bridge represented links between humans, society and the individual. It was seen as a solution to a problem, (and) a method of conquering or overcoming an obstacle" (p. 208). Twelve variables are considered.

• Kramer Art Therapy Evaluation Scale

With Edith Kramer's permission and funded by Accessible Arts, Inc., of Kansas City, Kansas, and Illinois State University, Frances Anderson (assisted by Maureen Craighill Moran) developed a quantifiable scale to evaluate child change in art therapy based on the Kramer Art Therapy Evaluation (KATE) (Kramer & Schehr, 1983). This procedure requires that a client complete three free (open-ended) art-based tasks; a drawing, a painting, and a clay sculpture. The client is not given any specific direction, but is asked only to make whatever he/she desires in each of the three media. Structured procedures require that each task be completed in a specific order: 1) drawing, 2) painting, and 3) clay. There is also consistency in the set-up and provision of the media and tools to be used. The KATE procedure can provide information on a client's strengths, weaknesses, and potential for benefiting from art therapy.

Results have been analyzed and a series of mostly forced-choice items that might lead to some more quantifiable data were developed. The KATE scale, still under development, has been used by art therapy students at Illinois State University and Florida State University reviewing a pre- and post-treatment pilot study of 24 children.

For more information contact:

Frances Anderson, EdD, A.T.R., HLM
Art Department
Illinois State University
Normal, IL 61764

• Levick Emotional and Cognitive Art Therapy Evaluation and Assessment (LECATA)

The LECATA is based on cognitive research by Levick (1983). The procedure is currently used in assessing students in various socio-economic situations (SES) in the Dade County Public Schools in Miami, Florida, and is ready to be used in research assessing normal students. Collaborations are from all normal and SES populations.

For additional information contact:

Myra Levick, PhD, A.T.R., HLM
or
Janet Bush, MA, A.T.R., Dept. Chairperson,
Clinical Art Therapy Program
1450 N.E. Second Avenue, Suite 736
Miami, FL 33132

• Manning (1987), A Child's Environment

Manning (1987) uses one art-based task to assess a physically abusive environment. She has subjects draw a "favorite kind of day" as both a projective technique and a diagnostic tool. She uses three rating measures (weather, size, and movement) to assess the child's environment. Supporting Parciak, Winnik & Shmueli (1975), Manning (1987) observed that violent content in drawings is reflected in movement of the wild forces of nature (weather). She reports that the "draw your favorite kind of day" is simple to administer and easy to rate.

For additional information contact:

Trudy Manning, MA, A.T.R.
Eastern Virginia Medical School
P.O. Box 1980
Norfolk, VA 23501

• Silver Tests (1979)

Over the last 15 years, Silver has been developing and standardizing art-based tests to test the cognitive and creative skills of children. Currently, she has three tests available through Ablin Press in New York. The three tests are:

> • The Silver Drawing Test of Cognitive and Creative Skills (Silver, 1983) has been found useful in evaluating ability to receive, process, and express concepts. The instrument includes three drawing tasks and stimulus drawing cards. The three drawing tasks are: 1) Draw from Imagination—Children are requested to select two images from stimulus cards and combine them into a drawing that tells a story. Responses are scored on the basis of content, form, and creativity; 2) Drawing from Observation—Children are asked to draw an

arrangement of a large pebble and three cylinders of different sizes. Responses are scored for ability to represent accurately the various relationships, horizontally, vertically, and in depth; 3) Predictive Drawing—Children are asked to show how a house would look on a steep mountain slope, and how a tilted bottle would look if half-filled with water. This test is standardized and is available through Ablin Press, New York.

• Draw-A-Story, Screening for Depression and Emotional Needs (Silver, 1988).

• Stimulus Drawings and Techniques, (Silver, 1982) (revised edition). Please contact:

Rawley Silver
3332 Hadfield Green
Sarasota, FL 34235

• Troeger Art Skills Assessment for Special Education Students

The Troeger Art Skills Assessment (Troeger-Clifford, 1981) identifies an individual's own learning and maturation. It allows the examiner to assess the learner's competencies in manipulating art materials (drawing, painting, cutting paper, and use of clay) and in developing symbolic representation. It is based on inventory developed by Brigance (1978) which focused on the early development (six months to six years) of fine motor skills and behaviors. The Art Skills Assessment has been empirically tested.

For additional information, please contact:

Betty Jo Troeger, EdD, A.T.R.
Department of Art Education
Florida State University
Tallahassee, FL 32306-3014

• Wadeson and Epstein—Effect of Amphetamine in Hyperkinesis

In a single-case study, Wadeson studied the changes in the art of a six-year-old hyperactive boy while "blind" to the varying doses of amphetamine administered by Epstein (Wadeson & Epstein, 1976). At each session he was directed to complete tasks using pastels and water paint at both table and easel and to make a self-portrait. Her observations indicated correlations between drug dosage and aggression, self control, and mood.

D. JUNGIAN ART-BASED PROCEDURES

• Arrington's Visual Preference Test

The Visual Preference Test (VPT) (Arrington, 1985; 1986) is a structured, art-based task developed as an initial step in establishing a normative baseline of visual constructs. Art therapists, who collectively had viewed hundreds of thousands of graphic images and constructs, selected 56 graphic signs and symbols that appeared frequently in the art drawn or selected by their clients. The visual constructs, presented on black and white cards, were initially judged by three art therapists and three Jungian therapists as to the universality of their meanings. The cards represent four Jungian categories: Feminine, Masculine, Self (Sense of Self), and Transformation (Change) concepts. In the long version of the instrument, participants select and rank the cards in three categories—most-preferred, neutral, and least-preferred. In the short version of the instrument, participants select and rank the five most-preferred and the five least-preferred. The instrument, although not standardized, has been empirically tested with 128 women (ranging in age from 21 to 73) with a high level of participation in community-based women's activities; 90% were Caucasian and 93% were married with one or more children. Participants are solicited to research both normal (noninstitutionalized) and institutionalized populations.

For additional information contact:

> D. Arrington, EdD, A.T.R.
> College of Notre Dame
> Belmont, CA 94002

• MARI Card Test

The term *mandala* was first used by Jung (1964) to describe a circular form he spontaneously produced in one of his paintings. For the past 25 years, Kellogg (1980, 1978) has used the mandala for psychological assessment and treatment in the process of self-realization. During therapy sessions she asked her patients to color with oil pastels a pencil outlined, 10½-inch diameter circle. She used these drawings as a monitor of change or progress during the course of therapy and interpreted them on the basis of color, movement, and symbols.

Beginning in 1969, after reviewing hundreds of drawn mandalas at different institutions and in private practice, she began to notice recurring images, patterns, and shapes. She organized these images into a circular design with 13 basic structures which she calls the "Archetypal Stages of the Great Round of Mandala."

The MARI Card Test is the result of Kellogg's years of research. The test is composed of 26 design cards embossed in black on clear plastic. The designs represent two versions of each of the 13 stages. There are 38 colored cards made of paperstock. The client is asked to select five design cards which appeal to him/her for any reason. The participant is then asked to select a color card for each design chosen. The resulting five design cards, each with a selected color, are ranked according to preference.

Training courses are offered in various parts of the country by nine licensed MARI instructors. Although the instrument is not standardized, it has been empirically tested in a variety of settings.

For additional information and research opportunities, contact:

Carol T. Cox, MA, A.T.R.,
Art Therapy Program
The George Washington University
2129 G Street, N.W., Building L
Washington, DC 20052

• Old Masters Series

Ratcliffe (1977, 1975), an art historian and family therapist, developed a test similar to the Thematic Apperception Test (TAT) but without some of its limitations. The individual is asked to select a most and least preferred picture from a collection of 2,000 postcard reproductions of Old Masters. These are used as stimuli for self-reflection. Next, the subject is instructed to spread the postcards face up on the floor and to select about 20 to which the subject had either a strong positive or a strong negative response. The subject is then asked to think about the cards and to attempt to discover the reason each card was selected. Then the subject is asked to arrange the cards in a "meaningful collage representing the self" and to verbally describe the collage to another subject. This art-based instrument addresses archetypal symbolic material. It has been used in empirical research.

• Shoemaker's Rainbow Phenomenon

Through a long interest in color phenomena, Shoemaker (1983) developed the Rainbow Phenomenon. The procedure consists of one drawing that can be administered in a group art therapy session or in an individual session. Materials consist of 18 x 24-inch white drawing paper (20 lb.) and a box of 36 oil pastels. Participants are asked to:

> "Place the paper in front of you, with the box of colors above the paper. Sit quietly looking at the colors. Pick the color that you like the best. Use it first, until you feel finished. Make a

small mark at the corner of the page to keep a record of which color you used first. Continue on with the next color, picked the same way, and continue with the next and the next, until you feel that you have used all the colors that you need to feel good and complete about your rainbow image. Remember to mark the order of the colors used" (Shoemaker, 1983).

A manual is available and courses are offered to explore the material. To obtain a manual describing how to collect Rainbow samples for this collaborative project write:

Roberta Shoemaker-Beal
306 Margon Ct.
Slidell, LA 70458

Discussion

Although art and visual projective tests have been used as instruments to assess conscious and unconscious thoughts and attitudes since before 1900, due to a lack of standardized tools, few of the instruments or procedures have been used as the primary indicators of organicity or pathology. Within the field of art therapy, there is an urgent need to develop standardized art-based assessment procedures and instruments for use in research.

A careful assessment or evaluation is essential to create a plan for art therapy treatment. This information is shared with team members. With appropriate releases and planning, information gained in treatment could also provide valuable data for art therapy research. Assessment procedures and materials used in treatment are varied according to the age and the general condition of the individual being assessed. Research assessment procedures and materials, although varied, may need to be more constant in order to elicit specific data and to test predictive hypotheses.

Naumburg (1958) identified the fundamental differences between projective drawings obtained in psychological tests and those produced in art therapy sessions as spontaneous art products. With emerging data, however, two separate but simultaneous lines of investigation have developed. One line continues to use free and spontaneous art-based tasks and the other line uses structured art-based tasks.

Art therapists, long plagued with problems of establishing and demonstrating reliability and validity, have learned that validation is a long process, rather than a single event. This understanding has resulted in art therapy assessment procedures that, whether free and spontaneous or structured, can be replicated, producing concurrent and predictive content validity.

Conclusion

Art-based procedures and instruments described in this chapter are based on the writings of pioneers within the fields of art therapy, art education, or psychology. It is understood that persons employing art-based instruments and procedures do so within the fields of education, research, and/or therapy. Permission of the developer or publisher may also be necessary.

The details of background materials, methods, or results for each investigation are available in the original sources or through the developer or publisher.

References

Agell, G., & Ulman, E. (1989). The Ulman personality assessment procedure [Abstract]. *Painting portraits: Families, groups & systems* (The Proceedings of the 20th Annual Conference of the American Art Therapy Association). Mundelein, IL: American Art Therapy Association.

Anderson, F. (1983). A critical analysis of a review of the published research literature in arts for the handicapped: 1971-81, with special attention to the visual arts. *Art Therapy: Journal of the American Art Therapy Association, 1*(1), 26-40.

Arrington, D. (1985). Arrington Visual Preference Test (AVPT). (Available from D. Arrington, College of Notre Dame, Belmont, CA 94002).

Arrington, D. (1986). A Jungian-based study of selected visual constructs preferred by women. Unpublished dissertation, University of San Francisco. (University Microfilms No. 87-13, 271.)

Bender, L. (1946). *A Bender Motor Gestalt Test*. (Cards and manual of instructions.) Washington, DC: The American Orthopsychiatric Association.

Brigance, A. (1979). *Brigance Diagnostic Inventory of Early Development*. Woburn, MA: Curriculum Associates.

Buck, J. N. (1978). *The House-Tree-Person technique* (rev. ed.). Los Angeles, CA: Western Psychological Services.

Burak, R. (1982). Conjoint family drawings: A family interaction assessment tool. In A. Di Maria, E. Kramer, and I. Rosner (Eds.), *Art therapy: A bridge between worlds*. The Proceedings of the Twelfth Annual Conference of the American Art Therapy Association, (p. 95). Falls Church, VA: American Art Therapy Association.

Burns, R. (1990). *A guide to Family-Centered Circle Drawings (F-C-C-D) with symbol probes and visual free association*. New York, NY: Brunner/Mazel.

Burns, R., & Kaufman, S. (1970). *Kinetic Family Drawings (K-F-D): An introduction to understanding kinetic drawings*. New York, NY: Brunner/Mazel.

Burns, R., & Kaufman, S. (1972). *Actions, styles & symbols in family drawings (K-F-D)*. New York, NY: Brunner/Mazel.

Buros, O. K. (1978). *Eighth mental measurement yearbook*. Highland Park, IL: Gryphon Press.

Cohen, B., Hammer, J., & Singer, S. (1988). The diagnostic drawing series: A systematic approach to art therapy evaluation and research. *The Arts in Psychotherapy, 15*, 11-21.

Gantt, L. (1990). A validity study of the Formal Elements Art Therapy Scale (FEATS) for measuring diagnostic information through assessing formal variables in patients' drawings. Unpublished dissertation, University of Pittsburgh, Pittsburgh, PA.

Goodenough, F. (1926). *Measurement of intelligence by drawings*. New York, NY: Harcourt, Brace, & World.

Hammer, E. F. (1958). *The clinical application of projective drawings*. Springfield, IL: Charles C Thomas.

Harris, D. (1963). *Children's drawings as measures of intellectual maturity*. New York, NY: Harcourt, Brace, & World.

Hays, R. (1981). The bridge drawing: A projective technique for assessment in art therapy. *The Arts in Psychotherapy, 8*, 207-217.

Hays, R. (1982). Dot-to-dot: Rationale for a "new projective" for children under ten. In L. Gantt & A. Evans (Eds.), Focus on the future. *The Proceedings of the Tenth Annual Conference of the Art Therapy Association* (pp. 116-120). Falls Church, VA: American Art Therapy Association.

Jung, C. (1964). *Man and his symbols*. Garden City, NY: Doubleday.

Kellogg, J. (1978). *Mandala - path of beauty*. Clearwater, FL: Mandala Assessment and Research Institute.

Kellogg, J. (1980). *MARI Card Test*. Clearwater, FL: Mandala Assessment and Research Institute.

Kramer, E., & Schehr, J. (1983). An art therapy evaluation session for children. *American Journal of Art Therapy, 23*(1), 3-12.

Kwiatkowska, H. (1978). *Family therapy and evaluation through art.* Springfield, IL: Charles C Thomas.

Landgarten, H. (1987). *Family art therapy: A clinical guide and casebook.* New York, NY: Brunner/Mazel.

Levick, M. (1983). *They could not talk and so they drew: Children's styles of coping and thinking.* Springfield, IL: Charles C Thomas.

Lowenfeld, V. (1947). *Creative and Mental Growth.* New York, NY: Macmillan.

McGlashan, T., Wadeson, H., Carpenter, W., & Levy, S. (1977). Art and recovery style from psychosis. *Journal of Nervous Mental Disorders, 164,* 182-190.

MacGregor, J. (1989). *The discovery of the art of the insane.* Princeton, NJ: Princeton University Press.

Machover, K. (1949). *Personality projection in the drawing of the human figure.* Springfield, IL: Charles C Thomas.

Manning, T. (1987). Aggression depicted in abused children's drawings. *The Arts in Psychotherapy, 14,* 15-24.

Murray, H. A. (1943). *Thematic Apperception Test manual.* (Ages 4 and over.) Cambridge, MA: Harvard University Press.

Naumburg, M. (1958). Art therapy: Its scope and function. In E. Hammer (Ed.), *The clinical application of projective drawings.* Springfield, IL: Charles C Thomas.

Parciak, R., Winnik, H.Z., & Shmueli, M. (1975). Aggression in painting Painting as a means of release of aggression. *Mental Health Society, 2,* 225-237.

Ratcliffe, E. (1975). The Old Masters Art Collage as an instrument of learning about oneself. Unpublished master's thesis, California State University, Hayward, CA.

Ratcliffe, E. (1977). The Old Masters Art Collage: An art therapy technique for heuristic self-discovery. *Art Psychotherapy, 4,* 29-32.

Reber, A. (1985). *Dictionary of psychology.* New York, NY: Penguin Books.

Roby, N. & Pastushak R. (1979). The significance of the first product in art therapy: Redefinition of Shoemaker's art assessment categories and evaluation grid. In L. Gantt, G. Forrest, D. Silverman, & R. Shoemaker (Eds.), *Art therapy: Expanding horizons. The Proceedings of the Ninth Annual Conference of the American Art Therapy Association*, (pp. 84-89). Baltimore, MD: American Art Therapy Association.

Rorschach, H. (1921). *Psychodiagnostics* (Hans Huber Verlag, transl., 1942). Berne: Bircher.

Rubin, J. (1986). From psychopathology to psychotherapy through art expression: A focus on Hans Prinzhorn & others. *Art Therapy: Journal of the American Art Therapy Association, 3,* 27-33.

Rubin, J. (1984). *Child art therapy: Understanding and helping children grow through art* (2nd ed.). New York, NY: Van Nostrand & Reinhold.

Shoemaker, R. (1978). The significance of the first picture in art therapy. In B.K.Mandel, R.H.Shoemaker, & R.E.Hays (Eds.), *The dynamics of creativity. The Proceedings of the Eighth Annual Conference of the American Art Therapy Association* (pp. 156-162). Baltimore, MD: American Art Therapy Association.

Shoemaker, R.J. (1983). *The rainbow booklet: A look at the psychology, physiology, and physics of color.* Wisconsin: Renewing Visions Press.

Silver, R. (1982). *Stimulus drawings and techniques.* New York, NY: Ablin Press.

Silver, R. A. (1983). *Silver drawing test of cognitive and creative skills.* Seattle: Special Child Publications.

Silver, R. (1988). *Draw-A-Story: Screening for depression and emotional needs.* Mamaronek, NY: Ablin Press.

Troeger-Clifford, B. (1981). *Development of a model to include art in the Individualized Education Program for physically handicapped and health impaired students.* Dissertation, North Texas State University. University Microfilms International, Ann Arbor, MI.

Ulman, E. (1975). A new use of art in psychiatric analysis. In E. Ulman & P. Dachinger (Eds.), *Art therapy in theory and practice.* New York, NY: Schocken.

Wadeson, H. (1971). Characteristics of art expression in depression. *Journal of Nervous and Mental Disease, 153,* 197-204.

Wadeson, H. (1973). Art techniques used in conjoint marital therapy. *American Journal of Art Therapy, 12,* 147-164.

Wadeson, H. (1980). *Art psychotherapy.* New York, NY: John Wiley & Sons.

Wadeson, H., & Bunney, W., Jr. (1969). Manic-depressive art: Tested graphic characteristics and psychodynamic implications. *Journal of Nervous and Mental Disease, 150,* 215-231.

Wadeson, H. & Carpenter, W. (1976). Subjective experience of acute schizophrenia. *Schizophrenic Bulletin,* 2, 302-316.

Wadeson, H., & Epstein, R. (1976). Intrapsychic effect of amphetamine in hyperkinesis. *Mental Health in Children, 3,* 35-60. Westbury, NY: PJD Publications.

Chapter 15

TABULATION OF DRAWING BATTERIES FOR ASSESSMENT

Nancy Knapp, PhD, A.T.R.

The following information is presented as a useful format to provide a large amount of material for reference. This was originally one part of a literature review for research for a doctoral dissertation (Knapp, 1989).

This information includes only art-based assessment procedures which are designed with a battery of several drawing tasks, and is divided into four segments: 1) Identifying Information and Reference (which includes bibliographical material); 2) Purpose (which describes the author's intent in the use of the battery); 3) Procedures and Materials; and 4) Evaluation System (which describes the scoring procedure).

House-Tree-Person (H-T-P)

Identifying Information and Reference
Designed by John N. Buck 1948, revised in 1966.

Buck, John N. (1973). *The house-tree-person technique/revised manual.* Los Angeles, CA: Western Psychological Services.

Purpose
A technique designed to give the clinician insight about an individual's "sensitivity, maturity, flexibility, efficiency, degree of personality integration, and interaction with the environment." (Buck, 1973, p.1)

Procedures and Materials

Phase I, Step 1: Three freehand pencil drawings in sequence of a house, a tree and a person. Step 2: Subject asked to define, describe, associate to, and interpret his or her drawings. Phase II, Step 1: Three freehand drawings in crayon of a house, a tree and a person. Step 2: Repeat of apperceptive, verbal descriptions of the crayon drawings.

Materials include standard white paper forms (8½" X 14" folded to form 8½" X 7") used and labeled horizontally for the house and vertically for the tree and person, a #2 lead pencil with an eraser and a box of eight crayons.

Evaluation System

Detail, proportion and perspective considered best for differentiation between drawings at different levels, items were designated GOOD or FLAW. Sixty primary questions about the drawings are classified as eliciting pressure of personality issues (P), associations (A), and reality testing (R). These are analyzed with the recorded sequence of drawn parts, pauses, comments, behavior, total time, placement of drawing, etc. Different levels of classification are based upon Buck's original test groups and include intelligence levels and the categorization of parts as pathoformic, pathological, and pathognomonic. Complex process allows qualitative extension of the quantitative scores.

Ulman Personality Assessment Procedure

Identifying Information and Reference

Developed by Elinor Ulman during the 1960's at the District of Columbia General Hospital, this battery consists of four drawings.

Ulman, E. (1975). A new use of art in psychiatric diagnosis. In E. Ulman & P. Dachinger (Eds.), *Art Therapy in Theory and Practice*. New York, NY: Schocken Books.

Purpose

Originally used for diagnosis of patients, this procedure has been developed as a personality assessment.

Procedures and Materials

Individual sessions with drawing boards and easels, 18" x 24" paper, and standard spectrum of 12 "NuPastels." The request for the first drawing is: "Please use these materials to make a picture." Before the second picture, the patient is directed in a movement exercise as if drawing in the air with circular and linear strokes, afterwards he or she is asked to "record those movements on paper." The third picture is a request to do a "Rhythmic scribble on the paper with the eyes closed." The fourth drawing is a choice between a free picture as in the first procedure or another scribble drawing.

Evaluation System

A definitive evaluation system is still evolving with collaboration from Gladys Agell (Agell & Ulman, 1989). As developed, evaluation relies upon the clinical skills of the interpreter for observing and analyzing indicators for assessment.

Kwiatkowska Structured Family Art Therapy Interview/Evaluation

Identifying Information and Reference

Designed by Hanna Kwiatkowska at the National Institute of Mental Health, Adult Psychiatry Branch.

Kwiatkowska, Hanna Yaxa (1978). *Family therapy and evaluation through art.* Springfield, IL: Charles C Thomas.

Purpose

Evaluation of all nuclear family members as part of research on family relations and etiology of mental illness, especially schizophrenia.

Procedures and Materials

During the family session the following tasks are given sequentially: (1) A free picture; (2) A family portrait; (3) An abstract family portrait; (4) A picture started with the help of a scribble; (5) A joint family scribble; and (6) A free picture. Drawing is done on folding floor easels. Materials used are 18" x 24" drawing paper and a box of square, semi-hard pastels for each participant. Following each picture, family members comment spontaneously and with encouragement from the therapists. Session is conducted by the art therapist with notes taken by a participant observer who is also involved in the ongoing therapy. Sessions are held soon after admission of family members to a hospital and about six months later for comparison. A family of four or five will require $1^{1/2}$ to 2 hours.

Evaluation System
A comparison is made of the first and last pictures and of the drawings in the session with an eye toward change or lack of it. Comparison of the individual scribble drawing and the joint family scribble looks at individual versus collective pathology. Titles are requested for all pictures and are looked at for relevance or irrelevance, idiosyncratic or symbolic meaning, and concreteness. Family dynamics, relations, and perceptions are all noted in the art, other non-verbal and verbal exchanges and interactions. Evaluations are done in a standardized, clinical way but with no structured quantitative 'score' or evaluation form.

The Dent-Kwiatkowska Study

Identifying Information and Reference
Collaboration of James K. Dent and Hanna Kwiatkowska at the Clinical Center of the National Institute of Mental Health.

Kwiatkowska, Hanna Yaxa (1978). *Family therapy and evaluation through art.* Springfield, IL: Charles C Thomas.

Purpose
Systematic statistical research of 1,514 pictures from 269 members of 63 families.

Procedures and Materials
As listed above structured Family Art Therapy Interview/Evaluation.

Evaluation System
Rating Manual was compiled, modified, and seen as continuing to change. Items were based upon salient characteristics of drawings gathered during several years from family interviews and existing literature on features of pictures from specific subject with psychopathology. According to the author "Most of the ratings describe form, but a few, such as Comprehensibility, Meaningfulness of Title, Emotional feeling, Pleasing or Displeasing Qualities, and Content Code deal with the clarity for quality of the communication made

by the pictures" (Kwiatkowska, 1978, p. 186-187). Pictures were anonymous and rated with additional check ratings to resolve differences. Sixty-five items of discrimination of form and content were rated without interactional material. (Kwiatkowska included copies of the Rating Manual and forms in her book's Appendix IV.)

Kwiatkowska-Mosher Twin Study

Identifying Information and Reference
Part of Twin and Sibling Studies at Adult Psychiatry Branch, the National Institute of Mental Health. Conducted by Hanna Yaxa Kwiatkowska and Loren Mosher.

Kwiatkowska, Hanna Yaxa (1978) *Family therapy and evaluation through art.* Springfield, IL: Charles C Thomas.

Purpose
To rate interactional as well as pictorial material as part of the investigation of the quality and style of transactions and role attribution in families with twins concordant and discordant for schizophrenia.

Procedures and Materials
Evaluative tasks and materials as outlined for the Family Art Evaluation.

Evaluation System
Art evaluated by "blind" raters on a 5 point scale for 12 variables. Evaluations looked at: (I) Integration, understandability and color use of #1 and #6, free pictures; (II) Body image in #2, family portrait and levels of abstraction for #3, abstract family portrait; (III) Creative resources, imagination and expression in #1 and #6; and (IV) Quality and style of family interactions and role attribution in #5 a joint family scribble. Raters looked at family individuation, involvement, alliances, ability to work at joint tasks, and their own subjective reactions. Forms & scoring sheets comprise Appendix V of Kwiatkowska's book.

The Projective Drawing Battery (H-T-P-P)

Identifying Information and Reference

Presented by Emanuel Hammer as a clinical model from his practice at Psychiatric Clinic Court, Child Guidance League and New York State Psychiatric Institute and Lynchburg State Colony, Virginia.

Hammer, Emanuel F. (1980) The projective drawing battery: A case illustration (Chapter 18) In: E. Hammer (Ed.) *Clinical Application of Projective Drawings*. Springfield, IL: Charles C Thomas.

Purpose

To provide a comprehensive combination of projective devices for practical clinical use.

Procedures and Materials

Employs a combination of Buck's and Machover's devices (hence the H-T-P-P designation) by including a drawing of a house, tree, and person of both sexes, with both achromatic and chromatic stages. This follows administration of the Rorschach and selected TAT cards. It may be supplemented with other projective drawings are added, for example, the Unpleasant Concept Test, Draw-A-Family, Drawing Completion Test, Draw An Animal, and the Eight Card Redrawing Test. Hammer estimates the H-T-P-P to take 45 minutes, excluding time spent on other procedures. Re-test results were presented using the same battery following 50 hours of therapy during a three-and-one-half-month period. Materials are standard #2 pencil with eraser, a box of eight crayons for chromatic stage of H-T-P-P, and standard 8½" X 11" white paper.

Evaluation System

Evaluation is global and done in the context of the case history and behavioral information with the background of psychodynamic theory and clinical experience. Subjective reaction and frank speculation is also employed and identified as such. Objective criteria are used to illustrate improved condition on re-test examples following treatment.

Rubin Diagnostic Art Interview

Identifying Information and Reference
Developed at the Pittsburgh Child Guidance Center as a diagnostic and treatment tool.

Rubin, Judith Aron. (1978) *Child art therapy. Understanding and helping children grow through art.* New York, NY: Van Nostrand Reinhold.

Purpose
To develop a standardized 60-minute format for use in diagnosis and treatment decision making for clinical or educational use. Initial goal was to combine both free and assigned tasks in a non-threating way, employing open choice diagnostically.

Procedures and Materials
Completely free choice of media, including sculptural material. Format became developed into unstructured free choice for the subjects, comparable to a play therapy interview with art. Therapist only intervenes in supportive way when the person seems unable to start. Typically the subject may do four or five art projects and associate to them or answer open ended questions such as "Can you tell me about ----?"; "Does it have a story?"; or "Could you speak for it as if it were a puppet?"

Evaluation System
There is no quantitative scoring system *per se*, but a structured approach is used to "Decode the symbolic messages" and to construct an understanding of the personality. Evaluation includes verbal and nonverbal behavior, interactions and attitude toward adults, the choice and approach to materials, the form and content of the products, common themes, self-representation, and the sequence of products and associations.

Wadeson Drawing Battery for Research

Identifying Information and Reference
Studies were done in the Psychiatric Assessment Section of the Clinical Center at the National Institute of Mental Health, directed by William Carpenter, M.D.

Wadeson, Harriet. (1980). *Art psychotherapy.* New York, NY: John Wiley and Sons.

Purpose

The goal was to use art expression to gain understanding of the subjective phenomenology of the acute schizophrenic episode.

Procedures and Materials

18" X 24" paper on easels with pastels were used. Sessions were structured with five drawing requests: free choice, self-portrait, picture of the psychiatric illness, picture of hallucinations experienced, and picture of delusions experienced. Process was done close to admission and prior to medication, prior to discharge, and at a one-year follow-up. Sixty-two patients were evaluated. Sessions were tape recorded.

Evaluation System

Emerging data were analyzed for commonalities, recurring themes, and other information as it applied to the acute schizophrenic experience.

Silver Drawing Test of Cognitive and Creative Skills

Identifying Information and Reference

Developed by Rawley Silver and supported by U.S. Department of Education, The National Institute of Education and the New York State Department of Education.

Silver, Rawley A. (1983). *Manual, Silver drawing test of cognitive and creative skills.* Seattle, WA: Special Child Publications.

Silver, Rawley A. (1986). *Stimulus drawings and techniques in therapy, development, and assessment* (3rd ed.). Mamaroneck, NY: Trillium Books.

Purpose

To identify children and adults with intellectual abilities that escape detection in traditional tests of intelligence or achievement.

Procedures and Materials

Three tasks are designed to assess levels of ability in conceptual, spatial and sequential thinking: (1) A Predictive Drawing tests a child's ability to figure out what will happen to liquid in a container at different angles; (2) Drawing from observation requests a drawing of an arrangement of three different cylinders and a stone to check spatial thinking and perception; and (3) Drawing from imagination, begins with a selection of two stimulus elements and combines them into a narrative drawing with a title. The drawings are on 8½" X 11" paper with a #2 lead pencil with an eraser.

Evaluation System
Drawings scored on scale of zero to five, based on developmental stages as demonstrated in experiments by Piaget, Bruner, and associates. Ability to select, combine and represent in creative tasks is pertinent.

Texas Research Institute in Mental Science (TRIMS)

Identifying Information and Reference
Developed by Felice Cohen, et al, at TRIMS, Harris County, Texas.

Cohen, Felice and Phillips, Randy. (1985). Incest markers in children's artwork. *The Arts and Psychotherapy, 12,* 265-284.

Purpose
To determine whether children's art reveals markers of incest or suspected incest, to design an evaluation protocol for scoring drawings of children identified as victims of incest, and to implement research.

Procedures and Materials
At intake, three drawings were collected: an H-T-P, a drawing of a family engaged in some activity, and a free drawing. Standardized paper, markers and pencils.

Evaluation System
Coding form counting 12 features on each of the three drawings. An additional 10 features were added. Rating was performed by both experienced and naive raters. Coding system continues to be revised.

Zierer Creative Analysis

Identifying Information and Reference
Developed at Hillside Hospital, Glen Oaks, New York, and other psychiatric hospitals in New York and Connecticut by Dr. Ernest Zierer.

Zierer, Edith (1987). Creative analysis involving multidisciplinary evaluations of a case study. *Art Therapy, 4,* 113-125.

Purpose

Designed to provide a flexible testing instrument to validate, question, or accommodate individual treatment goals and for related diagnostic and treatment decisions in emotional disorders. The authors saw it as a way to tap conscious, preconscious, and unconscious motivations. The authors stated that the painting tests "serve multiple purposes since the experimental conditions replicate past developmental vicissitudes as well as activate current stressful situations."

Procedures and Materials

The patient is given a battery of structured but not 'explicitly directive' therapeutic painting tasks. For example, if the patient were restricted to an achromatic painting, other choices such as motif and style remain with the patient. Different tests have different purposes, e.g., Reactivation. The number of components can be great; in the study presented there were 168 projects.

Evaluation System

The results of the tests are integrated on a graph to form a Psychogram.

Art Psychotherapy Family Systems Diagnostic Procedure

Identifying Information and Reference

Developed by Helen Landgarten at Cedars-Sinai Medical Center and Thalians Community Mental Health Center.

Landgarten, Helen. (1987). *Family art psychotherapy: A clinical guide and casebook*. New York, NY: Brunner/Mazel.

Purpose

To provide the family and the therapist opportunity to focus on the family's functioning, their interactional process, and communication patterns for diagnosis and treatment.

Procedures and Materials

Described as 'quasi-art experiences,' three standardized, structured, tasks are given to the family: (1) a Nonverbal Team Art Task, in which the family works in two teams, drawing without speaking, signalling or writing to each other. Each member use a single different colored marker through out; (2) a Nonverbal Family Art Task, has the entire family work on one piece of paper.

After both, the products are titled; and (3) a Verbal Family Art Task and may use either plasticine or colored paper construction, during which talking is permitted.

Evaluation System

The therapist observes the above process. Author cites 17 evaluation points which look at initiation, participation, involvement, space use, symbolic contact, dependence, independence, working style, roles, and emotions to be addressed in addition to verbal and nonverbal interchanges.

Diagnostic Drawing Series (DDS)

Identifying Information and Reference

Developed at Mt. Vernon Hospital in Alexandria, Virginia, by Barry Cohen. Newsletter available for collaborating clinicians and researchers.

Cohen, Barry M., Hammer, Jeffrey, & Singer, Shira. (1988). The Diagnostic Drawing Series: A systematic approach to art therapy evaluation and research. *The Arts in Psychotherapy, 15,* 11-21.

Purpose

To study the relationship between drawing and diagnosis in the field of art therapy for assessment, treatment and research.

Procedures and Materials

Drawings are done on 18" X 24" of 60 lb. white drawing paper with standard 12 pack of chalk pastels. Three directives are requested, as follows: "Make a picture with these materials", "Draw a picture of a tree," and "Make a picture of how you are feeling using lines, shapes and colors."

Evaluation System

Evaluation is linked to the Diagnostic & Statistical Manual, 3rd Ed. (DSM III). Developments include protocol handbook, an optional Drawings Inquiry, a Drawing Analysis Form, rating handbook, computer software and computer-compatible rating form. Quantitative systems evaluates use of paper, colors, shapes and related elements. Extensive library of categorized examples is being compiled.

Harbor/UCLA Diagnostic Art Battery

Identifying Information and Reference
Developed in 1983 at Harbor/UCLA Department of Psychiatry. (unpublished).

Purpose
Battery was put together in order to standardize initial art therapy sessions, to provide a baseline for presentation of material in case conferences, and to assist in diagnosis and treatment planning. Initial goals included obtaining the series at the beginning of treatment and at subsequent stages. They have also been used in court hearings for adults and Individual Education Plans (IEP's) for school-aged children.

Procedures and Materials
Materials are free choice within standardized spectrum of wax-pastels, fine- or broad-tipped markers, and pen or pencils on 8" X 11" white paper. Requests are made for four drawings based upon traditional projective drawing techniques, the Name Embellishment (NE), House-Tree-Person-Modification (H-T-P-M), Kinetic-Family-Drawing-Modification (K-F-D-M), and Free Choice, Titled (F-C-T).

Evaluation System
Evaluation system coupled with a standard psychiatric intake and mental status form. The results were evaluated in the context of case material, behavior, and treatment needs and response.

References

Agell, G. (1989). The Ulman personality assessment procedure [Abstract in conference program]. *Painting portraits: Families, groups, and systems.* The 20th Annual Conference of the American Art Therapy Association, Inc., San Francisco, CA.

Buck, John N. (1973). *The house-tree-person technique/revised manual.* Los Angeles, CA: Western Psychological Services.

Cohen, Barry M., Hammer, Jeffrey, & Singer, Shira. (1988). The Diagnostic Drawing Series: A systematic approach to art therapy evaluation and research. *The Arts in Psychotherapy, 15,* 11-21.

Hammer, Emanuel F. (1980) The projective drawing battery: A case illustration (Chapter 18) In: E. Hammer (Ed.) *Clinical Application of Projective Drawings*. Springfield, IL: Charles C Thomas.

Knapp, N. (1992). Tabulated review of diagnostic use of art as a resource for research with Alzheimer's disease. *American Journal of Art Therapy*.

Knapp, N. (1989). Comparison of diagnostic drawings from normal and Alzheimer's subjects. Unpublished doctoral dissertation. United States International University. San Diego, CA.

Kwiatkowska, Hanna Yaxa (1978) *Family therapy and evaluation through art*. Springfield, IL: Charles C Thomas.

Landgarten, Helen. (1987). *Family art psychotherapy: A clinical guide and casebook*. New York, NY: Brunner/Mazel.

Rubin, Judith Aron. (1978) *Child art therapy. Understanding and helping children grow through art*. New York, NY: Van Nostrand Reinhold.

Silver, Rawley A. (1983). *Manual, Silver drawing test of cognitive and creative skills*. Seattle, WA: Special Child Publications.

Silver, Rawley A. (1986). *Stimulus drawings and techniques in therapy, development, and assessment* (3rd ed.). Mamaroneck, NY: Trillium Books.

Ulman, E. (1975). A new use of art in psychiatric diagnosis. In E. Ulman & P. Dachinger (Eds.), *Art Therapy in Theory and Practice*. New York, NY: Schocken Books.

Wadeson, Harriet. (1980). *Art psychotherapy*. New York, NY: John Wiley and Sons.

Zierer, Edith (1987). Creative analysis involving multidisciplinary evaluations of a case study. *Art Therapy: The Journal of the American Art Therapy Association, 4*, 113-125.

Chapter 16

COMPUTERS AND RESEARCH IN ART THERAPY

Frances E. Anderson, EdD, A.T.R., H.L.M.
David Cox, B.S.
Maxine Crouch, MA , A.T.R.
Carol Cox, MA , A.T.R.

INTRODUCTION

Frances E. Anderson, EdD, A.T.R., H.L.M.

Less than a decade ago if someone had mentioned the word "computer" most of us would have thrown up our hands in dismay and visualized the ugly spectre of a *Brave New World* where Big Brother would be watching over us, and we would think that all semblance of creativity would be lost or gobbled up by the inhumanity of new technology.

Some art therapists and artists may still feel this way. However, in reality, what has happened is that computers have become powerful tools not just in terms of word processing, data analysis, and even as media for art therapy (Anderson, 1992; Canter, 1987, 1989), but also as an invaluable tool in basic art therapy research. Computers have become more and more invaluable in assisting art therapy scholars in their library literature searches and reviews of related research.

Over two decades ago when I was in the throes of writing my doctoral dissertation at Indiana University, all of my research data had to be analyzed on the large university mainframe computer. The only time when we lowly graduate students could do our data runs was between midnight and five in the morning (the rest of the computer time was allocated to faculty and departmental usage). What a difference two decades of software and personal computer development has made. It was estimated that by 1985, one out of every two households had a personal computer (Anderson, 1985; White, 1983). Now researchers do not have to be linked (tied down) to a university mainframe computer; they can analyze data at home on their own personal computer.

This chapter of the *Guide to Conducting Art Therapy Research* opens with a segment on basic computer terminology written by David Cox. This section is followed by descriptions of software packages that permit one to do basic statistical analyses on personal computers by Maxine Crouch and of the SPSSX software package, which enables one to do data analysis on the IBM personal computer, by Carol Cox.

Finally, a section is devoted to descriptions of several major computerized databases and how computerized literature searches can be conducted. Appendix V contains excerpts from four actual computerized searches executed by Sr. Dorothy McLaughlin and Dr. Winnie Ferguson.

COMPUTER TERMINOLOGY

David H. Cox, B.S.

Computer terminology is as arcane as that of any other field and can be just as intimidating. The following is a brief explanation of such terms, with an emphasis on those concerning personal computer technology.

File: A way of organizing information for a computer. A file can represent a program or data; it is a named unit of information.

Program: A set of instructions that a computer can execute. Typically, a program will read input data, and use that information to generate output data.

Data: The other type of information, besides programs, that makes sense to a computer. For instance, in a program that calculated your weekly wages, a line in a file that contained this information: "$12.50/hr 32 hours" would be input data.

Mainframe: The original, large-scale computer.

Mini-computer: A deceptive term, this refers to computers that are smaller than mainframes but still larger than a refrigerator. The typical mini-computer example is a Vax 11/780, made by Digital Equipment Corporation.

Micro-computer: This refers to an individual sized computer. There are two main types: IBM-PC and Macintosh. There are many different models of each type, and for the former, there are many different companies that made compatible computers that, generally speaking, run the same programs that were written for an IBM-PC; thus this type of technology is considerably cheaper. This is unfortunate, because the Macintosh operating system is more user friendly, especially for computer neophytes.

Basic: A computer language that is used to write programs. A specific way, narrowly defined, of describing what instructions a computer program will execute. There are many other computer languages besides Basic, such as Fortran, Cobol, and Pascal.

Chip: The brain of a computer; the central area where instructions are interpreted and carried out. (There are many other parts, mainly concerned with moving data from one place to another).

ROM: Read Only Memory, "burnt into" a computer's chip(s) permanently. This represents information that a computer needs to perform its upper level tasks; the most often used information, since it is stored in a place that is accessible quickly. In computer media (different ways of storing files) there is a tradeoff between price and speed of access.

RAM: Random Access Memory; a computer uses this area to execute programs. Anything in here when the computer is turned off is lost; that is why it is sometimes called volatile memory. Thus, if a program generates information that the user wants to save, it will be written to some type of permanent storage, such as fixed or floppy disks.

Hard Disk: Rotating metal platters, covered with magnetic oxide particles, that contain information using the same technology as the tape player in a home stereo. This is usually a permanent, internal part of a computer, along with the hard disk drive, and can store a lot of information (20-40 megabytes). The drive is used to read the information off the disk; it spins the disk around and moves a device with read/write heads (like the heads in a tape deck) to different portions of the disk. A hard disk is also called a fixed disk.

Floppy Disk: A flimsy disk in a square housing, that can be stored outside of a computer. It is inserted into a floppy disk drive in order for the computer to read the information on it. It is cheaper than a hard disk, can store less information (360 kilobytes - 1.2 megabytes), and is slower to access. Most micro-computers today will have both kinds of disk drives, fixed and floppy. There are two kinds of floppy disks, 3½-inch, and 5¼-inch. Floppy disks can be formatted to hold different amounts of information, with confusing terms such as "double density" or "high density", depending on the type of floppy disk drive and the quality of the floppy disk.

Byte: A measurement of computer information storage, which refers to a consecutive group of 8 bits. In a data file, it takes one byte to represent one character. A kilobyte is 1024 bytes, abbreviated as simply "k." A megabyte is a million bytes, often referred to as a "meg."

Bit: This is a physical unit in a computer that can represent one of exactly two states, depending on the amount or direction of current flow. Bit is short for binary digit.

Dump: A term used in several ways; it generally refers to the act of writing data to a file in such a way that the file can be carried over and read into another computer (sometimes referred to as an "ASCII dump", ASCII, pronounced AS-key, being the generic method of representing data among different computers.) In a mainframe (large) computing environment, a dump can refer to a printout of a program as it appeared in RAM that is used by experts to debug the program.

Extended memory: Additional RAM capacity that is helpful for large programs, or programs that use large amounts of data.

Keyboard: Similar to typewriter keys, where information is fed into the computer. It sometimes has a numerical pad in addition to the alphabet.

Format: Making a floppy disk compatible with the disk drive it will be used in; a way of organizing how the readable space on the disk will be used. This also needs to be done with the fixed disk of some computers. (It always has to be done by someone; sometimes it is done at the factory, sometimes by you, and may need to be done again if there are problems.)

Software: A term used to refer to **programs** in contrast to the actual physical components of a computer, which are known collectively as **hardware**. Software can be user or vendor-written.

Operating System: A program that determines how the computer accomplishes all the different tasks it has to do. This is the program in charge of everything. Some of it is in ROM, and some of it is usually on the fixed disk. (In essence, the main program executes other programs in order to carry out different functions.)

Modem: A device used to send information between computers, or between a computer and a terminal, over telephone lines. The speed of transmission is described as so many "baud," as in a 1200 baud modem. Typically, a modem is used to connect a micro-computer to a mainframe or mini; and in such a case, the latter computer is called the "host." In this case, the PC is emulating a terminal, which is a device that can do nothing on its own, but is useful in talking to a large computer. "Talking" in this sense refers to the exchange of information between a human and a computer, such as typing in an operating system command or displaying the contents of a data file. One may also want to transfer files from the PC to the host ("uploading") or the other way around ("downloading").

Peripherals: Hardware that is not part of the main computer system, but is attached by cables or cords to special "ports" in the computer (computers, external disk drives, etc.).

Cable: A cord-like device with pins in the plug that are designed to fit into computer hardware. The cable conducts information between the computer and various peripherals.

Serial Port: Refers to the fact that information is sent bit by bit, serially, one after the other.

Parallel Port: With this type of cable, information is sent a whole byte (or more) at a time, with all the little bits lined up parallel to one another. Different types of peripherals require a specific port type, and it is necessary to match the computer ports, cables, and peripheral types correctly.

Monitor: The cathode ray tube, or screen, used by a computer to display information. Sometimes referred to as a CRT.

COMPUTER PROGRAMS FOR RESEARCH

Maxine Crouch, M.A., A.T.R.

There are a number of programs available for research which are capable of saving a great deal of time computing data, categorizing, plotting correlation of variables, determining reliability of research data, or printing graphs or tables. Some of these are designed for scientific research or social sciences. The best known program is SPSSX. The majority of these programs require a fair amount of time to learn the commands necessary to execute the programs. Prices range from $99 to several thousand dollars. Most include graphics which enable the researcher to display a more visual overview of their research results.

A number of statistical programs were rated by *PC Magazine* (March, 1989) in five different areas, one of which was social science statistics. The best according to the editors were *SPSS/PC+*, *Systat with Sygraph*, and *Statgraphics*, with prices ranging from $795 to $895 (p. 127, 1989). The *SPSS/PC+* has a good rating but requires 12MB (megabytes) of memory due to 42 disks needed to run the entire program. The manuals are rated well, and the cost is $795 with options extra (p. 116). *Systat with Sygraph* has an excellent rating, requires 640K RAM and can be purchased separately for $495 and $595 respectively or $795 as a package (p. 156). *Statgraphics* has a requirement of a minimum of 512K RAM, with 640K needed for certain functions, and a hard disk is recommended. The editors state that the graphics are excellent and it is a well-rounded program. The cost is a little more at $895 (p. 148).

Some of the scientific graphing and presentation programs were also rated by *PC Magazine*. Two-dimensional programs that were editors' choices were *Grapher* at $199 and *Sigma-Plot* at a price of $395, the latter having more features for the extra money. Grapher did not have the capability of some two-dimensional plotting functions, such as error bars and polar plotting (p. 268). Two 3-dimensional programs they cited were *Surfer* at $499, and *SDS* at $995. The higher priced one could not perform arithmetic and neither could calculate standard deviations (pp. 268-9).

There are shareware and freeware programs available for minimal cost or free for the writing, and some computer bulletin boards such as Compuserve have programs users can plug into for the fee of the service, but a modem is required for this function.

The computer hardware and specifications required for each individual program vary from program to program, and whether one buys the hardware or software first, they need to be compatible with each other. Most PC's now are compatible with one another, with regard to language. For example, computers now usually state that they are capable of using IBM-PC compatible software. Shopping around can save several hundred dollars for computer equipment and software. The basics (a monitor, computer, disk drive, keyboard, and printer, capable of expandability) could cost as little as $900. The middle range for the above, plus a hard disk drive and expanded memory, is about $1500. The upper range is from $2000 to several thousand dollars more for a personal computer.

For more extensive information, refer to the March, 1989, issue of *PC Magazine*. This portion of the *Guide* provides but a brief overview of their extensive review of the many statistical programs available on the market, and many are constantly being revised and updated.

THE STATISTICAL PACKAGE
FOR THE SOCIAL SCIENCES (SPSS)®

Carol T. Cox, M.A., A.T.R.

Many art therapists have excellent research ideas but are intimidated when it comes to implementing a project and tabulating data because of a lack of knowledge in research procedures and statistics. Research procedures and a basic understanding of statistics can be easily learned; the statistics themselves can be handled with ease by using the *SPSS®*.

SPSS®

SPSS (the Statistical Package for Social Sciences)® is a comprehensive data analysis system. *SPSS-X* is designed for mainframes and supermini's and can be accessed by modem with an IBM-compatible computer. *SPSS/PC* is a software package available for IBM-PC/XT's and compatible microcomputers, such as the COMPAQ PLUS. *SPSS®* is an easily comprehensible program which can be used with minimal training by persons with no computer experience. Several manuals for *SPSS®* are available which have been developed in collaboration with McGraw-Hill.

Data and File Management

SPSS/PC is capable of processing large data files of up to 200 variables and has extensive and convenient facilities for transforming data and files. New variables can be created and existing variables can be modified. Numeric values can be recoded, cases can be selected conditionally and made into subsets, selected values can be counted, and cases can be weighed differentially. Missing values can be processed in a variety of ways. In addition, a special procedure is available for transferring and reading files which have been stored in other mainframe statistical programs (e.g., SAS).

Example of Recoding:
In a normative study of color usage, my demographic form asked for the following information:

Indicate what art experience or formal art training you have had (circle applicable numbers):

(1) No formal art education
(2) Grade school art classes
(3) High school art classes
(4) College or professional art classes
(5) College minor in fine arts
(6) College major in fine arts or professional art degree
(7) Graduate art classes
(8) Graduate degree in fine arts
(9) Post-graduate formal art training
(10) Other (please specify)

When filing the data, the largest number each person indicated was recorded. A recoding into the following four categories:

(1) No formal art education
(2) Grade school art
(3) High School art
(4) Post-secondary school art

was entered as a command and then processed by the computer so that each subject would have a new numerical value for the category, art education. Similarly, actual ages of subjects which were filed originally were subsequently recategorized by a simple command into three groups:

(1) Young adult
(2) Mid-adult
(3) Mature adult

Descriptive Statistics

SPSS/PC DESCRIPTIVE provides descriptive and frequency procedures for summary statistics on one or more variables, including frequency counts and plots. These include: mean, standard error of mean, standard deviation, variance, kurtosis, skewness, range, minimum and maximum, sum, median, mode, percentiles and n-tiles, bar charts, and histograms.

Example of Frequency Distribution:

Figure 1 is an example of a frequency distribution with a bar chart from my normative study on color.

FIGURE 1.

VALUE LABEL	VALUE	FREQUENCY	PERCENT	VALID PERCENT	CUM PERCENT
NO FORMAL ART	1	30	20.0	20.0	20.0
GRADE SCHOOL ART	2	39	26.0	26.0	46.0
HIGH SCHOOL ART	3	25	16.7	16.7	62.7
POST SECD SCHOOL ART	4	56	37.3	37.3	100.0
	TOTAL	150	100.0	100.0	

```
NO FORMAL ART          ------------------------30
GRADE SCHOOL ART       -------------------------------39
HIGH SCHOOL ART        --------------------25
POST SECD SCHOOL ART --------------------------------------------56

                0...........12.........24...........36.............48.............60
```

FREQUENCY

VALID CASES 150   **MISSING CASES** 0

Categorical Data Analysis

Multi-way contingency tables and measures of association and significance tests are available by entering CROSSTABULATION or cross-classification commands. Many options include: up to 10-way contingency tables, row, column, and total percentages, observed and expected frequencies, residuals, chi-square, Lambda, contingency coefficient, uncertainty coefficient. A hierarchical loglinear program can be used for more complex categorical analysis.

Example of Crosstabulation:

Subjects in my normative study on color usage were asked to draw a rainbow according to art therapist, Roberta Shoemaker's guidelines for drawing a "personally expressive rainbow" (Shoemaker, 1983). The rainbow drawings were evaluated for several data categories including the SHAPE of the rainbow: (1) arc, (2) elaborated arc, and (3) non-arc.

FIGURE 2. Cross Tabulation of Art Education by Shape

ART EDUCATION	SHAPE ARC	ELAB.ARC	NON-ARC	ROW TOTAL
NO FORMAL ART	27	2	1	30 20.0
GRADE SCHOOL ART	26	6	7	39 26.0
HIGH SCHOOL ART	14	7	4	25 16.7
POST SECD SCHOOL	20	15	21	56 37.3
COLUMN TOTAL	87 58.0	30 20.0	33 22.0	150 100.0

CHI-SQUARE	D.F.	SIGNIFICANCE	MIN E.F.	CELLS WITH E.F.< 5
27.35247	6	.0001	5.000	NONE

NUMBER OF MISSING OBSERVATIONS = 0

Figure 2 is an example of a crosstabulation of the shape of the rainbow drawings by the level of art education of the subjects.

The column totals give the frequencies and percentages of subjects who drew arcs, elaborated arcs, or non-arcs. The row totals give the frequencies and percentages of subjects who fall within the different levels of art education. There was a total of 150 subjects, so the frequencies equal 150 and the percentages equal 100.

The numbers in the boxes represent the number of cases or frequency. For example, 27 subjects who had no formal art education drew a traditional arc for the shape of their rainbows (see top row). In the same art education category, only 2 drew an elaborated arc, and only one subject drew a non-arc. Of those subjects who had post-secondary school art education (see bottom row), 20 drew a traditional arc, 15 drew an elaborated arc, and 21 drew a non-arc.

The chi-square test of independence measures the extent of association between two variables, or how likely (or unlikely) the variables are independent of one another. This is a complicated statistical procedure which is automatically computed by the *SPSS®*. For this research project, the typical research chi-square level of significance of .05 or less was established, meaning that there is a 5% chance or less that the results are due to marginal probabilities of random scatter. A highly significant level of significance is considered .01 or less.

In this example, the chi-square level of significance is .0001 (highly significant) in the crosstabulation of shape of the rainbow by art education. In other words, the degree of art education a person has significantly affects the outcome of the shape of the rainbow. This, of course, makes sense, i.e., that the more art education a person has, the more apt he or she will be to employ a more creative and less traditional approach in the rendering of a rainbow drawing.

Group Comparisons

SPSS/PC offers group comparisons (with independent and paired samples) with a program called T-TEST. Another program called MEANS displays group means, standard deviations, and sums across groups of independent variables. ONEWAY is a program which performs analyses of variance procedures for multiple comparison tests. ANOVA provides factorial analyses of variances with optional covariates, allowing for up to 10 independent variables. Multiple comparison procedures protect against calling too many differences significant.

Multiple Linear Regression Analysis

Multiple Regression is another feature of *SPSS/PC* which offers residual analysis for a wide variety of applications. The following procedures are included: descriptive statistics, correlation matrices and significance levels, covariance matrices, cross-product deviations, regression statistics and coefficients, standard error of estimate, and 95% confidence interval, among many others.

Example of Multiple Regression:
An excellent example and description of how art therapists used the multiple regression analysis of the linear probability model is cited in "The Diagnostic Drawing Series: A Systematic Approach to Art Therapy Evaluation and Research" (Cohen, Hammer, and Singer, 1988).

Graphs and Plots

A full array of display facilities for every purpose is possible with the *SPSS/PC*, eliminating the need to employ a graphic artist or programmer to produce charts or graphs of research results. Quality graphs and charts can be generated directly from data for submitting to professional journals. Pie charts, bar charts, maps, contour plots, line graphs, and scatter plots are among the many possible ways to graphically illustrate data and results. The *SPSS-X* has a color graphics option as well.

Graphs and Plots

SPSS® has simplified research procedures for the novice. Withthis software package it is possible for a non-statistician tocreate sophisticated research reports. This package organizes,analyzes, and presents data in an efficient and professional manner.

For further information, contact SPSS, Inc., 444 N. Michigan Ave., Chicago IL 60611; (312) 329-2400.

COMPUTERIZED DATABASES AND COMPUTERIZED LITERATURE SEARCHES

Frances E. Anderson, Ed.D., A.T.R., H.L.M.

Prior to 1967, anyone conducting research for a master's thesis or doctoral dissertation or engaged in writing a grant had to rely on hand searches of the literature to determine what research on a particular topic (or closely related to that topic) had already been done. I am one of those dinosaurs who had to do just that during my graduate study. The review of related literature for my doctoral study was the section that took the longest time (six months) and this was facilitated because I had access to a major library collection. Even so, waiting for interlibrary loans of those pesky few citations that "seemed" to be relevant (but when given the opportunity for a hands-on perusal often proved irrelevant) also slowed down the whole research process.

Computerized databases have changed all of this. Most libraries now have access to the major computerized databases. Also, most libraries have these databases on compact discs which enable users to do their own literature searches. The computerized databases that may be of greatest relevance to art therapy research are *Educational Resources Information Center (ERIC)*, *Psychological Abstracts Information Service (PsychINFO)*, and *Medline*. *Medline* covers articles from 3,200 journals and includes all references from the *Index Medicus* which covers all psychiatry and some psychology journals. *Medline* coverage is from 1983 to the present and is updated monthly (Perspectives, 1989).

PsychINFO, initiated in 1967, is a department of the American Psychological Association in Washington, DC. *PsychINFO* covers over 330,000 citations. Currently, a part of this database is on compact disc (from 1974 to the present) called *PsychLIT* and researchers can do their own literature search "in house." *PsychINFO* is updated monthly. *PsychLIT* contains psychology abstracts of articles from 1400 journals, 1000 of which are in English. One of the newest developments in databases in psychology is *Psybooks*. *Psybooks* includes abstracts of 1300 books that are published annually in psychology. Currently, it is in the form of a five-volume set of hard cover books indexed by subject. Future plans are to have this database put on compact disc (Anderson, Ash, & Gambach, 1982; Perspectives, 1989).

There are also two major parts to the *ERIC* database: *Current Index of Journals in Education (CIJE)* and *Research in Education (RIE)*. *ERIC* goes back to 1969 and *RIE* to 1966. As of June 1989, *CIJE* covered about 780 periodicals in education and related fields, representing 403,353 articles. As of June 1989, *RIE* contained 315,503 research reports, conference presentations, and final grant reports (Anderson, Ash, & Gambach, 1982; Perspectives, 1989).

In 1981, these two major computerized databases (*ERIC* and *RIE*) were used to assist in conducting a comprehensive review of the published research literature in all the arts for the handicapped (Anderson, Ash & Gambach, 1982). This project was sponsored by the National Committee, Arts for the Handicapped (since renamed Very Special Arts) in Washington, DC. The project had an extremely short time frame in which to work (only three months) and were it not for the *ERIC* and *RIE* computerized databases, it could not have been completed in the time allotted. These two databases enabled us to search over 400,000 articles, research reports, technical documents, and books. Because the databases included brief (100-word) abstracts of the articles and reports, it enabled the project staff to quickly determine which research study fit the criteria for inclusion and warranted the effort to locate, read and condense into one- to three-page abstracts for the project publication. In this way, 53 studies were identified that fit our criteria ("empirical research [Eisner, 1972] that employed appropriate educational and psychological research methodology that resulted in 'hard data'") (Anderson, Ash, & Gambach, 1982).

The Very Special Arts literature project used a third computer database, the *Comprehensive Dissertation Index (CDI)*. The *CDI* is part of a larger database called *Dissertation Abstracts Online (DAO)*. Also included in the *DAO* are contents of the publications of *American Doctoral Dissertations, Dissertation Abstracts International* and *Masters Abstracts International*. As of July 1989, there were one million entries in the *CAO*. *DAO* contains subject, title, and author guide to most American dissertations completed at accredited institutions since 1861. About 3500 entries are made monthly. When students opt to have their dissertations included in *Dissertation Abstracts*, these abstracts are included in the *DAO* system. However, not all students exercise this option, so there are some citations in the *DAO* with no accompanying abstract. Within the last several years, the *American Dissertation Index (ADI)*, another dissertation database, was added. The *ADI* only includes bibliographic citations and no abstracts.

As noted above, computerized databases have become more accessible through their becoming available on compact discs. The *PsychLIT* compact disc database covers material from 1974 to the present and the *ERIC* compact disc database covers material from 1966 to the present. It should be noted that these compact disc data files are not as complete as the original files that are part of the mainframe dialog system.

Another compact disc database that may contain information of interest to art therapists is *The Social Sciences Index* which covers 300 periodicals including social work, sociology, and urban studies.

Computerized databases are of great assistance not only to scholarly research, but also to grant writing. In submitting a grant for scholarly research, it is essential to include a current and complete overview of research that pertains to the topic of the proposed grant. In many instances the related research part of a grant is a specific category that grant reviewers rate in terms of its comprehensiveness and current coverage of research and related studies that have been accomplished to date (Anderson, 1991; Anderson and Arrington, 1986).

In Appendix V are the initial pages of four computerized literature searches. The searches are limited by the key search words entered into the computer and the inclusive dates of the items in the specific databases. In using a computer to assist with literature search, hand searches of the most current journal issues must always be entered in the database. Hand searches also permit serendipitous discoveries of information, which were always an added bonus when one had to do a "hands on" search of library shelves and bound (and unbound) periodicals. Some of the excitement of this "treasure hunt" has been lost in the emergence of the computerized literature search, but perhaps this has been more than offset by the timesaving and convenience of computerization of data.

Many electronic searches are available in most college and library settings. Four of these are *ERIC, Dissertation Abstracts, PsychINFO*, and *University Microfilms International*. Information that they provide includes complete bibliographical reference and descriptions or abstracts of content. The best way to learn to use these systems is to visit your librarian, ask questions shamelessly, and practice on available computers.

References

Anderson, F.E.; 1992. *Art for all the children: Approaches to art therapy for children with disabilities* (2nd ed.). Springfield, IL: Charles C Thomas.

Anderson, F.E. (1990). *Courage! Together we heal: Mural messages from incest survivors to incest survivors* (A report on a pilot project on the development and implementation of an art therapy short-term ceramics group for incest survivors). Normal, IL: Illinois State University Press.

Anderson, F.E. (1985). Electronic media, videodisc technology, and the visual arts. *Studies in Art Education*, 26(4) 221-231.

Anderson, F.E., & Arrington, D. (1986). Grants: Demystifying the mystique and creating job connections. *Art Therapy: The Journal of the American Art Therapy Association*, 3(1), 34-37.

Anderson, F.E., Ash, L., & Gambach, J. (1982). *A review of the published research literature on arts and the handicapped*, 1971-1981. Washington, DC: National Committee, Arts for the Handicapped.

Canter, D.S. (1987). Art therapy and computers. In H. Wadeson, J. Durkin, & D. Perach (Eds.). *Advances in art therapy*. New York, NY: John Wiley.

Cohen, B., Hammer, J., & Singer, S. (1988). The diagnostic drawing series: a systematic approach to art therapy evaluation and research. *The Arts in Psychotherapy, 15*, 11-21.

PC Magazine (1989). Scientific graphing and presentation graphics software: Summary of features, 8(5), 268-269.

Perspectives (1989). Compact disc databases. Normal, IL: Illinois State University. 6,1-4.

Shoemaker, R.J. (1983). *The rainbow booklet: A look at the psychology, physiology, and physics of color*. Wisconsin: Renewing Visions Press.

White, D. (Ed.). (1983). Mini-issue on computers and art. *Art Education, 36*(4).

Chapter 17

GRANTS: A STRUCTURE FOR RESEARCH

Doris Arrington, EdD, A.T.R.
Frances Anderson, EdD, A.T.R., H.L.M.

This section on grants is included in the *Guide* because art therapists have found that grants can provide funding for research projects. Funding sources often require a research component as well.[1]

The success of grant writing is presenting the right idea to the right source at the right time. Following are key points in grant writing:

1. Tailor your grant to fit the specific agency.

2. Find out the person in charge and direct your grant to that person.

3. Do your homework. Research the funding source. What are the funding priorities of the agency? What are the corporate pet projects?

4. Give out only the "abstract" (but have the rest of the grant in your pocket, just in case).

5. Use the corporate language so the funding source understands your proposal.

6. Use the corporation forms and format.

---

[1] This excerpt is from Anderson, F.E., & Arrington, D.B. (1986). Grants - demystifying the mystique and creating job connections. *Art Therapy, 3*(1), 34-38. It is reprinted here in an abridged form with the permission of the authors and the publisher.

7. If you are unsure, team up with someone who knows the proper jargon.

8. Review grants written for the same type of corporation or agency.

9. Forego the ego trip and team up with a Project Director, (a person who gets grants and will lend his/her name to your grant).

10. If you fail, try again.
In writing the proposal, you should remember two key points:

"K.I.S.S.! = Keep it short and simple!"
"If you cannot scan it, can it."

Outline for Grant Proposals

Most grants should be no longer than 10 pages. No one wants to wade through pages and pages of text. All grant proposals include the following general categories. Some may be called by another title.

1. INTRODUCTION/ABSTRACT
Limit this to one page and use LARGE type. It will be helpful to begin with the following statement as an INTRODUCTION.
(You fill in the blanks!)

(You)_____(Your hospital or institution) seek $ _____ from _____Corporation for_____ (Specify what: a program, an evaluation, etc.): for the time period _____to_____. Matching funds will come from _____ (Examples: Board contributions, NCAH, California Arts Council). This project follows _____number of years of successful programs, etc.

2. PROBLEM STATEMENT
This is sometimes called the "Rationale" or "Needs Assessment." You are solving some societal problem. It is even better if you have several. You may want to establish the problem by citing research that relates to the issue. Or you may want to clearly document a specific need. If you intend to establish a specific NEED, then you may have to conduct a survey or poll (i.e., a needs assessment) of agencies or clientele.

3. GOALS/OBJECTIVES

It will be important to state goals in quantifiable terms. It will be essential to use objectives that are easy to measure.

4. CAPABILITY STATEMENT

Sometimes this section is combined with the "Problem Statement" described earlier. This statement is essentially why you should get money. Show how your project will be cost effective. It also will be important to indicate how long you have been doing this sort of activity. Evidence, such as demand for the program and your services, and other testimonials would be appropriate here. Also, if you are submitting a proposal for your institution, corporations are extremely concerned about your institution's management structure. Is it a good structure, i.e., one which can carry out the programs for which you are requesting funds?

5. DETAILED PROGRAM DESCRIPTION

Sometimes this section is called "Methods." In this section you would include: Plan of Action, Treatment Plans, and Time Line for accomplishing the project. It would be very important to briefly describe week by week what you intend to do.

6. EVALUATION

Justification for your project is essential because you have to be accountable for the effectiveness of your project to laypersons who are not convinced that art therapy has value. It will be important to provide some pre/post measures.

You also should include how you will disseminate information about your research. You might remember that the funding agency wants to see some tangible outcome of its funding of your research. You want to provide good public relations for art therapy, your specific research and the funding agency or corporation.

7. FUTURE FUNDING

It also will be important to include plans for future funding of this kind of research. Future funding might be via clientele fees, grants from other agencies, or corporation grants.

8. BUDGET

Give a detailed accounting of all items. Be sure that you check on actual costs of items and briefly explain why you have included the items in your budget. It will also be important to list the value of "in-kind" contributions (any support other than actual dollars such as provision of space, use of office equipment, secretarial help) after the rest of the budget. Do not hesitate to include ALL possible in-kind contributions. This accounting makes your project look better, that is, the agency knows that you are really giving them something.

9. FINANCIAL STATEMENTS

This section is important only if you represent a nonprofit institution asking for a grant. If you are submitting your proposal through some agency, you should include the agency's Internal Revenue Service tax exempt statement. It will be important to establish the "financial soundness" of the agency through which you are submitting your grant proposal. No agency or corporation will give monies to an institution that is not financially sound.

10. REFERENCES

You should include FULL bibliographic citations for all studies and/or experts cited in each and every part of your proposal narrative. You should find out what style manual (i.e., Turabian, American Psychological Association Manual, etc.) is preferred by the funding agency and use that format.

11. LETTER OF APPROVAL FROM AGENCY

This is necessary only if you are submitting your grant via an agency. Your grant proposal should then include a letter from the agency saying they approve of your proposed project.

12. PROMOTIONAL MATERIALS

Again, this would be important if you are submitting your grant through an agency.

13. LETTERS OF SUPPORT

Get testimonials from "neutral", highly visible persons. It will be very important to find out what impresses the agency/corporation to which you are submitting the proposal. If this is a Federal agency, try to get congress-persons to send letters. If the project is an individual submission, get letters from state arts councils, the American Art Therapy Association, or other related professional organizations such as the American Association of Mental Deficiency, Easter Seals, or the local chapter of the Muscular Dystrophy Association.

Other Helpful Hints

In writing a grant proposal, should you ask for more funding than you think you can get? Do not hesitate to be as realistic and honest as you can in your proposal. It is usually a wise idea to plan a program that will cost a little more than you think the agency might fund. Often projects are approved, but for 10 to 20 percent less monies than are requested. If you have to cut your budget, be sure you also eliminate a part of your proposed research. Generally, most Federal agencies cut budgets as a usual practice.

If you are a little unsure in writing a grant, team up with someone who may know the jargon of the corporation or agency and work with that person. It may also be helpful to get a highly visible expert or professional who is already known in the field to serve as the Project Director, purely as an honorary title with no actual time spent on the project.

Most colleges and universities have a grants office with lists and books of corporations, foundations, and agencies that give out funds. These books are divided by geographic location and by topics/areas in which they award funds. A rule of thumb is that the closer you or your agency is to the funding source geographically, the easier it is to get your project funded. Sometimes it is easier to go for a smaller grant that is funded by a local group or business than to go for a huge project that would be funded by a Federal agency.

It also is very helpful to peruse a funded grant or two written for the same type of corporation or agency for which you are planning a proposal. It is always easier to follow someone else's successful model.

If you fail, try, try again. The competition for grant funds is tough and one out of 10 or 20 gets funded. Also, know that, at least for Federal grants, the funding agency will send you the reviewers' comments on your proposal so you can "clean up your act."

Resources

The following resources are listed in priority order, not in alphabetical order:

1. Someone with grant writing experience.
2. T. W. Tenbrunsel, 1982. *The fund raising resource manual.* Englewood Cliffs, NJ: Prentice-Hall.
3. J. Flanagan, 1982. *The grass roots fundraising book: How to raise money in your community.* Chicago, IL: Contemporary Books.

Excellent references that may be found in any library are:

1. *The Foundation Directory* (specializing in foundations).
2. *The Catalogue of Federal Domestic Assistance* (listings of governmental funding programs).
3. *The Annual Register of Grant Support* (a comprehensive register).

For information on periodical literature, newspapers, library materials, institutional grants offices, and subscription information services, an excellent source is:

V.P. White, 1975. *Grants, how to find out about them and what to do next.* New York, NY: Plenum Press.

Note: The authors have compiled a Grants Manual to assist professionals in their grant writing. For more information about this booklet, contact F.E. Anderson, Ed.D., A.T.R., H.L.M., Art Department, Illinois State University, Normal, IL 61761 or Doris Arrington, Ed.D., A.T.R, Art Therapy Program, College of Notre Dame, Belmont, CA 94010.

Chapter 18

ANNOTATED BIBLIOGRAPHY

Nancy Knapp, PhD, A.T.R.

The following annotated bibliography presents some of the standard resources which have been useful guides for a variety of research projects and classes. References are presented in categories sequenced roughly as they might be used in research: idea generation, literature searches, research methodology, ethics of research, statistical presentation, writing style, and publication. Although there is some overlap in purpose and content in this assortment, they are all generally accepted and readily available. Complete bibliographic information, a brief, broad description, and in most cases, specific utility for art therapists is presented.

For Planning and Searching the Literature

The following are useful sources for preliminary searches of pertinent literature which may generate, solidify or eliminate nascent research projects. They also provide continuously updated information throughout the research process, since a researcher is responsible for being aware of everything which is current in his or her area of interest; this may be no small feat, for example, 150 articles a month are being published related to Alzheimer's Type Dementia alone.

ABSTRACTS

Publications of abstracts of all published research are available in most libraries. They provide a quick reference in a standardized format with many cross references which are likely to coincide with topics for art therapy researchers.

• Gantt, Linda, and Schmal, Marilyn, 1974. *Art Therapy: A Bibliography*. Rockville, MD: National Institute of Mental Health.

Description

The first publication of an annotated bibliography of literature of art therapy from 1940 through June, 1973. It contains 1,175 abstracts.

Potential Use for Art Therapists

This publication continues to be a precedent and a model as well as a resource for historical information in the field of art therapy.

• Moore, Rosanna W., 1981. *Art Therapy in Mental Health*. National Clearinghouse for Mental Health Information, Literature Survey Series, No.3. Rockville, MD: U.S. Department of Health and Human Services.

Description

The third in a series of references to the literature on subjects of interest to users of the National Clearinghouse for Mental Health Information. This comprehensive collection includes 392 abstracts and an author and subject index for art therapy literature from June, 1974, through 1980.

Potential Use for Art Therapists

This should be a standard source for any overview or literature search in the field of art therapy.

• *Psychological Abstracts* (ongoing publication). Executive Editor, Dennis Auld. Arlington, VA: American Psychological Association, Inc.

Description

A collection of non-evaluative abstracts of world-wide literature in psychology and related topics. Published monthly with semi-annual volume indexes and 3-year cumulative index.

Potential Use for Art Therapists

Information in the abstract will often refer to the use of art in a study even though it may not have been evident from the title itself.

Additional abstracts with similar format and utility include the following self-explanatory topics which may interface with art therapy: *Child Development Abstract and Bibliography, Cumulated Index Medicus, Education Index, Exceptional Child Education Abstracts, Social Sciences*

Index, Sociological Abstracts, and *Women Studies Abstracts.* There is also a Bibliographic citation list generated by *MEDLARS II* and the National Library of Medicine's *National Interactive Retrieval Service.*

GUIDES FOR PUBLISHED TESTS AND ASSESSMENT TOOLS

In the relatively uncharted ground of art therapy, correlational studies are useful. The following books have almost infinite amounts of information to assist the search for appropriate tools. In a short time a researcher can extract different measures to fit studies which compare, contrast, or correlate with art therapy research interests.

• The *10th Mental Measurements Yearbook,* Jane Close Conoley and Jack J. Kramer, Eds., 1989 (published frequently since 1933). Lincoln, NE: The Buros Institute of Mental Measurements.

Description
Organized to be used like an encyclopedia, this reference provides descriptive information, critiques, references, reviews, synopses, and commentary on all commercially published, English language tests and measures used in education, psychology and personality evaluation.

Potential Use for Art Therapists
This is a reliable and convenient way for art therapists to find tools which are appropriate for specific measures as part of a design incorporating the use of art in research

• *Tests in Print III: An Index to Tests, Test Reviews, and the Literature of Specific Tests,* James V. Mitchell, Ed., 1983. Lincoln, NE: The Buros Institute of Mental Measures.

Description
A comprehensive directory, bibliography, title index, indexed directory for test authors and publishers, classified by test subjects and populations.

Potential Use for Art Therapists
This is particularly useful for beginning research designs for people who have not been trained in testing but wish to incorporate standardized measurements along with an art experience.

ELECTRONIC SEARCH TOOLS

See Chapter 16 for additional information on the dazzling variety of computerized programs and other electronic wizards now available for art therapists and other researchers. Initially, older researchers may long for the seemingly simpler task of running our fingers down the tattered columns of *Psychological Abstracts*; however, the current mother lode of information systems is worth mining.

All academic libraries have access to major systems and generally newly trained, enthusiastic staff eager to guide a novice in the appropriate use of their particular network. If a researcher is not friendly with computers, s/he should make friends with someone who is. Following are some of the reference books which describe such computer systems and are commonly available.

The growth of the information industry seems overwhelming, yielding staggering amounts of material to be sifted. The American Society for Information Services (ASIS) is one resource to make information more accessible. Additionally, the APA has numerous tools, such as the Psychological Abstracts Information Services, available via Psych INFO. A variety of related services such as Psych INFO Databases are also available on machine-readable tapes or disks.

• *Bibliodata Fulltext Sources Online: for Periodicals, Newspapers, Newsletters and Newswires.* Summer 1989. Ruth M. Orenstein, Ed. Needham Heights, MA: Bibliodata.

Description
This publication covers topics including science, technology, medicine, law, finance, business, industry, and the popular press. They provide both subject index and cross references; the vendor list includes gateways for direct access. A periodical listing and glossary are helpful. A potential disadvantage of this resource is that it may be expensive since it supplies the full text.

• *Computer Readable Databases: A Directory and Data Sourcebook*, 7th ed., 1990. Kathleen Young Marcaccio, Ed. Detroit, MI: Gale Research, Inc.

Description
Fortunately, this general directory of databases provides simple directions on how to use the book to access the database industry. The user is provided statistical facts and trends, 4,200 databases and 4,042

entries. An indication of the continuous expansion for some topical listings is that sub-divisions are required in order to manage sheer quantity of material; there are several which cover AIDS, including separate entries for AIDS policy and AIDS law.

• *Dialog Database Catalogue*, 1990. Published by Dialog Information Service, Knight Ridder Company.

Description

This directory describes services and ways to connect with resources. The databases are provided by subject category which are described. Data types and providers and price lists are included and updated frequently.

• *Encyclopedia of Information Systems and Services*, 10th ed. Two volumes: I. Descriptive Listings; II. Indexes. Amy Lucas, Ed. Detroit, MI: Gale Research, Inc.

Description

This comprehensive and international guide describes more than 4,400 organizations, systems services involved in production and distribution of information in electronic form. It may include more than you ever wanted to know about the subject but both its specific information and its general descriptive statements of programs, their missions, purposes and functions can be very helpful.

• *The North American Online Directory*, 2nd ed. Scott D. MacFarland et al, Eds. 1987. New York, NY: R. R. Bowker Co.

Description

The directory includes Online information products and services, databases, database producers, vendors, telecommunication networks, library networks and consortia, information collection and analysis centers, information brokers, consultants, associations, online user groups, and a conference, course, and calendar section. (Obviously, the list is not current because of the 1987 publication). This was intended as a quick and concise reference tool describing products and services in US and Canada. They attempt to fill a gap in the turnover and change in the information industry including names and numbers of those in production, distribution, and support services.

Reminder:

Even as art therapists benefit from the seductive accessibility of these resources, we need to retain and renew our familiarity with earlier publications in our own literature which will not be harvested in an electronic search. For example, a literature review of art therapy with incest victims should include Naumburg's case "Images and Hallucinations of an Alcoholic Patient" (*Dynamically Oriented Art Therapy: Its Principles and Practice*, 1966. New York, NY: Grune and Stratton). Similarly, art therapy with drug abusers might refer to Betensky's histories of "Lee" and "Jack" (*Self-Discovery Through Self-Expression*, 1973. Springfield, IL: Charles C Thomas).

Subject indexes in our standard publications, art therapy journals, and AATA Proceedings from Annual Conferences still provide us with entry to useful information. Even when they seem uneven in quality compared to products of current methods and knowledge, both our heritage and our future are weaker if we neglect our own classic references.

Research Methods

The following selection provides standard books used in research classes as well as for personal guidance when formulating or conducting research. They include both basic and sophisticated information which may be either preventive or curative when a researcher is faced with some of the more subtle dilemmas in research.

GENERAL RESEARCH METHODS

- Barber,Theodore X., 1985. *Pitfalls in Human Research, Ten Pivotal Points*. New York, NY: Pergamon Press, Inc.

Description
Based upon the principle that, as a product of fallible individuals, research has as many pitfalls as other human endeavors. This book provides both specific do's and don'ts and also has an extensive reference section.

Potential Use for Art Therapists
A good dose of Barber might well be the best preventive medicine that an art therapist could take in the germinal stage of research. All ten points are potentially pertinent for research including art.

• Campbell, Donald T., and Stanley, Julian C., 1966.
Experimental and Quasi-experimental Designs for Research. Chicago, IL:
Houghton Mifflin.

Description
Presents overview of validity of different experimental design.

Potential Use for Art Therapists
Models suggested are particularly good for novice researchers using
art because they provide valid research constructs; legitimate but with
paradigms which may differ from the standard laboratory experiment.

• Christenson, Larry B. 1988. *Experimental Methodology*, 4th ed. Boston,
MA: Allyn and Bacon, Inc.

Description
A comprehensive, well received textbook which provides everything
a beginning researcher should know from paradigms through debriefing
interviews to the research report.

Potential Use for Art Therapists
The bulk of this book is pertinent for basic training for art therapists.
Sections which are probably not pertinent (eg.,the APA Guide to Care of
Laboratory Animals) are easily ignored.

• Cook, Thomas D., and Campbell, Donald T., 1979.
Quasi-Experimentation: Design and Analysis Issues for Field Settings.
Chicago, IL: Rand-McNally College Publishing Company.

Description

Comprehensive survey of quasi-experimental designs with the emphasis on field settings.

Potential Use for Art Therapists

Variety of valid designs which are appropriate in art therapy settings, with art therapy techniques.

• Campbell, William, 1978. *Form and Style: Theses, Reports, Term Papers*, 5th ed. Boston, MA: Houghton Mifflin.

Description

Designed as a guide for academic writing.

Potential Use for Art Therapists

Useful because of orientation toward research which can be done in classrooms and similar settings where art therapists might be particularly active.

• Isaac, Stephen, and Michael, William B., 1977. *Handbook in Research and Evaluation*. San Diego, CA: EDITS Publishers

Description

A small handbook especially for the design and evaluation of studies in education and behavioral science. Its particular aim is for students and occasional researchers who desire a summary of alternatives, an exhibit of different models and an overview of strengths and weaknesses of different types of research.

Potential Use for Art Therapists

Both the goal of this book and its format fit the needs of art therapists, especially for initial research.

• Kerlinger, Fred N., 1986. *Foundations of Behavioral Research*, 3rd ed. New York, NY: Holt, Rinehart and Winston.

Description

651 pages of basic information provide a crash course on every phase of the fine art of research from design to analysis. The book includes appendix and references to other resources.

Potential Use for Art Therapists

Useful and inclusive source for filling in the gaps between most art therapy education and research models. Kerlinger's orientation is appropriate for the art therapy admixture; he begins his preface with "Some ACTIVITIES command more interest, devotion, and enthusiasm than do others. So it seems to be with science and with art." (p. vii)

• Massaro, Dominic W., 1989. *Experimental Psychology: An Information Processing Approach*. New York, NY: Harcourt Brace, Janovich.

Description
Inclusive guide to experiments with cognitive research. Numerous additional references are provided.

Potential Use for Art Therapists
Section on mental processing and perception as they relate to art are potentially useful. His descriptions of methods of psychological inquiry are readily understood and adapted to use with art.

ETHICS OF RESEARCH

Enlightenment increases both awareness and expectations, but rules are needed to enumerate the demands that demonstrate that enlightenment. The following references provide both philosophical and practical guidelines for ethics in the context of research.

• American Psychological Association, 1982. *Ethical Principles in the Conduct of Research With Human Participants*. Washington, DC: American Psychological Association.

Description
A manual based upon APA ethical principle 9, research with human participants it provides both an inclusive philosophical overview of and an explicit guide to the use and understanding of ethical principles in all phases of the conduct of research.

Potential Use for Art Therapists
Both the spirit and the letter of this book are consistent with AATA. This is perhaps the most universally accepted guide which is readily applicable or adaptable to research which includes human subjects doing art.

- Ansell, C., 1987. *Ethical Practices Workbook*. CA: A.A.T.B.S. Publ.

Description
Based upon 1981 APA "Ethical Principles of Psychologists" to provide guidelines for ethical decision making. This is pertinent for research design and preventive training.

Potential Use for Art Therapists
This supplement may be appropriate for clarification of judgment when art therapists design research with problematic or ambiguous features involving human participants.

- Pence, G., 1990. *Classic Cases in Medical Ethics*. New York, NY: McGraw-Hill Publishing Co.

Description
Subtitled "Accounts of the Cases That Have Shaped Medical Ethics, with Philosophical, Legal, and Historical Backgrounds", this book includes all of that and more. It is well organized and accessible reading.

Potential Use for Art Therapists
This contains particularly helpful information for art therapists who wish to do research in medical or rehabilitation settings or with subjects for whom health issues are pertinent.

WRITING FORM AND STYLE

The following books are reliable and consistent helpmates in spite of changes in preferred style and form. They are in virtually every library but you will thank yourself for having a personal copy to solve the inevitable midnight quandaries.

- *A Manual of Style*, 13th ed. 1982. Chicago, IL: University of Chicago Press.

Description
Good cornerstone reference for writing.

Potential Use for Art Therapists

Particularly useful for details which need judgment calls because research data or format is somewhat eccentric, or different from standard research without art.

- American Psychological Association, 1983. *Publication Manual of the American Psychological Association*, 3rd ed. Washington, DC: Author.

Description

This is the basic manual for publication in psychological journals provides a standardized guideline for mechanics as required by most publications as well as academic institutions.

Potential Use for Art Therapists

From this accessible reference it is especially good for tables, graphs, etc., where the creativity of the researcher might lend itself to idiosyncratic format rather than more helpful standardized presentation.

- Tallent, Norman, 1983. *Psychological Report Writing*, 2nd ed. Englewood Cliffs, NJ: Prentice Hall.

Description

This book is an inclusive and authoritative reference for a variety of purposes. It includes valuable guidelines for organization and structure but also more subtle issues such as orientation and flavor when presenting conclusion. Recommended readings for reference and assessment are also presented.

Potential Use for Art Therapists

This author provides a useful bridge for art therapists who have not a surplus of experience in rigorous clinical training but aspire to be clinically proficient.

- Turabian, K., 1973. *A Manual for Writers of Term Papers, Theses, and Dissertations*, 4th ed. Chicago, IL: University of Chicago Press.

Description

Useful, all-purpose handbook, based on *A Manual of Style*.

Potential Use for Art Therapists

As with other standard and reliable resources, this manual may be particularly helpful in master's thesis work.

• Webb, Eugene J., et al. 1981. *Nonreactive Measures in the Social Sciences*, 2nd ed. Boston, MA: Houghton Mifflin Company.

Description
Previously published as *Unobtrusive Measures: Nonreactive Research in the Social Sciences*.

Potential Use for Art Therapists
The inherent nature of this work and the paradigms which are presented lend themselves to a variety of studies which could evaluate art experiences.

MISCELLANEOUS RESOURCES

The following references do not fit into a congruent category but they provide particular information which may be helpful in designing a sound research project. The purpose of the books vary greatly but they have all proved useful for art therapists.

• Henry, William E., 1973. *The Analysis of Fantasy*. Huntington, NY: Robert E. Krieger Publishing Company.

Description
This book is designed to help interpret data from the Thematic Apperception Technique (TAT). The emphasis is on understanding variations in the presentation of basic data and the analysis of it in relationship to characteristics of the stimuli.

Potential Use for Art Therapists
Henry's schema to put large amounts of fascinating but amorphous material into a meaningful interpretative format can be as useful in art products as it is in TAT responses.

• Schmid, C., 1983. *Statistical Graphics: Design Principles and Practice*. New York, NY: Wiley.

Description
Illustrations of good graphic presentations.

Potential Use for Art Therapists
Both useful and encouraging in art therapy writing where graphics should be great in number and high in impact.

Guidelines for Publication

Although different publication needs dictate different specifications, the following resources are among those which provide standard information which is easily accessed and usually pertinent for art therapy use.

• Day, Robert A., 1979. *How to Write and Publish A Scientific Paper*, 2nd ed. Philadelphia, PA: ISI Press.

Description
One of many manuals with similar missions, but as one of the series from the Institute for Scientific Information designed to improve the communication skills of professionals and students, it is particularly worthy of attention.

Potential Use for Art Therapists
Art therapists can easily benefit from this benign glimpse at a potentially intimidating topic.

ART THERAPY JOURNALS

The following art therapy journals provide guidelines for prospective publications in each volume. See the title pages for specific instructions. These journals all welcome original art therapy manuscripts. Because some of the requirements for reporting and publishing art therapy research are singular, representatives of these art therapy journals can provide specific help which may vary from requirements in more general publications.

• *The American Journal of Art Therapy*, Vermont College of Norwich University, Montpelier, VT 05602.

• *The Arts in Psychotherapy*, Pergamon Press, Maxwell House, Fairview Park, Elmsford, NY 10523.

• *Art Therapy: Journal of the American Art Therapy Associaion*. The American Art Therapy Association, 1202 Allanson Road, Mundelein, IL 60060.

RELATED JOURNALS

The following suggestions for potential publications for art therapists have been submitted by Phoebe Dufrene:

• *Art Education*, 1990. National Art Education Association: 1916 Association Drive, Reston, VA 22091.

Description
"Manuscripts are welcome at all times and on any aspect of art education. Please send three double-spaced copies, prepared in accordance with the *Publication Manual* of the American Psychological Association (1983) to the Editor, Dr. Jerome J. Hausman, 1501 Hinman Ave., Apt. 7A, Evanston, IL 60201.

To facilitate the process of anonymous review, the author's name, title, affiliation, mailing address and phone number should be on a separate sheet. Retain a copy of anything submitted. An Author's Guidesheet giving further information may be obtained by sending a stamped self-addressed envelope to the Editor at the above address. Authors are encouraged to submit black and white photographs with their manuscripts."

• *Journal of Multicultural & Crosscultural Research in Art Education.*

Description
"...will consider for publication articles on all aspects of multi-cultural and cross-cultural research in art education." Manuscripts should be addressed to:

Dr. Rogena M. Degge, Editor
Dept. of Art Education
School of Architecture and Allied Arts
University of Oregon
Eugene, OR 97403

• *School Arts*, 1990. Davis Publications: SchoolArts, Portland Street, Worcester, MA 01608.

Description
"Manuscripts will be handled with care but the Magazine assumes no responsibility for them. The editors reserve the right to edit and adapt materials for use in SchoolArts. Unsolicited manuscripts must be

accompanied by a self-addressed, stamped envelope. Microfilm and Microfiche copies available from University Microfilm, Ann Arbor, MI 48106."

- *Studies in Art Education.*

Description

"*Studies in Art Education* invites manuscripts for a professional art education audience that report empirical, historical, and philosophical research with implications for art education, or that explore theoretical and practical growth, curriculum and learning program and other educational dimensions of visual art. *Studies* welcomes manuscripts that show the applicability to art education of methods and concepts in the literature of related fields such as anthropology, education, philosophy and psychology. *Studies* encourages interdisciplinary authorship dealing with research, theoretical, methodological, and political problems shared by the broader educational field."

Send manuscripts (in APA style) to:

National Art Education Association
1916 Association Drive
Reston, VA 22091-1590
(703)860-8000

These should be typed doublespaced on 8-1/2" x 11" or word processed on MacIntosh MicroSoftWord (Versions 3.0, 3.1, 3.2, or 4.0) MacWrite (4.5) or Microsoft Works (1.1) and submitted with a 3.5 diskette. Reference style is APA or Chicago Manual. Original manuscript and three Xerox copies. Black and white glossy photos or camera-ready charts made with India ink on white paper accepted.

EXCERPTS FROM THE AATA CODE OF ETHICS

The following excerpts from the Ethical Code of the American Art Therapy Association are particularly applicable for research with human subjects:

Confidentiality

Art therapists have a primary responsibility to respect client confidentiality and safeguard verbal and visual information about an individual or family that has been obtained in the course of their practice, investigation or teaching.

A. Information shall be revealed only to professionals concerned with the case. Written and oral reports only disclose data relevant to the purpose of the inquiry. Every effort is made to avoid undue invasion of privacy.

B. Art therapists are responsible for informing their clients of the limits of confidentiality.

C. Art therapists obtain written permission from clients involved before any data, visual or verbal, is divulged. All identifying information about the individual is adequately disguised.

D. Art therapists reveal information without the consent of their clients when there is clear and immediate danger to any individual or to society, or as mandated by law. Such information is revealed only to the appropriate professional workers, public authorities or others designated by law.

E. Art therapists make provisions for maintaining confidentiality in storage and disposal of records and art expression.

Welfare of the Art Therapy Client

Art therapists respect the integrity, protect the welfare of the person, family and/or group with whom they work, and understand that the art expression is the privilege of the client.

A. Art therapists terminate or transfer clients when it is reasonably clear that the client is not benefiting from a therapeutic relationship.
B. Art therapists make financial arrangements that are clearly understood by their clients and that safeguard the best interests of the client and the profession.
C. Art therapists employed by another person or agency suggest clientele of the employer or agency leave to come to their private practice when there is mutual agreement between the art therapist and the employer or agency. Such a change is made only in the client's best interest.

Public Use and Reproduction of Client Art

Art therapists are responsible to their clients for any public use and reproduction of client art expressions.

A. The identity of the client is protected by withholding the name, address, date of hospitalization or treatment, and other specific information which may disclose the person's identity to the public. Any part of the art expression which may reveal client identity is disguised.
B. Art therapists display client art expressions with the written consent of the client or his/her legal representative. Consent is obtained with the recognition of the client's freedom of choice and appraisal of conditions that may limit freedom of choice.
C. Art therapists display client art expressions in a manner upholding the dignity of both client and the profession.
D. Art therapists have the responsibility to interpret client art expressions fairly and accurately in a manner that minimizes the possibility of misleading the public and other professionals.

APA PRINCIPLE 9

Principle 9 from the existing "Ethical Principles of Psychologists" is reproduced here with permission from the American Psychological Association. It is consistent with the ethical guidelines of AATA and is potentially useful for art therapists aspiring to do research with human subjects.

APA Principle 9: Research with Human Participants

The decision to undertake research rests upon a considered judgment by the individual psychologist about how best to contribute to psychological science and human welfare. Having made the decision to conduct research, the psychologist considers alternative directions in which research energies and resources might be invested. On the basis of this consideration, the psychologist carries out the investigation with respect and concern for the dignity and welfare of the people who participate and with cognizance of federal and state regulations and professional standards governing the conduct of research with human participants.

a. In planning a study, the investigator has the responsibility to make a careful evaluation of its ethical acceptability. To the extent that the weighing of scientific and human values suggests a compromise of any principle, the investigator incurs a correspondingly serious obligation to seek ethical advice and to observe stringent safeguards to protect the rights of human participants.

b. Considering whether a participant in a planned study will be a "subject at risk" or a "subject at minimal risk", according to recognized standards, is of primary ethical concern to the investigator.

c. The investigator always retains the responsibility for ensuring ethical practice in research. The investigator is also responsible for the ethical treatment of research participants by collaborators, assistants, students, and employees, all of whom, however, incur similar obligations.

d. Except in minimal-risk research, the investigator establishes a clear and fair agreement with research participants, prior to their participation, that clarifies the obligations and responsibilities of each. The investigator has the obligation to honor all promises and commitments included in that agreement. The investigator informs the participants of all aspects of the research that might reasonably be expected to influence willingness to participate and explains all other aspects of the research about which the participants inquire. Failure to make full disclosure prior to obtaining informed consent requires additional safeguards to protect the welfare and dignity of the research participants. Research with children or with participants who have impairments that would limit understanding and/or communication requires special safeguarding procedures.

e. Methodological requirements of a study may make the use of concealment or deception necessary. Before conducting such a study, the investigator has a special responsibility to (i) determine whether the use of such techniques is justified by the study's prospective scientific, educational, or applied value; (ii) determine whether alternative procedures are available that do not use concealment or deception; and (iii) ensure that the participants are provided with sufficient explanation as soon as possible.

f. The investigator respects the individual's freedom to decline to participate in or to withdraw from the research at any time. The obligation to protect this freedom requires careful thought and consideration when the investigator is in a position of authority or influence over the participant. Such positions of authority include, but are not limited to, situations in which research participation is required as part of employment or in which the participant is a student, client, or employee of the investigator.

g. The investigator protects the participant from physical and mental discomfort, harm, and danger that may arise from research procedures. If risks of such consequences exist, the investigator informs the participant of that fact. Research procedures likely to cause serious or lasting harm to a participant are not used unless the failure to use these procedures might expose the participant to risk of greater harm, or unless the research has great potential benefit and fully informed and voluntary consent is obtained from each participant. The participant should be informed of procedures for contacting the investigator within a reasonable time period following participation should stress, potential harm, or related questions or concerns arise.

h. After the data are collected, the investigator provides the participant with information about the nature of the study and attempts to remove any misconceptions that may have arisen. Where scientific or humane value justify delaying or withholding this information, the investigator incurs a special responsibility to monitor the research and to ensure that there are no damaging consequences for the participant.

i. Where research procedures result in undesirable consequences for the individual participant, the investigator has the responsibility to detect and remove or correct these consequences, including long- term effects.

j. Information obtained about a research participant during the course of an investigation is confidential unless otherwise agreed upon in advance. When the possibility exists that others may obtain access to such information, this possibility, together with the plans for protecting confidentiality, is explained to the participant as part of the procedure for obtaining informed consent.

EXPERIMENTAL SUBJECT'S BILL OF RIGHTS

All people requested to consent to participate as subjects in research studies or who are requested to consent on behalf of another have the following rights:

1. Be informed of the nature and purpose of the experiment.
2. Be given an explanation of the procedures to be followed in the experiment, and any drug, device, or procedure ot be utilized.
3. Be given a description of any attendant discomforts and risks reasonably to be expected from the experiment.
4. Be given an explanation of any benefits to the subject reasonably to be expected from the experiment, if applicable.
5. Be given a disclosure of any appropriate alternative procedures, drugs or devices that might be advantageous to the subject, and their relative risks and benefits.
6. Be informed to the avenues of medical treatment, if any, available to the subject after the experiment if complications should arise.
7. Be given an opportunity to ask any questions concerning the experiment or the procedure involved.
8. Be instructed that consent to participate in the experiment may be withdrawn at any time and the subject may discontinue participation in the experiment without prejudice.
9. Be given a copy of any signed and dated written consent form used in relation to the experiment.
10. Be given the opportunity to decide to consent or not to consent to an experiment without the intervention of any element of force, fraud, deceit, duress, coercion, or undue influence on the subject's decision.

Appendix IV

SAMPLE CONSENT FORM

When research is conducted under the auspices of an educational, treatment or research institute, a Human Subjects Committee will have established a standard procedure. The following is a sample consent form which was used in a comparative study of drawings with early stage Alzheimer's patients and age-matched controls. It fulfills criteria for informed consent as outlined in Chapter 5. An identical form was reviewed with each subject in both study groups.

Name of sponsoring facility if applicable_____Date of approval for use_____

Date after which it is void_____

HUMAN SUBJECTS CONSENT FORM

Subject's Name _____   Date _____
Code_____

1. **The purpose of this research is** to review, evaluate, and compare four drawings to see if there are differences in the drawings by people with and without Alzheimer's Disease.

2. **If I participate in this research the following will be done:** I will be asked to draw four pictures and I will be asked a few questions about my drawings. The process will take about one-half hour. The drawings will be kept by the investigator, and coded and evaluated without my name being attached to the drawings.

3. **The following are the treatments and procedures which are experimental in this study:** For the purpose of this study, all procedures are experimental although these picture techniques have been used many times before.

4. The following are the risks and discomforts which reasonably may be expected (including the likely result if the experimental treatment does not work): Many people who do not draw often may feel a little uncomfortable, frustrated or embarrassed. Some pictures remind people of either good or bad memories and may stir up feelings. If I begin to feel uncomfortable I should talk with my worker and I may stop at any time.

5. The following are benefits which reasonably may be expected:

    A. To myself: None
    B. To humanity: Information may become apparent about how disease and aging affects the way we draw.

    I understand that these benefits may not occur and that unexpected feelings of discomfort may also develop.

6. The following are the alternative procedures which might be of help to me if I do not participate in this research: My care will proceed in the usual fashion.

7. The results of this research may be published for the information of others. My drawings and answers to questions may be published but my name or my records will not be given out without my consent.

8. I understand that a committee of medical and non-medical people periodically reviews and approves this research for scientific and ethical merit. I will be told of any new information which may affect my willingness to continue in this research. I may leave this research at any time. Such a decision will not affect my future medical care. I understand my questions will not be answered at any time.

9. If this research causes me any injury, emergency medical care will be available. This care will **not** necessarily be free of charge. Financial compensation for any injury from this research is not available. If I am injured as a result of this research, I should first try to contact the principal investigator, who is listed below. If I don't reach the investigator, I may call_____.

10. I have participated in the research studies listed below within the past three months. (Describe the studies):

11. I acknowledge that I have fully reviewed and understood the contents of this consent form. I have been given a copy of this consent form and the Experimental Subject's Bill of Rights.

Subject's signature_____   Date_____

Witness to Subject's signature_____   Date_____

12. If subject is a minor, or otherwise unable to sign, complete the following:

a) Reason subject is unable to sign:_____

b) Signature of Authorized Person_____

Relationship and Basis of Authorization to Give Consent

_____

For the Investigator or Designee

13. I certify that I have reviewed the contents of this form with the person signing above, who, in my opinion, understood the explanation. I have explained the known side effects and benefits of the research.

Principal (Investigator or Authorized Representative)_____

Telephone Number_____

Date_____

14. For all in-patient research studies, to insure that patients receive coordinated care from the investigator and the primary physician, the primary physician must sign this form indicating he/she has knowledge of the research study. If the patient has no primary physician, the physician treating the patient is considered the primary physician.

Primary Physician_____

15. I certify that I am the principal investigator and am responsible for this study, for ensuring that the subject is fully informed in accordance with applicable regulations, and for advising the Human Subjects Committee of any adverse reactions that develop from the study.

Principal Investigator_____ Date_____

SAMPLES FROM COMPUTER SEARCHES

On the following pages are excerpts from actual computer searches (see Chapter 16 for a discussion of the use of computers in research). Dorothy McLaughlin and Winnie Ferguson conducted these searches.

This material is printed by permission of the data base owners and cannot be reproduced without their specific written permission.

The dissertation titles and abstracts contained on pages 256-258 are published with permission of University Microfilms International, publishers of Dissertation Abstracts International (copyright 1980-1989 by University Microfilms International), and may not be reproduced without their prior permission.

Copies of the dissertations may be obtained by addressing your request to:

> University Microfilms International
> 300 North Zeeb Road
> Ann Arbor, Michigan 48106

or by telephoning (toll-free) 1-800-521-3042.

A. A Sample from ERIC Using a DIALOG Retrieval System
Dorothy McLaughlin, R.S.M., Ed.D., A.T.R.

```
PRINTS SUMMARY    User:032029  . File 1
                  TITLE:DIALOG
```

```
File(s) searched:

File   1:ERIC - 66-89/DEC.


Sets selected:

Set     Items    Description
 1      14213    ART/DE  (BROAD TERM FOR THE PROCESSES AND
                 RESULTS OF ...)
 2       5098    THERAPY/DE
 3        102    ART/DE(W)THERAPY/DE
 4     123663    RESEARCH/DE  (SYSTEMATIC INVESTIGATION,
                 COLLECTION, AND AN...)
 5          8    ART(W)THERAPY/DE AND RESEARCH/DE
 6     177567    RESEARCH  (SYSTEMATIC INVESTIGATION,
                 COLLECTION, AND AN...)
 7         16    S3 AND RESEARCH
 8      25206    METHODOLOGY
 9      25569    PURPOSE
10          3    S3 AND (METHODOLOGY OR PURPOSE)
11         17    S10 OR S7
12      20348    ART  (BROAD TERM FOR THE PROCESSES AND
                 RESULTS OF ...)
13       7942    THERAPY
14     177567    RESEARCH  (SYSTEMATIC INVESTIGATION,
                 COLLECTION, AND AN...)
15          1    ART(W)THERAPY(W)RESEARCH
16         17    S11 OR S15

Prints requested   ('*' indicates user print cancellation) :

Date  Time       Description
04jan 10:02EST   P155: PR 16/5/6-17

Total items to be printed: 12
```

A. A Sample from ERIC Using a DIALOG Retrieval System
(continued)

PRINTS User:032020   04jan90   P155: PR 16/5/6-17
DIALOG

DIALOG File 1: ERIC - 66-89/DEC.

ED263306   CE042562
Expressive Therapists in Long-Term Care Settings.
Palmer, Mary Kay
Nov 1985
20p.; Papers presented at the National Conference of the American Association for Adult and Continuing Education (Milwaukee, WI, November 6-10, 1985).
EDRS Price - MF01/PC01 Plus Postage.
Language: English
Document Type: POSITION PAPER (120); CONFERENCE PAPER (150)
Geographic Source: U.S.; Wisconsin
Journal Announcement: RIEAPR86
Expressive therapists (in art, music, and dance) possess the techniques necessary for working with older adults who need assistance in making productive use of their leisure time. Therapeutic expressive activities for long-term care residents promote creativity, self-expression, communication, and understanding of oneself. The purpose of the activities refers to the therapeutic process of the art making; the person and the process become the most important aspect in therapy. In long-term care settings, expressive therapy is important as a means for residents' self-expression, mental stimulation, and social interaction. Progressive activity departments offer a variety of activities to meet residents' needs based on diagnoses. Motivating each resident individually to attend activities is vital when a resident lacks desire to continue his/her emotional or educational growth. The expressive therapist needs to (1) learn about the resident's background and special interests; (2) create an atmosphere of warmth, concern, sociability, and interesting activities; (3) explain the program and encourage questions; and (4) respect each resident's dignity, choice, and individual characteristics. (Appendixes contain four sample lesson/session plans.) (YLB)
  Descriptors: Adult Education; Adult Programs; *Art Therapy; *Dance Therapy; *Motivation; *Music Therapy; Nursing Homes; *Older Adults; *Residential Care; Residential Institutions; Therapeutic Recreation; Therapists
  Identifiers: *Expressive Therapy

ED248282   UD023758
Children's Human Figure Drawings: Clinical and Cultural Considerations.
Thakur, P. S.
1982
132p.; Printed by Community College of Rhode Island, Lincoln.
EDRS Price - MF01/PC06 Plus Postage.
Language: English
Document Type: REVIEW LITERATURE (070); NON-CLASSROOM MATERIAL (055)
Geographic Source: U.S.; Rhode Island
Journal Announcement: RIEJAN85
Target Audience: Teachers; Counselors; Practitioners
This paper considers the psychological aspects of children's drawings. The utility of the Draw a Person Test (DAPT) for different types of pscyhological research is discussed, and

---

A. A Sample from ERIC Using a DIALOG Retrieval System
(continued)

the non-intellectual and cultural factors of the DAPT are described. Suggestions on the administration, scoring, and interpretation of drawings are given. The next two sections focus on using drawings for particular purposes: gauging a child's mental development and discerning specific emotional indicators. The history of art therapy is briefly outlined, and its advantages are explained. The second half of this paper consists of sample children's drawings, with captions that offer tentative psychological readings. Sixteen drawings are uncaptioned; they may be used for exercise in interpretation. (KH)

Descriptors: *Art Therapy; Child Development; *Children; *Childrens Art; Cognitive Processes; Cognitive Tests; Cultural Differences; Elementary Secondary Education; Psychological Characteristics; *Psychological Evaluation

Identifiers: *Draw a Person Test

ED235398   CG016931
Increased Challenge with the Elderly.
Wilson, Helen
Apr 1983
15p.; Paper presented at the Annual Convention of the Rocky Mountain Psychological Association (Snowbird, UT, April 26-30, 1983). Research made possible by a grant from the Billings Clinic Foundation.
EDRS Price - MF01/PC01 Plus Postage.
Language: English
Document Type: RESEARCH REPORT (143); CONFERENCE PAPER (150); TEST, QUESTIONNAIRE (160)
Geographic Source: U.S.; Montana
Journal Announcement: RIEMAR84
Target Audience: Researchers
Research has shown that too little stress or stimulation can increase health risks. To determine the effectiveness of mild stimulation on the depression levels and feelings of self-worth of the elderly, 24 withdrawn nursing home residents participated in a non-judgemental 6-month art expression group. Half the group were assigned to a control condition. The experimental group met twice a week for 2 hours a day. The mild stimulus was provided by a local program known as Growth Through Art. Socialization and discussion were encouraged equally with expression through art. Pre- and post-testing of both groups with the Cattell Depression Scale and attendants' notes and anecdotal reporting showed the art activity inhibited depression, which increased significantly in the control group. Activity levels of participants in both the experimental and control groups remained about the same and there were no significant changes in self-concept. (JAC)

Descriptors: Aging (Individuals); Alienation; *Art Expression; Art Therapy; *Depression (Psychology); Gerontology; Motivation; *Older Adults; *Program Effectiveness; Self Concept; *Stimulation; Withdrawal (Psychology)

B. A Sample from Ecer/Except Child
Dorothy McLaughlin, R.S.M., Ed.D., A.T.R.

PRINTS   User:032029   04jan90   P154: PR 11/5/6-34
DIALOG

DIALOG File 54: ECER/EXCEP CHILD - 66-89/NOV

EC122200
Art Therapy as a Modality for Crisis Intervention: Children Express Reactions to Violence in Their Community.
Landgarten, Helen And Others
Clinical Social Work Journal v6 n3 p221-9 Fal 1978; 1978-Fa 9P.
EDRS: NOT AVAILABLE
DOCUMENT TYPE: 143;

Ten days after the Symbionese Liberation Army's ""shoot out,'' a team of three psychotherapists began art therapy with a group of 21 third grade Black children who lived in the neighborhood where the incident occurred. The purpose of the program was to help the children ventilate their reactions to the event. The resulting drawings expressed the children's anxiety and wish for law and order as well as denial and counterphobic reactions. (PHR)

DESCRIPTORS: *Emotional Problems; *Crisis Intervention; Educational Research; *Art Therapy; Psychotherapy; Elementary Education; *Adjustment (to Environment); *Responses; Black Students; Violence;

EC122189
Creative Arts for the Severely Handicapped. Second Edition.
Sherrill, Claudine, Ed.
1979- 286P.
Available from Charles C Thomas, 301-327 E. Lawrence Ave., Springfield, IL 62717 ($15.50)
EDRS: NOT AVAILABLE
DOCUMENT TYPE: 020; 130;

Designed for professionals working with handicapped children and youth, the resource book provides an interdisciplinary approach to integrating the arts into special education delivery systems. The following titles and authors are included: ""Personnel Preparation in Creative Arts for the Handicapped--Implications for Improving the Quality of Life'' by C. Sherrill and R. Cox; ""Public Law 94-142 (the Education for All Handicapped Children Act) and the Arts'' by Sherrill; ""Self Expression Through the Arts--A Human Right'' by W. Perks; ""The Severely Handicapped--Who Are They? What Can They Do?'' by Sherrill; ""Mainstreaming Severely and Profoundly Handicapped Children in Creative Arts'' by J. Moran; ""Sensitivity in Recreation Programming, Not Tokenism'' by M. Lord; ""Advocating for Mentally Retarded People'' by P. Roos; ""The Dance of Childhood--Focus on Wellness, Not Emotional Disturbance'' by L. Fuller; ""Fabrics, Balls, and Pillows in Dance and Movement Discovery'' by W. Delaney; ""Square Dancing for Ambulatory Severely Mentally Retarded Children'' by O. Brown; ""Where There's a Will--Adapting Wheelchair Dance to the Severely Disabled'' by. W. Rainbolt; ""Dance for the Deaf'' by P. Wisher; ""Aesthetic Awareness Through a Multisensory Approach to the Integrated Arts'' by L. Routon; ""So Much Pleasure from Mere Touch--Arts for the Visually

B. A Sample from Ecer/Except Child
(continued)

Handicapped'' by S. Ervin; ""Creating a Children's Theatre for the Deaf'' by C. Robertson; ""Drama for the Mentally Retarded'' by Routon and M. Schneider; ""Orff-Schulwerk--An Adaptation for Drama for Retarded Participants'' by D. Morgan; ""A Dynamic Recycling of Film--Markamation'' by M. Reid; ""Creative Use of the Stuff Box'' by B. Ross; ""Realism in Permitting the Profoundly Retarded Citizen His Right to Creative Arts Expression'' by Ross; ""Music as Therapy for the Developmentally Delayed'' by M. Reesing; ""The Arts as Learning and Socialization Experiences for the Severely Handicapped'' by E. Uhler; ""Research in Creative Arts for the Handicapped'' by Sherrill; ""BCP (Behavioral Characteristics Progression) Strands for Evaluating Changing Behaviors in Music and Rhythms and Arts and Crafts'' by D. Russell; ""Observation and Rating of Motor Creativity'' by Sherrill et al.; ""Motion Photography--A Tool for the Analysis of Movement Patterns in the Creative Arts for the Severely Handicapped'' by M. Hinson and T. Lawton; and ""Drum Beating to Improve Overarm Throwing--Photographic Analysis as an Evaluation Technique'' by Hinson et al. A list of addresses of organizations concerned with arts, special education, and arts for the handicapped; and bibliographies in the areas of creativity, art, dance, drama, and music are appended. (PHR)

DESCRIPTORS: *Severe Disabilities; *Creativity; *Creative Art; Creative Dramatics; Art Therapy; Creative Expression; Photography; Evaluation Methods; Resource Materials; Federal Legislation; *Self Expression; Art Activities; Mainstreaming; Motion; Emotional Disturbances; Visual Impairments; Dance Therapy; Deafness; Multisensory Learning; Music; Handicrafts; Behavior Patterns; Motor Development; Quality of Life; Recreational Programs;
   IDENTIFIERS: Education For All Handicapped Children Act;

EC121404
Choosing an Appropriate Candidate for Art Therapy among Emotionally Disturbed-Mentally Retarded Children.
   Roth, Ellen A.
   1978-Oct   26P.
   NOTE: Paper presented at the Annual Conference of the American Art Therapy Association (9th, Los Angeles, CA, October 25-29, 1978)
   Available from American Art Therapy Association, Inc., 428 E. Preston Street, Baltimore, MD 21202 (Query price)
   EDRS: NOT AVAILABLE
   DOCUMENT TYPE: 143; 055;

   Focus of the paper is on the appropriate choice of a candidate for art therapy among emotionally disturbed, mentally handicapped children. Possible goals of art therapy are reviewed and choice of a good candidate for art therapy is illustrated with six case studies of children (ages 4 to 10) who benefited from the experience. It is explained that
                    (cont. next page)

DIALOG
INFORMATION SERVICES, INC.

C. A Sample from PsyAlert
Dorothy McLaughlin, R.S.M., Ed.D., A.T.R.

PRINTS SUMMARY User:032029 , File 140
TITLE:DIALOG

File(s) searched:

File 140:PSYCALERT / FEB 22,1988
         (Copr. Am. Psych. Assn.)

Sets selected:

Set	Items	Description
1	129	GROUP PSYCHOTHERAPY/DE
2	1553	CHILDREN/DE
3	685	ADOLESCENTS/DE
4	7	GROUP PSYCHOTHERAPY/DE AND (CHILDREN OR ADOLESCENTS)/DE
5	7	S4 AND DT=JOURNAL ARTICLE
6	7	S5 AND PY=1982:1988
7	2026	S2 OR S3
8	8	S7 AND ART THERAPY/DE
9	8	S8 AND DT=JOURNAL ARTICLE
10	8	S9 AND PY=1982:1988

Prints requested   ('*' indicates user print cancellation) :

Date	Time	Description
25feb	19:20EST	P455: PR 10/5/1-8
25feb	19:20EST	P456: PR 6/5/1-7

Total items to be printed: 15

C. A Sample from PsyAlert
(continued)

DIALOG File 140: PSYCALERT / FEB 22,1988 (Copr. Am. Psych. Assn.)

2030654
735141009
Employing a modified positive peer culture treatment approach in a state youth center.
Tannehill, Ronald L.
Youth Ctr at Larned, KS, US
Journal of Offender Counseling, Services & Rehabilitation,
1987 Fal-Win Vol 12(1) 113-129
Coden: OFREDJ
ISSN 01956116
Languages: ENGLISH
DOC TYPE: JOURNAL ARTICLE
Descriptors: GROUP PSYCHOTHERAPY; PROBLEM SOLVING;
ADOLESCENTS; JUVENILE DELINQUENTS

2028214
732182008
Model for the group treatment of eating disorders.
Hendren, Robert L.; Atkins, Darlene M.; Sumner, Calvin R.;
Barber, Joan K.
U New Mexico, Children's Psychiatric Hosp, Albuquerque, US
International Journal of Group Psychotherapy,
1987 Oct Vol 37(4) 589-602
Coden: IJGPAO
ISSN 00207284
Languages: ENGLISH
DOC TYPE: JOURNAL ARTICLE
Descriptors: GROUP PSYCHOTHERAPY; SCHOOL AGE CHILDREN;
ADOLESCENTS; ANOREXIA NERVOSA; BULIMIA; APPETITE DISORDERS

2028213
732182007
Therapeutic issues of adolescent children of alcoholics (AdCA) groups.
Rogdaniak, Roman C.; Piercy, Fred P.
Community Outreach, Prevention & Education Inc, Niles, IL,
US
International Journal of Group Psychotherapy,
1987 Oct Vol 37(4) 569-588
Coden: IJGPAO
ISSN 00207284
Languages: ENGLISH
DOC TYPE: JOURNAL ARTICLE
Descriptors: OFFSPRING; ADOLESCENTS; GROUP PSYCHOTHERAPY;
ALCOHOLISM; PARENTS

2024163
728004031
Treatment of a 7-year-old boy with Obesity-Hypoventilation (Pickwickian Syndrome) on a psychosomatic inpatient unit.
Boxer, Gary H.; Miller, Bruce D.
National Jewish Ctr for Immunology & Respiratory Medicine,
Pediatr'- Psychosomatic Inpatient Unit, Denver, CO
Jour   of the American Academy of Child & Adolescent

D. A Sample from PsychINFO
Dorothy McLaughlin, R.S.M., Ed.D., A.T.R.

PRINTS SUMMARY User:032029 . File 11
TITLE:DIALOG

File(s) searched:

File 11:PSYCINFO - 67-88/JAN
(COPR. AM. PSYCH. ASSN.)

Sets selected:

Set	Items	Description
1	4495	GROUP PSYCHOTHERAPY/DE
2	53324	CHILDREN/DE
3	22847	ADOLESCENTS/DE
4	418	GROUP PSYCHOTHERAPY/DE AND (CHILDREN OR ADOLESCENTS)/DE
5	345	S4 AND DT=JOURNAL ARTICLE
6	119	S5 AND PY=1982:1988
7	69119	S2 OR S3
8	134	S7 AND ART THERAPY/DE
9	125	S8 AND DT=JOURNAL ARTICLE
10	39	S9 AND PY=1982:1988

Prints requested ('*' indicates user print cancellation) :

Date	Time	Description
25feb	19:19EST	P453: PR 6/5/21-95
25feb	19:19EST	P454: PR 10/5/21-39

Total items to be printed: 94

D. A Sample from PsychINFO
(continued)

PRINTS   User:032029   25feb88   P453: PR 6/5/21-95
          DIALOG

DIALOG File 11: PSYCINFO - 67-88/JAN (COPR. AM. PSYCH. ASSN.)

74-11084
 Group therapy with friends of an adolescent suicide.
 Saffer, Jerry B.
 Adolescence, 1986 Fal Vol 21(83) 743-745 CODEN: ADOLAO
ISSN: 00018449
 Journal Announcement: 7404
 Language: ENGLISH Document Type: JOURNAL ARTICLE
 Describes the time-limited, specifically focused therapy
with a group of adolescents after their mutual friend
committed suicide. The purpose of the group was to discuss the
feelings engendered by the suicide. The setting of the group,
an explanation of the victim's difficulties, and issues dealt
with by the group are described. (PsycINFO Database Copyright
1987 American Psychological Assn, all rights reserved)
 Descriptors: GROUP PSYCHOTHERAPY .(21810); ADOLESCENTS
.(00950); SUICIDE .(50620); PEERS .(37154); ADOLESCENCE
.(00920)
 Identifiers: group therapy, adolescents whose mutual friend
committed suicide
 Section Headings: 3313 .(GROUP & FAMILY THERAPY)

74-11064
 A parental paradigm for co-therapists in boys' latency
groups.
 Fineberg, Beth L.
 Community Hosps of Indianapolis, Gallahue Mental Health Ctr,
IN
 Journal of Clinical Child Psychology, 1986 Sum Vol 15(2)
172-173 CODEN: JCCPD3 ISSN: 0047228X
 Journal Announcement: 7404
 Language: ENGLISH Document Type: JOURNAL ARTICLE
 Suggests that cotherapists (especially male-female dyads) in
boys' group therapy can form a special relationship within the
group analogous to the parental relationship within a family.
The concepts and techniques of structural family therapists,
especially S. Minuchin (1974), are discussed, and suggestions
for maintaining balanced therapeutic relationships are made.
(1 ref) (PsycINFO Database Copyright 1987 American
Psychological Assn, all rights reserved)
 Descriptors: GROUP PSYCHOTHERAPY .(21810); COTHERAPY
.(12047); PSYCHOTHERAPEUTIC TECHNIQUES .(42060); CHILDREN
.(08830); HUMAN MALES .(23490)
 Identifiers: parental paradigm for co-therapists, males in
group therapy
 Section Headings: 3313 .(GROUP & FAMILY THERAPY)

74-08362
 Terapijski rad dnevne bolnice Zavoda za zastitu mentalnog
zdravlja djece i omladine u Zagrebu. (Therapeutic work of the
Day Hospital at the Institute for Child and Youth Mental
Health in Zagreb.)
 Gruden, Zdenka
 U Zagreb, Medical Faculty, Yugoslavia
 Psihijatrija Danas, 1985 Vol 17(3) 255-257 CODEN: AZMZB7
ISSN: O   !538

Journal Announcement: 7403
Language: Serbo-Croatian Document Type: JOURNAL ARTICLE
Discusses the background, theoretical aims, and practical content of programs for children and youths aged 11-18 yrs. Individual and group psychotherapy, occupational and recreational therapy, and group family therapy are provided. The personality problems characteristic of adolescence are reviewed, and specific goals of psychotherapy are examined with reference to the theories of A. Freud, Blos, Vlatkovic-Prpic, and Piaget. (PsycINFO Database Copyright 1987 American Psychological Assn, all rights reserved)
Descriptors: SCHOOL AGE CHILDREN .(45540); ADOLESCENTS .(00950); PARTIAL HOSPITALIZATION .(36775); INTERDISCIPLINARY TREATMENT APPROACH .(26030); FAMILY THERAPY .(19290); RECREATION THERAPY .(43420); GROUP PSYCHOTHERAPY .(21810); OCCUPATIONAL THERAPY .(35100); PSYCHOTHERAPY .(42110)
Identifiers: psychotherapy & occupational & recreational & group family therapies, day hospitalization, 11-18 yr old patients, Yugoslavia
Section Headings: 3379 .(HOSPITAL PROGRAMS & INSTITUTIONALIZATION)

74-08027
The use of early recollection drawings in children's group therapy.
Nelson, Anne
Southern Arizona Mental Health Ctr, Tucson
Individual Psychology: Journal of Adlerian Theory, Research & Practice, 1986 Jun Vol 42(2) 288-291 ISSN: 02777010
Journal Announcement: 7403
Language: ENGLISH Document Type: JOURNAL ARTICLE
Discusses the use of art therapy activities with a group of 6-8 girls (aged 10-13 yrs) who must deal with issues of late latency. Activities, which include encouragement exercises, symbolic drawings, and family pictures, are presented as vehicles for promoting interpersonal skills by providing opportunities to explore new behaviors in a safe setting. The case report of a 12-yr-old female's adjustment to the group through the expression of a painful recollection in a drawing is discussed. (PsycINFO Database Copyright 1987 American Psychological Assn, all rights reserved)
Descriptors: ART THERAPY .(03820); GROUP PSYCHOTHERAPY .(21810); INDIVIDUAL PSYCHOLOGY .(24880); SOCIAL SKILLS .(48395); SCHOOL AGE CHILDREN .(45540); CHILDHOOD .(08750)
Identifiers: early recollection drawings in Adlerian-based group therapy, interpersonal skills, 10-13 yr old females
Section Headings: 3313 .(GROUP & FAMILY THERAPY)

74-08026
Otpori u grupnom radu sa porodicom adolescenta. / Resistances in the group work with the adolescent's family.
Mrevlje, Gorazd
Faculty of Medicine, Ljubljana, Yugoslavia
(cont. next page)

AN UNIVERSITY MICROFILMS ORDER NUMBER ADG18-36520. 8912.
AU KELLEY-CAROL-HUNTER.
IN 1031 M.A. 1989, 187 PAGES.
TI ART THERAPY USED IN THE REHABILITATION OF ADULTS WITH TRAUMATIC HEAD INJURY:
DRAWING THE LOSSES.
SO MAI V27 (04) PP534.

2

AN UNIVERSITY MICROFILMS ORDER NUMBER ADG13-36518. 8912.
AU OTCASEK-MONICA-MARY.
IN 1031 M.A. 1985, 105 PAGES.
TI AN ART THERAPY PROGRAM AS AN ENHANCEMENT OF SELF-ESTEEM IN AN INNER CITY
    SCHOOL.
SO MAI V27(04) PP432.

3

AN UNIVERSITY MICROFILMS ORDER NUMBER ADG13-36517. 8912.
AU MURDOCK-MARCI-RUBIN.
IN 1031 M.A. 1988, 161 PAGES.
TI PEDIATRIC ART THERAPY: AN EFFECTIVE COUNSELING MODALITY IN THE
EXPRESSION OF FEELINGS AND REDUCTION OF FEARS IN MEDICALLY HOSPITALIZED CHILDREN.
SO MAI V27-(04) PP535.

4

AN UNIVERSITY MICROFILMS ORDER NUMBER ADG88-21940. 8902.
AU VENDETTI-THOMAS-ANTHONY.
IN THE UNION FOR EXPERIMENTING COLLEGES AND UNIVERSITIES (0557) PH.D. 1988,
    384 PAGES.
TI CRAYON COUNSELING: A GROUP THERAPY EXPERIENCE DESIGNED FOR THE CHRONICALLY
    EMOTIONALLY - DISABLED POPULATION, EMPHASIZING THE RELATIONSHIP BETWEEN
    COLOR DRAWING AS A PROJECTIVE MODALITY AND SELF-EXPRESSION.
SO DAI V49-(08), SECB, PP3426.

5

AN UNIVERSITY MICROFILMS ORDER NUMBER ADG88-18104. 8901.
AU BRAKARSH-JONATHAN.
IN CALIFORNIA SCHOOL OF PROFESSIONAL PSYCHOLOGY-BERKELEY/ALAMEDA (0039) PH.D.
    1988, 261 PAGES.
TI THE CHILD'S FAMILY DRAWING AS A MEASURE OF STRESSFUL FAMILY
ENVIRONMENT.
SO DAI V49(07), SECB, PP2844.

6
UNIVERSITY MICROFILMS ORDER NUMBER ADG88-16876. 8901.
WILSON-DEAN-ARMSTRONG-JR.
UNITED STATES INTERNATIONAL UNIVERSITY (0229) PH.D. 1983, 110 PAGES.
AN EXPLORATION OF FAMILY REACTIONS TO VIDEO FEEDBACK IN FAMILY ART THERAPY.
DAI V49-9(07), SECB, PF2879.

7
UNIVERSITY MICROFLIMS ORDER NUMBER ADG88-15990. 8812.
BROWN-NANCY.
COLUMBIA UNIVERSITY TEACHERS COLLEGE (C055) ED.D 1988, 252 PAGES.
AN EXPLORATION OF THE USE OF CHILDREN'S IMAGERY IN THE PROMOTION OF HEALTH: AN
INTERDISCIPLINARY STUDY.
DAI V49(06), SECA, PP1367.

8
UNIVERSITY MICROFILMS ORDER NUMBER ADG88-14139. 8812.
JOHNSON-ROBERT-MARLOW.
THE UNION FOR EXPERIMENTING COLLEGES AND UNIVERSITIES (0557) PH.D. 1988, 402
PAGES.
THE TRANSPERSONAL EXPLORATION OF UNCONSCIOUS PROCESSES THROUGH A CENTERING AND
PROJECTIVE ARTFORM.
DAI V49(06), SECA, PP1351.

9
UNIVERSITY MICROFILMS ORDER NUMBER ADG88-09607. 8812.
MCINTYRE-BARBARA-BETKER.
THE UNION FOR EXPERIMENTING COLLEGES AND UNIVERSITIES (0557) PH.D. 1987, 171
PAGES.
THE USE OF ART THERAPY WITH BEREAVED CHILDREN.
DAI V49(06), SECA, PP1376.

10
UNIVERSITY MICROFILMS ORDER NUMBER ADG88-06724. 8809.
COHEN-ILANA.
THE UNION FOR EXPERIMENTING COLLEGES AND UNIVERSITIES (0557) PH.D. 1986, 284
PAGES.
CREATIVITY IN OLD AGE.
DAI V49(03), SECB, PP909.

11
UNIVERSITY MICROFILMS ORDER NUMBER ADG87-18517. 8712.
MINES-STEPHANIE-M.
THE UNION FOR EXPERIMENTING COLLEGES AND UNIVERSITIES (0557) PH.D. 1986, 177 PAGES.
THAT FEELING OF NOT BEING SEEN AS WHOLE: HOLISTIC THERAPY AND PEOPLE WITH DISABILITIES (REHABILITATION).
DAI V48(06), SECB.

12
AN UNIVERSITY MICROFILMS ORDER NUMBER ADG87-11429. 8708.
AU WITLIN ROY.
IN TEMPLE UNIVERSITY (0225) ED.D. 1987, 199 PAGES.
TI THE USE OR NON-USE OF ART THERAPY - ART PSYCHOTHERAPY BY
    GENERAL HOSPITALS AND PSYCHIATRIC FACILITIES IN THE UNITED STATES.
SO DAI V48(02), SECA, PP350.

13
AN UNIVERSITY MICROFILMS ORDER NUMBER ADG86-22688. 8701.
AU KURINSKY-DIANE-PINE.
IN UNIVERSITY OF MASSACHUSELTTS (0118) ED.D. 1986, 654 PAGES.
TI THE DEVELOPMENT AND CLINICAL FIELD TEST OF A STRUCTURAL/DIRECTIVE FAMILY ART
    ASSESSMENT TOOL (FAMILY   THERAPY, STRUCTURAL FAMILY THERAPY, FAMILY ART
    THERAPY).
SO DAI V47(07), SECB, PP3114.

14
AN UNIVERSITY MICROFILMS ORDER NUMBER ADG86-17263. 8611.
AU KUNKLE-MILLER-CAROLE-LOIS.
IN UNIVERSITY OF PITTSBURGH (0178) PH.D. 1985, 196 PAGES.
TI COMPETENCIES FOR ART THERAPISTS WHOSE CLIENTS HAVE PHYSICAL, COGNITIVE OR
    SENSORY DISABILITIES (HANDICAPPED, EXPRESSIVE, CREATIVE, REHABILITATION).
SO DAI V47(05), SECB, PP2170.

15
AN UNIVERSITY MICROFILMS ORDER NUMBER ADG86-05922. 8607.
AU CORBIT-IRENE-ELIZABETH.
IN THE UNION FOR EXPERIMENTING COLLEGES AND UNIVERSITIES (0557) PH.D. 1985,
    481 PAGES.
TI VETERANS' NIGHTMARES: TRAUMA, TREATMENT, TRUCE (POST-TRAUMATIC STRESS
    DISORDER, DREAMS, ART THERAPY).
SO DAI V47(01), SECB, PP369.

16
AN UNIVERSITY MICROFILMS ORDER NUMBER ADG85-22008. 8602.
AU KAPLAN-FRANCES-FISHER.
IN NEW YORK UNIVERSITY (0146) D.A. 1985, 121 PAGES.
TI LEVEL OF EGO DEVELOPMENT AS REFLECTED IN PATIENT DRAWINGS (ART THERAPY).
SO DAI V46(08), SECA, PP2166.

17
AN THIS ITEM IS NOT AVAILABLE FROM UNIVERSITY MICROFILMS
     INTERNATIONAL ADG05-55450. 8504.
AU WALLACE-JAMES-IRWIN.
IN UNIVERSITY OF SOUTHERN CALIFORNIA (0208) PH.D. 1984, 1 PAGE.
TI EFFECTS OF RELAXATION AND PHYSICAL CONDITIONING PROGRAMS UPON IMPULSIVITY IN
     THIRD - AND FOURTH-GRADE MALES.
SO DAI V45(10), SECA, PP3100.

CONTRIBUTORS

Editor

Harriet Wadeson, PhD, A.T.R., developed and directs the Art Therapy Graduate Program at the University of Illinois at Chicago as well as its Annual Summer Institute at Lake Geneva, Wisconsin. Previously she directed the Art Therapy Graduate Program at the University of Houston at Clear Lake. She is author of *Art Psychotherapy, The Dynamics of Art Psychotherapy,* and editor of *Advances in Art Therapy,* all published by John Wiley. She has published over 50 articles and numerous chapters in psychology texts. She has served AATA as a member of the Board of Directors for six years (as Research Chair, 1987-1989, and Publications Chair, 1983-1987). She was Chair of the Board of Ethics and Professional Practice and the Ad Hoc Committee on Funding, and served on the Editorial Board of *Art Therapy: Journal of the American Art Therapy Association.* She has received the AATA Research Award (1978), the Rush Scientific Exhibit Bronze Medal Award from the American Psychiatric Association, a Resolution of Commendation from the Illinois State Legislature, and numerous art awards. She is an international guest lecturer and maintains a private practice in Chicago.

Authors

Pat B. Allen, PhD, A.T.R., has taught at the University of Illinois, Vermont College, and at the School of the Art Institute of Chicago. She has served on the AATA Board of Directors as Publications Chair (1987-1989) and continued to serve in that capacity for another year when the Board was reorganized. She is a member of the editorial boards of both the *American Journal of Art Therapy* and *Art Therapy: Journal of the American Art Therapy Association.* She currently maintains a private practice in River Forest, Illinois.

Frances E. Anderson, EdD, A.T.R., H.L.M., is founding member of both The American Art Therapy Association and the Illinois Art Therapy Association. She has had multiple articles published, has received 26 grants, and made over one hundred conference presentations. She has written or contributed to ten monographs and has completed a second edition of *Art for All the Children* (Charles C Thomas, Springfield, IL). In 1989, she was named

Outstanding University Researcher by her home campus, Illinois State University. In 1980, she was invited to conduct the first comprehensive review of the research literature in all the arts for the handicapped by Very Special Arts in Washington, D.C. A critical review of this research was published in the first issue of *Art Therapy: Journal of the American Art Therapy Association* (October, 1983). Dr. Anderson has served on the AATA Research Committee, the AATA Education and Training Board and as a Contributing Editor for *Art Therapy: Journal of the American Art Therapy Association*.

Doris Arrington, EdD, A.T.R., is Director of the Art Therapy Programs at the College of Notre Dame. She has been elected to three terms as a member of the Board of Directors (as Chair of the Professional Standards Committee, 1987-1989, and as a Director, 1989-1991 and 1991-1993). In 1984, she chaired the Nominations Committee. Doris has presented at conferences and universities, both nationally and internationally since 1975 and has published in art therapy journals. Currently she consults with educational and mental health agencies throughout the San Francisco Bay area. She co-founded the "In Touch Through Art" art therapy show, the first art therapy museum show in the country. Doris and her students have received numerous art therapy grants.

Richard Carolan, M.A., A.T.R., is presently a doctoral candidate working on a dissertation concerning art therapy related outcome research. He has worked as an artist, art teacher, and art therapist, and is a Registered Psychological Assistant. He specializes in work with adolescents as well as with adolescent sexual abuse survivors and perpetrators. Richard also has developed a program integrating art therapy with experiential wilderness education.

Carol Thayer Cox, MA, A.T.R., is an Adjunct Assistant Professor for the Graduate Art Therapy Program of The George Washington University. She is an art therapist at Child Art Therapy Services in Bethesda, Maryland, and the Maryland Institute for Individual and Family Therapy in College Park, Maryland. She is also a licensed MARI Instructor in mandala assessment. She has conducted a number of art therapy research projects which have primarily focused on color and/or the MARI Card Test. A frequent presenter at national conferences, she has also co-authored a chapter on working with the somatic patient with art in *Advances in Art Therapy,* (H. Wadeson, Durkin and Perach, Eds.).

David Cox is a Computer Scientist at the Naval Surface Warfare Center in Dahlgren, Virginia. He has been working with computers, from PC's to mainframes, for over 10 years, and has provided technical assistance to art therapist Carol Cox in her research projects.

Maxine Crouch, MA, A.T.R., is an art therapist at the Strafford Guidance Center in Rochester, New Hampshire. One area of her expertise is the use of computers in art therapy research.

Pamela Diamond, A.T.R., is currently a doctoral candidate in Educational Psychology at the University of Texas at Austin where her area of specialization is Quantitative Methods. She is employed as a researcher at the Hogg Foundation for Mental Health where she is responsible for both policy and services research in conjunction with the Foundation's statewide Commission on the Community Care of the Mentally Ill. Ms. Diamond was the director and founder of the Art Psychotherapy Institute of Cleveland and the Indiana Center for the Arts in Therapy.

Winnie J. Ferguson, PhD, A.T.R., is a member of the graduate art therapy faculty at Wright State University, Dayton, Ohio. She has worked extensively with persons with special needs. She is former Executive Director of Very Special Arts, Ohio. In her faculty role she supervises art therapy graduate students. She was a public school educator and conducts workshops, lectures and presentations locally and nationally.

Linda Gantt, PhD, A.T.R., is active in art therapy research and has served on the AATA Board of Directors (as Publications Chair, 1977-1981; Research Chair, 1985-1987; President-Elect, 1987-1989; and President, 1989-1991). In addition to contributing several chapters to this *Guide* she has provided both editorial guidance and technical services. She is a Visiting Faculty Member of the Graduate Art Therapy Program at Vermont College of Norwich University, Montpelier, Vermont.

Maxine Borowsky Junge, PhD, L.C.S.W., A.T.R., is Director and Associate Professor, Department of Marital and Family Therapy (Clinical Art Therapy) Loyola Marymount University, Los Angeles, California. She served on the AATA Board of Directors as Chair of the newly established Clinical Committee, 1986-1987, and on the Educational and Training Board. She is in private practice specializing in family work and organizational development and is the author of a forthcoming history of art therapy in the United States to be published by AATA.

Nancy Mayer Knapp, PhD, A.T.R., is an Assistant Professor in the Division of Psychology and Special Education at Emporia State University where she teaches both psychology and art therapy. She was Research Chair for AATA (1989-1991) and has worked on both Ethics and Professional Standards committees. She is past president of Southern California Art Therapy Association and worked for 10 years at Harbor/UCLA Department of Psychiatry. She has been elected to a term on the AATA Board of Directors (1991-1993).

Debra Linesch, A.T.R., MFCC, is Associate Director and Assistant Professor, Department of Marital and Family Therapy (Clinical Art Therapy) Loyola Marymount University, Los Angeles, California. She is the author of *Adolescent Art Therapy* (published by Brunner/Mazel, 1988) and editor of the forthcoming *Art Therapy with Families in Crisis* (also published by Brunner/Mazel).

Cathy A. Malchiodi, MA, A.T.R., is the Director of Art Therapy Graduate Studies at the University of Utah, Salt Lake City. She is the author of *Breaking the Silence: Art Therapy with Children from Violent Homes* (1990) and has given numerous national and international presentations on the use of art therapy with children and adults in trauma. She has also received many awards for her work in art therapy, including recognition from Very Special Arts, Kennedy Center, Washington, DC; Hong Kong Social Services; China Fund for the Handicapped; and Thomas Dee Foundation for her research in art therapy with children. She served on the AATA Board of Directors in the capacity of Membership Chair (1987-1989) and Secretary (1989-1991), and is the Editor of the professional journal *Art Therapy: Journal of the American Art Therapy Association.*

Dorothy McLaughlin, RSM, EdD, A.T.R., is Professor/Director of the Graduate Art Therapy Program at Marywood College, Scranton, Pennsylvania. Dr. McLaughlin also directs the art therapy program at the Catherine McAuley Center in Scranton, which sponsors several projects for homeless women and their children. She is a Sister of Mercy, an artist, author, teacher, and consultant.

Janie Rhyne, PhD, A.T.R., H.L.M., is the author of *The Gestalt Art Experience* as well as numerous articles. She is a practicing therapist, supervisor, and visiting lecturer in both the United States and Canada. She teaches nonverbal communication at the University of Iowa and teaches in the

Graduate Art Therapy Program at Vermont College of Norwich University, Montpelier, Vermont. She served on the AATA Board as Research Chair from 1981 to 1985.

Marcia Rosal, Ph.D., A.T.R., is an associate professor of art therapy at the University of Louisville where she teaches art therapy research and group art therapy. She is in private practice specializing in children with behavior disorders, sexual and physical abuse, and attention deficit disorders. She has served on the AATA Education and Training Board since 1988 and has been appointed for another term (1991-1993). She is also on the editorial board of both *Art Therapy: Journal of the American Art Therapy Association* and *The Arts in Psychotherapy.*

Acknowledgments

(Recognition to those who helped create this book in 1991):

Special Thanks to **Judy Rubin, PhD, A.T.R.,** for her long-term advocacy of this project, her thoughtful reading of the preliminary text and helpful suggestions.

Maria Lammers, B.A., has served as text coordinator and editorial aide. She has spent countless hours combining the separate portions of this book and has had the primary responsibility for combining several different computer styles as well as typesetting each chapter.

Additional Gratitude goes to Emporia State University's Division of Psychology and Special Education and Word Processing for the initial production of this book, especially **Robert Ault, A.T.R., David Dexter, Shari Parks, Martin Slimmer, Paul McKnab,** and **Billy Yates** without whose cooperation this *Guide* would still be in many pieces.

Note: Thanks to the AATA National Office for the subsequent rework and reprint of this publication.